Free the Land

T0270773

Land reform has been the most challenging social issue for China, which is in transition from an agricultural society to an industrialized country. As the initiator of "common-ownership trust," the author introduces trust theory into China's land reform, trying to settle the issues of land right verification and land circulation.

First, this book reflects on land circulation and common ownership theoretically. Then it reviews China's rural land system transition in history as well as its current circumstances and problems. Based on theoretical thinking and practice, this book proposes land trust and expounds on its nature and content. And finally, it interprets the "cloud trust + land trust" model, which combines science, technology, knowledge and capital with land to realize the intensive and overall development of land.

This book attempts to solve China's land problems with financial tools, which provide significant implications for not only land reform but also trust theory study.

Jian Pu is a senior economist and a graduate of Fordham University with a master's degree in business administration. He is the initiator of "common-ownership trust" and has over 20 years' work experience in financial institutions, particularly in the securities and trust fields.

China Perspectives

The *China Perspectives* series focuses on translating and publishing works by leading Chinese scholars, writing about both global topics and China-related themes. It covers humanities and social sciences, education, media and psychology as well as many interdisciplinary themes.

This is the first time any of these books have been published in English for international readers. The series aims to put forward a Chinese perspective, give insights into cutting-edge academic thinking in China and inspire researchers globally.

For more information, please visit www.routledge.com/series/CPH.

Regulating China's Shadow Banks
Qingmin Yan and Jianhua Li

Internationalization of the RMB
Establishment and Development of RMB Offshore Markets
International Monetary Institute of the RUC

The Road Leading to the Market
Weiying Zhang

Free the Land
A Study on China's Land Trust
Jian Pu

Forthcoming titles:

Peer-to-Peer Lending with Chinese Characteristics
Development, Regulation and Outlook
P2P Research Group Shanghai Finance Institute

Government Foresighted Leading
Theory and Practice of the World's Regional Economic Development
Yunxian Chen and Jianwei Qiu

Free the Land

A Study on China's Land Trust

Jian Pu

Routledge
Taylor & Francis Group

LONDON AND NEW YORK

First published 2017
by Routledge

2 Park Square, Milton Park, Abingdon, Oxfordshire OX14 4RN
52 Vanderbilt Avenue, New York, NY 10017

Routledge is an imprint of the Taylor & Francis Group, an informa business

First issued in paperback 2020

Copyright © 2017 Jian Pu

The right of Jian Pu to be identified as author of this work has been
asserted by him in accordance with sections 77 and 78 of the Copyright,
Designs and Patents Act 1988.

All rights reserved. No part of this book may be reprinted or reproduced or
utilised in any form or by any electronic, mechanical, or other means, now
known or hereafter invented, including photocopying and recording, or in
any information storage or retrieval system, without permission in writing
from the publishers.

Notice:
Product or corporate names may be trademarks or registered trademarks,
and are used only for identification and explanation without intent to
infringe.

British Library Cataloguing-in-Publication Data
A catalogue record for this book is available from the British Library

Library of Congress Cataloging-in-Publication Data
A catalog record for this book has been requested

ISBN: 978-1-138-22648-7 (hbk)
ISBN: 978-0-367-52285-8 (pbk)

Typeset in Times New Roman
by Apex CoVantage, LLC

Contents

List of illustrations

Figure

Tables

Introduction

Land is the basic means of human subsistence and "the source of all production and existence." Land reform has been the most challenging social issue ever since ancient times. Yet it is also the fundamental driving force of national development and transformation. At present, land issues still have a direct bearing on China's future. However, problems such as low land utilization efficiency, failure in optimizing the allocation of land resources and realizing land value appreciation are still widespread in China.

By introducing the trust theory in China's socialist market economy to realize land trust, we can solve the issues of land right verification and circulation. It represents a new thinking pattern to solve the most challenging social issues around land reform in China. Land trust, land circulation and value appreciation hold the keys to issues related to agriculture, rural development and farmers as well as national development. Land trust reform promises to achieve land circulation and realize value appreciation, thus overcoming the deep-rooted problem of rural development, which is the perpetual poverty of farmers despite sweat and toil. In this way, the challenging issue of land reform can be readily solved.

In this book, Jian Pu, a pioneer of China's trust industry and leading innovator of land trust in China, expounds on the nature and content of land trust. He provides pioneering and practical answers to the challenging issues revolving around land circulation.

Land trust reform should follow a dialectical and reasonable approach based on socialist "common ownership." It should strike a balance between fairness and efficiency and between the basic principles of socialism and market resource allocation. We should break from the dichotomy of public and private ownership. In this way, law-based separation of land ownership, rights of use and usufruct (the right to use and derive profit from a piece of property belonging to another) will be achieved. The attribute of state-owned land as financial capital can be activated. The relations of production between land capital and labor, featuring inclusiveness, can be established. This allows land to become a fluid asset which enables the transformation of agricultural production and allows for the sharing of the fruits of reform and development among farmers.

Foreword

A short while ago, a report on "the first project of land circulation trust launched in Suzhou" aroused my attention to the Chinese International Trust and Investment Corporation (CITIC) Trust. The issue of land is the crux of future development and reforms in China. It is an innovative and helpful exploration to settle the issues of land rights verification and circulation by introducing trust theory into the socialist market economy.

According to Jian Pu, president of the CITIC Trust, "The circulation should not cause land to be used for new purposes other than [those purposes] stipulated by law, and should not lead to farmers' loss of land. Land concentrated through circulation should maintain sustainable large-scale effect and keep up with technology." More importantly, though land in China is collectively owned, it should also possess the properties of capital and can be separated from farmers to become liquid assets. What's more, farmers should be able to constantly share the gains made from land and realize the transformation of production mode.

Having been engaged in reform for many years, I know well the headaches and interwoven interests surrounding the issue of land. Thus it is by no means easy to put into practice the land circulation plan described by Jian Pu.

The People's Republic of China was founded on the base of an agriculture-dominated economy. At that time, the first generation of leaders realized the limits of small-scale farming and launched the reform of traditional agriculture. The public ownership of land practiced in the 1950s suppressed the land disputes under private ownership policies; household-based farming operations were concentrated under the system of people's commune. However, such a system of rural collective production went beyond the level of the productive forces and against the will of farmers, violated their interests and dampened their enthusiasm for production.

The second generation of leaders carried out reform at a crucial period, when the contradiction between a large population and a shortage of land grew more salient, with imbalances in industrial development, a weak capability of job creation and the lack of social safety. The egalitarian practice of land proved to be a dead end, yet going in the direction of privatization meant that the ruling party would be confronted with insurmountable barriers.

Therefore, on the premise of maintaining public ownership of land, it was the optimal choice at that time to implement the household contract responsibility system by fixing farm output quotas.

Since 1978, the household contract responsibility system gradually replaced the people's commune system. Farmers began to contract land with a term of fifteen years. After the contract expired, farmers actively renewed the contract for another thirty years.

In March, 2003, the *Law of the People's Republic of China on Land Contract in Rural Areas* was promulgated, stipulating that farmers are entitled to the rights to use the land contracted and to reap the yields; more importantly, it confers to farmers the right to land circulation, providing that the right to farmland circulation belongs to the farmers rather than being collectively owned.

At a press conference in 2006, Premier Wen Jiabao said that the government should protect the right to manage land by farmers for a contract period of fifteen years and then for another thirty years and "that it should never be changed."

Over the past thirty-five years, based on the household contract responsibility system, a double-layer land management system combining unified management with independent management was implemented, which has unleashed massive gains in agricultural productivity. Within a short span of time, grain output grew by leaps and bounds, enabling over 1 billion people to have food on the table.

Compared with the people's commune system, the household contract responsibility system, with its economic success, significant grain output growth and humane design, won scholars' recognition at home and abroad.

Yet change is inevitable. Just as an ancient saying goes, "It is a general truism of this world that anything long divided will surely unite, and anything long united will surely divide." Still, we cannot solve existing problems by gaining new troubles.

In terms of production mode, the household-based land management system has many disadvantages, such as low efficiency, limited investment, weak risk resistance and slow application of new technology, which make it difficult to adapt to the modern market economy. The increasingly salient problem of small-scale production and a large market poses a great challenge for farmers. Meanwhile, against the backdrop of industrialization and urbanization, the rural labor force continues to flow to urban areas, leaving women and elderly people behind with the farmland. Moreover, due to the hard work and low returns of farming, the amount of farmland becoming deserted is constantly on the rise. Yet with a population of 1.3 billion, including 900 million farmers, managing the land to maintain self-sufficiency in grain supply is an issue of great concern.

While developed countries have already achieved a high level of agricultural modernization featuring factory farming, large-scale production, commercial operation and biotechnology application, factory farming will become normal practice in the future.

Without modern agriculture, there can be no modern economy. The fifth plenary session of the 17th CPC Central Committee put forward the idea of coordinated development of industrialization, urbanization and agricultural modernization, the key of which is the transformation of agricultural development mode.

To change the mode of agricultural development, we need to determine where to start and how to make breakthroughs.

Theory is pale and sometimes lags behind actual practice. Innovations are often created among the common people. I have noted that in recent years, many kinds of agricultural cooperatives emerged across the country. Farmers spontaneously shifted from decentralized operations to market-oriented modes and standardized production and went from struggling alone to uniting together in market competition.

It is another thorough change of agriculture in China.

Jian Pu and I have known each other for over ten years. A finance manager with a state-owned enterprise, he has led the CITIC Trust in scoring sound business performance for several consecutive years. He always reflects on some underlying social issues. Recently, he put forward the concept of "financial inclusion and capital sharing" and applying financial instruments and methods in exploring the rules governing the development of socialist market economies. This time, he leads the CITIC Trust in breaking the dichotomy of public and private ownership and exploring re-verification of land rights based on collective ownership. This exploration, with the purpose of making breakthroughs in the new rounds of rural reform, is pioneering because it addresses the major concerns of this administration and all the farmers.

Focusing on land trust, this book also puts forward Jian Pu's ideas of ownership, common prosperity and reform theories, especially his new thoughts on the knowledge of mankind, some of which might offer enlightenment for theorists.

As Jian Pu says in the Acknowledgments, the book bases its theory on practice and is the fruit of collective wisdom. After the project in Suzhou, Anhui Province, Jian Pu led his team to promote the new practice in larger areas including Jilin, Guizhou and Shandong provinces. I hope that their work accumulates more inspiring experience for further reform in China.

As an 84-year-old man, I have witnessed and participated in the whole process of China's reform and opening up. Over the past few decades, the Chinese people crossed the river by feeling the stones in their reform, enduring great hardships in their pioneering work. Now we are crossing deeper water, with no stones to rely on, which not only requires good decision-making and determination but also fine tools. I appreciate the courage of Jian Pu and his CITIC Trust for their efforts to solve the tough issues of land reform with financial instruments. I also hope more people of vision devote themselves to the exploration and practice of reform. You might be dissatisfied with the status quo, but we need to pool our wisdom for a better China.

Gao Shangquan
Honorary President of the China Society of Economic Reform
Former Deputy Director of the State Council Office for Restructuring the
Economic System

Prologue

To free the land is to free the mind and the forces of production. It is both a pressing task and a reform of far-reaching implications.

The intricacies of land reform not only manifest themselves in land use over the long course of history but are interwoven with changes in land ownership in modern times. The reform also involves ideological debates and a nation's development choices. For China, the greatest common ground in a socialist country is to seek common prosperity for the people. Meanwhile, we cannot afford to ignore the market forces created through agriculture that is modern, intensive and knowledge based. We should carry forward our fine traditions with Chinese characteristics while drawing on the best of global innovation. While addressing the salient problems in economic development, we should also be mindful of the final goal – rejuvenation of the Chinese nation. Our thinking is often hindered by entangled interests. We have to acknowledge that with limited rationality and incomplete information and knowledge, we are yet to solve such an extremely complex social issue as land reform. Therefore, we propose a framework called "transformation – innovation" to guide both theory and practice. Exploration and research should focus on two aspects: one covers the existing social system, namely, maintaining its internal structure while transforming and adjusting to new external systems or principles; the other is to explore underlying differences and create innovative practices based on a socialist theory with Chinese characteristics. Developing countries can serve as a mirror for China to view its own problems; indeed, China needs a global perspective and a spirit of independent innovation to fully understand and improve itself.

At the same time, we need to gain a complete understanding of the nature of land reform to realize the Chinese Dream. Without it, we risk emergence of paradoxes in our principles and methods, with an unclear boundary between power and the market. We also risk a land reform that is quickly set in motion without everyone fully recognizing its potential benefits.

Land is the basic means of human subsistence and "the source of all production and existence."[1] Land is fundamental for agriculture, guaranteeing the livelihood of the people and the nation. As the English economist William Petty said, "Labor is the Father and active principle of Wealth, as Lands are the Mother."[2] Thus, the nature of land circulation is that of wealth circulation. Land is a fundamental issue in rural China. As the country's land distribution is part of the most basic socio-economic system, land reform is the foundation for all other social reforms.[3] Under a socialist market economy, the land in China is either state owned or collectively owned, making it difficult to introduce an all-inclusive and pragmatic reform plan while remaining consistent with our current theory. In any attempt to change, we not only risk raising suspicion of our theory and ideology but also face the challenge of balancing immediate and long-term benefits. At the very least, in regard to land use, we need to keep in mind the need to share wealth, common prosperity, intensive land use, introduction of market forces, assets activation, value appreciation, land rights transfer, continuous benefits from the land and maintaining harmony between urban and rural areas. In fact, we are faced with a number of dilemmas that are testing our wisdom and courage. Land circulation involves complicated claims of rights and interests, thus only through reforms grounded in China's reality and based on the Constitution of the People's Republic of China and knowledge of the national structure can we work out the problems. Attempting to blindly follow the examples of capitalist countries in planning our future reforms is trapped in groundless assumptions of top-level design or the abstract "rationality principle," a result of incorrect theories and practices. As is said in the opening words of the *Great Learning* by Confucius, "What the Great Learning teaches, is to illustrate illustrious virtue; to renovate the people; and to rest in the highest excellence" (English translation: James Legge). For China, the "top-level design" already exists, namely, the socialist market economy with Chinese characteristics. The method we adopt to "illustrate illustrious virtue" is enlightening the people to develop the wisdom to solve the problems we encounter in moving forward. The requirement for "renovating the people" is to seek innovation and reform, with the "highest excellence," which rests in the pursuit of equality, justice and common prosperity.

As an old proverb observes, "sharp tools make good work." Reform also needs to be guided by powerful theories. Karl Max founded materialistic dialectics and developed Marxism based on his observations of a newly born capitalist society in an era symbolized by the steam engine. On this foundation laid out by Marx, Lenin applied materialistic dialectics and developed Leninism by analyzing social contradictions in the imperialist era. Building on the foundations of Marxism and Leninism, Mao Zedong applied materialistic dialectics and created the Mao Zedong Thought grounded in the realities of a semifeudal and semi-colonial China. Combining Marxism, Leninism and Mao Zedong thought, Deng Xiaoping applied materialistic dialectics and created the Deng Xiaoping theory to rebuild the country emerging from the disorder of the Cultural Revolution. Today, we adopt materialistic dialectics in studying land issues in a socialist market economy, with common prosperity as the ultimate goal. However, it remains a daunting task to understand social issues centered on land circulation from the perspective of land trust, yet we have no other choice but to press ahead.

As an important part of the current institutional land arrangement, land circulation – which exerts an enormous influence on improving productivity and the sustainable development of agriculture – is at the core of rural economic reforms. Throughout China's long history, land circulation was carried out in China in various ways under certain historical conditions and kept changing with the times. Rational, highly efficient and institutionalized land circulation not only has a direct bearing on all-around rural economic development, as well as development of the overall economy, but also helps ensure political stability and a harmonious society.

Over the past seventy years since the founding of the People's Republic of China in 1949, land in China has been divided and united four times, forming two different cycles. The first occurred in the early 1950s. Through expropriating land from landlords and redistributing it to the farmers, the farmers finally became masters of the land. Later, the collective ownership of land practiced by the people's commune resulted in reduced productivity and food and clothing scarcities. After the reform and opening up, the household contract responsibility system once again distributed land use rights to individuals, which resulted in better livelihoods for farmers. Today, land circulation reform involves a new type of intensive land use. As one ancient saying goes, "It is a general truism of this world that anything long divided will surely unite, and anything long united will surely divide." China has undergone two completely different cycles of dividing and uniting land over the past seventy years, each imprinted with distinctive era featuring and reflecting our cognitive choices. The type of land trust we are exploring might offer a new pattern or a clear path for land reform which is in line with the requirements of a socialist market economy with Chinese characteristics, and such a possibility cannot be ruled out.

Human power developed from knowledge attainment manifests itself in various forms. Economic power, affiliated to traditional ownership, is increasingly being transferred to an external power. Policy making as a representative form of knowledge is growingly specialized, with more and more scientists and professionals becoming involved. Traditional means of production are not only separated from the workers but also from capital products. While capitalism is slowly undergoing qualitative changes, the knowledge framework of socialism is also witnessing confusion in theory and practice. It is unjustified to determine the nature of society by the ownership of the means of production. Therefore, the theory of judging the nature of society by ownership-centered productive relations is also being enriched by scientific socialism on the principle to the effect that science and technology are the primary forces of production. Reviewing the penetrating remarks of Karl Max in the preface to *A Contribution to the Critique of Political Economy* will help us develop a research approach.

> At a certain stage of development, the material productive forces of a society come into conflict with the existing relations of production or – this merely expresses the same thing in legal terms – with the property relations within the framework of which they have operated hitherto. From forms of development of the productive forces these relations turn into their fetter. . . . No social order is ever destroyed before all the productive forces for which it is sufficient have been developed, and new superior relations of production never replace older ones before the material conditions for their existence have matured within the framework of the old society.[4]

Our successful past experiences and immediate challenges require us to rethink and put forward the questions concerning where socialism with Chinese characteristics comes from and where it is going. Without answers, we become prone to making the mistake of blindly following the example of capitalist countries in planning for our own future. To quote from the Taoist sage Lao-tzu, "Knowledge of the future is only a flowery trapping of Tao. It is the beginning of folly." The author hopes that new knowledge can be acquired through critical thinking on the ideas of land reform to draw new conclusions based on the logic of this book. Such explorations will certainly yield positive results and inspire those engaged in the promotion of land reform in China.

Acknowledgements

This book is the result of years-long trust practice and the collective wisdom of all CITIC Trust staff through learning from others and innovating. People show a mixed attitude toward the current development status of trust. The rapid development of trust is by no means accidental but illustrates the rationality of legal thinking, new types of economic relations and inclusive culture.

The book could not have been completed without a mature social economy or our reflection on the basic theories or the accumulated practice of socialist theory with Chinese characteristics. Allow me to express my gratitude to the times and to a number of like-minded colleagues with lofty ideals and a strong sense of responsibility. Among them, Dr. Zhou Ping contributed a lot to the data collection, text editing and coordination of the book; and Chen Yisong, Lu Jingsheng, Lu Junfang, Ma Chunguang, Zhang Zimei, Wang Daoyuan, Li Feng, Zhang Jisheng, Li Zimin, Bao Xueqin and Che Er enriched the book with expertise in their respective fields. Feng Weimin, Liu Xiaojun, Tu Yikai, Wei Enqiu, Wu Chaojie, Zhang Mingxi, Gu Bin, Zhou Qin, Li Shulin, Zhong Jie, Dong Yu and Wang Zhen offered valuable suggestions and cases for some chapters of the book.

I would also like to pay tribute to the late Professor Zhang Shunjiang, from whose original ideas and guidance I have benefited a lot. The book is also devoted to marking the sixth anniversary of his passing.

Last, but not least, I would like to acknowledge the support of my wife Xiao Rui and my daughter Pu Xiaoyi. When writing this book, I drew inspiration from discussions with my wife, and the admission of my daughter into Yale School of Architecture brought me joy and confidence. They both not only offered encouragement but also criticized me when needed. Their strong support made the completion of the book possible.

1 Critique of ideas

According to Karl Marx, "All knowledge involves a critique of ideas." Our study starts from the real world by exploring solutions to contradictions. Once the results of practice go against the theory, we should find the reasons not from the theory but from the critique of ideas. Thus, we should always remember the warnings of Lao-tzu, "Knowledge of the future is only a flowery trapping of Tao. It is the beginning of folly."

The study of people and land is an essential part of the study of land and land circulation, for it is the people who own, manage and benefit from the land. Therefore, the basic objective of the study of land and land circulation is to develop a correct and comprehensive understanding of people, with common prosperity as the ultimate goal. This objective has other implications; that is, China cannot become a modern nation without shifting from an agriculture-based society to an information-based one in both conceptual and practical senses, or without the change of the majority of the agricultural population turning into an urban population, or without fulfilling the historical mission of transforming specialized farmers into farmer-entrepreneurs.

How hard it is to understand human beings? What on Earth are they? How can they best be defined? Opinions vary on these questions.

According to Hegel, man is self-consciousness.

According to Cassirer, human beings are animals of symbol.

Jean-Paul Sartre states: "Man is nothing else but what he purposes. He exists only in so far as he realizes himself; he is therefore nothing else but the sum of his actions, nothing else but what his life is. He only has his own life. Man is nothing. He will not be anything until later, and then he will be what he makes of himself. Thus, there is no human nature, because there is no God to have a conception of it. Man simply is man."

As is noted in the French Enlightenment *Encyclopédie* of the eighteenth century, "Man is a kind of animal with feelings and the ability of thinking. He roams freely on the Earth. It seems that he rules other animals as the leader. Man is a social animal. He invents science and arts. He knows good and evil, chooses his master and makes the law. Man is made up of two essential parts: one is the spirit and the other is the flesh."

Marx considers man as "the ensemble of the social relations" in reality.

In cultural anthropology, man is defined as an animal that can invent and use language, form social organizations and develop technology; in particular, man can unite to make life purpose come true.

In ancient China, people consider man as an animal that has historical records and literature and can consciously take history as a mirror for self-reflection.

Lao-tzu asked, "How to integrate the body and the spirit and never make them separated?"

These definitions demonstrate people's understanding of the unity of opposites in man's inner world, that is, understanding of the unity of the spirit and the flesh; the definitions are also the understanding of the unity of opposites of the outside world, that is, the unity of environment and man. The definitions of man based on different logical deductions only prove that our understanding of ourselves is not as deep as that of the outside world, leaving a huge gap for people to fill in. The riddle of the Sphinx vividly displays the complexity of man: "What goes on four feet in the morning, two feet at noon, and three feet in the evening?" Among all the creatures in the world, it is the only one that walks with different number of feet. Yet it walks the slowest and the weakest with the greatest number of feet. The answer to the riddle is "man."

In today's world, with explosive population growth and globalization, man's unconstrained exploitation of nature has led to environmental degradation. We have realized that while asking for freedom from nature, we are sacrificing our inner freedom. What follows will be the confrontation and conflicts between individuals and societies as well as the invasion and deprivation of the minority against the majority, which will result in panic, alienation, isolation and feelings of imbalance among people. Such feelings will be reflected in the personality and nature of man through changes in our psychological mechanisms. If we fail to pay attention to the new characteristics and implications manifested by the existence and nature of man, which is determined by the changes of time and society and to develop new logics of cognition, then we cannot make breakthroughs or carry out innovation to improve ourselves. As an old saying goes, "Discover the rules of the ancient times to understand the current affairs. By knowing the beginning of all in ancient times, one will understand the whole system of Taoism."

The relationship between man and land is probably the most fundamental one among all the various relations in human society, which is all-inclusive. It should be the basic attitude of human beings to love and respect land. This love and respect is also the key to understanding land and is the prerequisite for harmonious relations between man and land and among all human beings. We need to view the land and nature in a comprehensive way instead of only from the perspectives of economic or other immediate interests. We need to re-examine the aesthetic and ethic significance of the land, take a scientific approach toward the land issue and protect its natural systems. We must fulfill our responsibility and exercise our rights to the land in a sacred way. We should also put in perspective the subordinate relations of the land with human beings instead of only greedily taking possession of it.

Nature came into existence before man and will last eternally into the future. Without the insured existence of nature and land into the future, there can be no future for human beings. Man is subordinate to and dependent on the land instead of being the other way round. The history of all countries is, to some extent, the history of the existence of the land and how man takes possession of it. Land offers immense potential for man, yet it never confers to man its ownership. Man can coexist with the land, but it cannot irrationally take possession of the land, especially, when it cannot be exclusively owned by man, who only has bounded rationality and limited life. As our study cannot avoid the ownership system, we should be fully aware of the fact that the way we explored by "feeling the stones when crossing the rivers" no longer fully fits the goals and tasks we are faced with in the new era of reform, which requires us to be logically consistent and find the right direction. We must firmly uphold the innovation spirit of a socialist market economy with Chinese characteristics, incorporate Marx's theory premise of "rebuilding individual ownership based on the common ownership of the means of production" into the macro framework of the study of land trust and integrate the land, man and ownership. Facts have proven that with the development of socialist market economics with Chinese characteristics, the connotation and denotation of "economy with different types of ownership" as a traditional concept have already undergone substantial changes. The practice of determining the nature of a system's ownership based on the dichotomy of being public or private, with no scientific boundary, can no longer meet the new requirements of social development. It is the reexamination of man himself as well as the need of reform to transcend the narrow concept of land possession, to make new interpretations of public and private ownership or land occupation and existence and to develop some revolutionary new ideas on the forms of ownership. Erich Fromm says in the book *To Have or to Be*, "When the personality structure of the dominant group experienced fundamental changes, a new society can then be built."[1]

It is the common aspiration of the Chinese people to integrate economic efficiency, social justice and individual freedom, which is reflected in the Chinese Dream. We are marching on the right path despite all the twists and turns. However, we cannot afford to confine ourselves to established modes or to guide future reform and innovation with theories inconsistent with the logics of our social system if we aim to translate constantly growing productivity into harmonious social relations and reasonable improvement of people's living standards. We are faced with similar dilemma and challenges in land ownership and circulation issues.

The essence of land value derives from its productivity, which manifests itself in three aspects: material productivity, social productivity and knowledge productivity. Land's material productivity is formed by the natural productive force combining the natural substances of the land itself and related natural environment. Land's social productivity is a kind of collaborative productive force formed by the land as the bond among productive relations, capital, markets, organizing power, and so one. The knowledge productivity is a twofold concept. On the one hand, man gains knowledge from land. On the other hand, the knowledge of man injects new vigor and vitality into land. Thus, a kind of dialectical relationship is built between knowledge and land. The result is that each time land value grows

and costs reduce, there is a change in the knowledge of man. This is the real contradiction in land circulation and urbanization.

The knowledge of man is the starting point of our understanding of any issue.
There is a special and dynamic relationship between knowledge and society as
when the control power of knowledge shifts, it will cause a shift in social and economic power. The means of production in the form of knowledge is increasingly
showing the feature of individual possession as knowledge is the product of the
brain. Yet in terms of organization and society, new knowledge is not created by
any individual but by the sharing of knowledge and expertise within communities
and society. It can offer a logic basis for rebuilding individual ownership and a
new perspective for the study of land trust by putting the thinking on land ownership within the context of the unity of opposites between knowledge sharing and
individual possession.

We need a new goal system with our new perspective. The goal system of
China's rural land circulation consists of three aspects: the first is the ideal, which
is to build a harmonious society consistent with the theory, logic and interests
of the path of socialism with Chinese characteristics and with shared governance, collective ownership and the sharing of fruits as the prerequisite and common prosperity as the goal. The second is the responsibility goal. We need to
squarely face the problems related to the issues of agriculture, farmers and rural
areas, explore and innovate in the formation mechanism, operation efficiency
and types of land wealth flow, and handle these issues through marketization,
urbanization and knowledge in a bid to improve the knowledge level of farmers
and technology using efficiency of farming to boost the dynamism of rural areas
and contribute to the ongoing reform in China. The third is interests. Against the
backdrop of imbalance caused by the urban-rural dual system, the widening gap
in the distribution of wealth between urban and rural areas, and the psychological
imbalance arising from the fact that most people cannot equally share the fruits of
economic growth (actually, relative wealth or income instead of the absolute one
affects the balancing of social psychology on wealth), the task of land reform is
to find a feasible way to tap the land potential, unleash its value and enable farmers to share the fruits of new types of land wealth creation in a secure, stable and
sustainable way.

Improve the rural land ownership system while maintaining the collective land ownership

It is a realistic goal of rural land reform in China to constantly improve the land
ownership system while maintaining the collective land ownership system. The
present system has many flaws. Due to the undefined main body of land ownership, the rights of farmers cannot be protected, which accounts for the misgivings
of farmers in making investment in the land. These issues hinder the efficient
use of land and its social security function. Thus, it is imperative to carry out
reform of the current rural land ownership system. We need to clarify the existing
mode of farmers' collective ownership, define and protect their land rights, so that

farmers have a sense of security in production and can better realize the comprehensive benefits of rural land. Entailed by rural productivity growth and national interests, this kind of reform paves the way for institutional changes.

Balance fairness and efficiency and improve social security

In the transition of China's market economy system, the major goal of land circulation is to let the land perform the function of social security and resource allocation. The former emphasizes social fairness, which reflects the nature of socialism; the latter stresses economic efficiency, which is the essence of a market economy. Other countries' experiences and China's reform over the past two decades prove that the market mechanism is the foundation to ensure maximum efficiency of resource allocation. Therefore, it is a necessity for building a well-off society in a balanced way to allocate rural land resources on the basis of the market mechanism. To this end, we should thoroughly examine all the constraints hindering rural land market development and explore innovative practices to ensure rapid and sustainable development of the agricultural economy.

Build the "land guardian" mechanism to realize the sustainable utilization of rural land resources

The key to implementing this strategy is the sustainable use of rural land resources. At present, Chinese people are shocked by the short-sighted practices in using rural land resources and the ecological imbalances caused by them. The root cause of this problem is that farmers do not treat the land as their own property. Thus, their predatory management results in the decline of farmland quality, grassland degeneration and desertification. Therefore, the key is to change farmers' attitudes towards the land (including forest land and grassland) to ensure that they treat the land property as their own and maintain and invest in it. To achieve this purpose, we need to encourage land circulation, offer incentives to farmers and look for the "land guardians" to eradicate short-sighted practices and encourage the sustainable use of rural land resources.

Push for the reform of rural construction land and avoid the emergence of new landlords

In the process of rural land circulation, we need to lay a strong institutional foundation for a market-oriented land trust mechanism, regulate the land value-added revenue distribution system and push for the reform of rural construction land. First, we should regulate the use and circulation of rural, collectively owned construction land and ban the unlawful trade of farmland for better protection. Second, we should build a land revenue distribution mechanism and facilitate land circulation by establishing a trade center for rural, collectively owned construction land. When conducting a land transfer deal, we need to clarify the use of construction land's added value through market means, improve the infrastructure of rural communities and public service and enable farmers to share the benefits to realize the reasonable distribution of land revenues. Third, we must curb the abusive requisition and use of rural, collectively owned construction land and farmers' land loss caused by the local governments' blind pursuit of economic growth.

Farmers must be entitled to share differential earnings from land and benefits of land marketization

The distribution of revenues from land rights and circulation between collective economic organizations and farmers must be regulated. We should gradually explore the shift of rural collective ownership from common ownership to co-ownership by shares, enact strict institutional control over the use of collective funds by collective economic organizations and maximize the part of revenue used for farmers' social security to ensure the long-term improvement of their livelihoods. At the same time, farmers should have access to differential earnings and added value of the land as well as the fruits of marketization, which is the direction of rural land circulation and the crux to increase farmers' income. Farmers' income growth includes not only labor remuneration but also the involvement of productive factors in distribution. To ensure farmers' income from land ownership, we need to provide legal and policy incentives for farmers to participate in farmland marketization with land as capital and offer tangible benefits by giving them a part of the differential earnings from land.

Apprehend moderate scale management and intensive management of the land

According to Karl Marx, "Ownership of the land is the foundation of individual independence and the necessary transition stage for the development of agriculture itself."[2] It means to recognize the transition from a fragmented management to large-scale intensive management. In practice, "Proprietorship of land parcels, by its very nature, excludes the development of social productive forces of labor, social forms of labor, social concentration of capital, large-scale cattle-raising, and the progressive application of science."[3] The large-scale management of rural land can raise the income of farmers and rural areas. By concentrating the fragmented land into the hands of the professional grain producers or industrial organizations and re-employing farmers, farmers can gain the rental income from the farmland and remuneration for their labor. The "farming factory" can not only increase the income per mu (fifteen mu = one hectare) for farmers but also help them get rid of the conventional farming modes and gain stable rental income from land circulation. Large-scale land management can invigorate rural land resources, push for industrial restructuring, change the farming structure in rural areas by shifting from growing grain crops exclusively to including cash crops and enable the agricultural industry to pursue a more standard and scientific path, thus changing the rules of proprietorship of land parcels put forward by Karl Marx – that is to say, "[the] perpetual fragmentation of means of production and separation of producers. There exists huge waste of manpower. Production conditions grow worse and means of production grow more costly."[4] Thus, we need to guide agricultural development with modern knowledge and ideas, promote the integration of factors of production, including land, capital, technology and labor, tap the potential of land resources, motivate farmers and free the productive forces to realize win-win results of agricultural development and income growth for farmers.

Finance for rural development and innovate rural financial systems

The crux of China's rural development is the dissymmetry and backwardness of financial services. The financial services targeted at rural areas should take capital as the bridge, facilitating coordination and division of labor. We need to innovate new financial instruments to enable balanced wealth distribution among members of different classes, enforce land assets capitalization through institutional arrangement and fully achieve financial inclusion and capital sharing. It can help farmers overcome local constraints and build a relationship between people and land; and among people, such a relationship could foster interdependence, mutual complementation and promotion. The financing demand is urgent in rural areas, where formal finance can only meet one-third of capital needs, with the rest relying on informal private finance. Therefore, to develop rural finance, we need to encourage private capital and innovate the rural financial system to achieve effective land circulation and large-scale management. Financial development will invigorate mortgage, trust, credit and other financial activities; only in this way can we accomplish the substantive development of large-scale land circulation and modern agriculture.

Reviewing the theories and practices about land study, we find that the attitude towards land varies in different civilization models. China's confidence in its development path, theory and social system all come from people's confidence. The history of malpractices in land business is painful, and the reality is alarming.

Large-scale management

Whether or not management logics borrowed from the manufacturing industry fits agricultural production has yet to be tested by practice. The rules governing agricultural and industrial production are not the same, with the former having different boundaries, binding forces and a natural dependence on soil texture, temperature, humidity, irrigation, climate and location. We should not simply pursue a generally intensive and large-scale management of land but adapt to local conditions and build a multilevel, moderate scale management system while considering the cost-efficiency. We should avoid blindly copying the United States or other foreign countries.

Capital's pursuit of profit

With large capital involved in the management reform of land circulation, we need to be wary of the potential plunder and externality brought by capital's pursuit of profit. Failure in identifying the underlying structural mismatching and moral defects will result in new conflicts between capital and labor. Therefore, the combination of capital and land should not spontaneously follow the cooperation order but be regulated by law and market legitimacy.

The choice of urbanization

China's urbanization must follow a path with its own characteristics, just like the theoretical choice of "encircling the cities from the countryside and taking the political power by armed forces." For China, a socialist agricultural country with a population of nearly 1.4 billion, any of its reforms in urbanization, the land and the issues of agriculture, farmers and rural areas is unprecedented in Chinese history. The law of quality and quantity interconversion tells us that the larger a country is, the lesser the influence of any citizen on his country is. In this way, we can draw little from the experience of small countries. Without answering this question, our actions will lack practical reason. We need to be the designers of the new common dream of China rather than the apprentices blindly following others. The history of the United States is shorter than at least seven of the dynasties in Chinese history. The reference data of urbanization rate and academic standards of modern agriculture, as well as the advanced experience of European countries and the Unites States, must be tested by China's specific reality and system and strike a balance between production efficiency and rural populations' employment, between capital's pursuit of profit and financial inclusion, between land capacity and the transformation of farmers' identity, between the priority of efficiency and people's livelihood and between rash advance and pragmatic results.

The balance between development and stability

Land circulation will inevitably bring about a new round of wealth redistribution. We would risk putting the cart before the horse if land circulation results in generating new interest groups, social instability or power-for-money deals or creating a hotbed for substantial "landlords," new poor people with urban *hukou* (household registration) or proletarians with home ownership.

Future practice will prove that only when farmers' knowledge grows significantly, when modern civilization reshapes them and when they are connected to the market with capital can we, without changes in ownership, translate the productivity of capital into social productivity and rebuild the farming economy and individual ownership.

2 Theoretical thinking on land circulation

Land circulation, in essence, is the flow of wealth, information and knowledge. The premise of the study of land circulation is the study of people and the relationship between people and nature and between individuals and their fellows. Therefore, our study needs to start from the people and their nature and proceed to the issue of land circulation. Just as Lao-tzu said in *Tao Te Ching*, "Everything in the universe has its origin, like the mother and the son. Knowing their origin enables us to know everything. In this way, we can live our life without danger."

Understanding the nature of man

Thoughts on the ownership system are actually thoughts on man: on man's liberation, freedom, independent activities and individuality as well as on the concepts that "[t]he free self-development of each would be the condition of the free self-development of all" and "[ma]n is man's highest essence."

According to Karl Marx, "The human essence is no abstraction inherent in each single individual. In its reality it is the ensemble of the social relations."[1] It is a basic way of examining human nature by Marx, not the same as the idea that "human nature is [the] ensemble of all relations." Marx said, "Free, conscious activity is man's species-character."[2] The free development of each individual is the precondition for the free development of all human beings. Therefore, to have a comprehensive understanding of humanity from both a historical perspective and reality, we are required to understand the general nature of man in social relations instead of denying it with the ensemble of the social relations.

Deng Xiaoping's "Science and Technology Constituting a Primary Productive Force" theory represents a breakthrough in Marxism. It pushes the idea of "man as the ensemble of social relations" to a higher level and thus lays the theoretical cornerstone for a socialism-based system with Chinese characteristics. Based on this concept, we can reveal the essences of the market, commodity and labor and re-examine and update the Labor Theory of Value to the Knowledge Theory of Value. In this way, we have a logical basis to rethink the ownership system and its essence under the socialist market economy as well as a new way of explaining the relationship between man and land.

Man has three innate attributes: materiality, sociality and intellectuality. In terms of man's needs, the material needs make man survive, the social needs (sex demand) preserve the system and the intellectual demand preserves the status quo (to rule all). The subjective mind of human beings is a beautiful flower nurtured at an advanced stage of material development. It is such a flower that decorates and connects man's common world of consciousness and separates man from the world of instinct-driven behavior found in other animals. The most salient feature of this common world of man is intellectuality, which is man's essential nature that nurtures the width and depth of man's development. In practice, man's thinking derives from intellectuality, and the behaviors stem from materiality and common practice from society. Our ultimate goal is to achieve the free and comprehensive development of human beings, which entails thorough understanding of our essential nature and recognition that intellectuality is the cause rather than result of development. To this end, we should explore the converging point between human nature and social system and the internal logic between intellectuality and the ownership system.

Human nature

"Know thyself" was inscribed onto the wall of the forecourt of Apollo's temple at Delphi in Greece. Socrates often talked about this motto to his disciples. Hegel quoted it in his *Lectures on the Philosophy of History* as a basis for why absolute spirit is used to analyze human nature through man's cognitive activities and define humans as they are. Humans have certain qualities that make them human, and these qualities are then internalized as human nature. Thus, the essence of human is the reason for humans to be what they are. It is also the internal factor behind human nature. It determines choices of human nature, the development of humans, and is the basis for the ultimate objectives of the development of modern society.

Human beings represent a perfect combination of body and mind. They possess materiality, sociality and intellectuality, of which materiality is their first nature; sociality is a nature in the real world and intellectuality an essential one. In real life, the nature of mankind is honed and upgraded from the interactions between man and nature, between man and society and among men. Ways to achieve such nature are based on the institutional arrangements of a time in history so that men develop homogeneously or heterogeneously and find out their self-identity in society.

Materiality is the first nature of mankind and implies man's autonomous and natural activity. It is realized through direct labor which naturally distinguishes mankind from other animals. The question of whether materiality is the first nature has always been a divide between materialism and idealism. Dante once said something to the effect that understanding is materialist in nature, and in the end, understanding is still about materials. The top priority in developing a socialist market economy with Chinese characteristics is to properly approach "the appreciation of the world of materials and the depreciation of the world of humans." As Karl Marx once said,

> In our days, everything seems pregnant with its contrary: machinery, gifted with the wonderful power of shortening and fructifying human labor, we behold starving and overworking it; the newfangled sources of wealth, by some strange, weird spell, are turned into sources of want; the victories of art seem bought by the loss of character. At the same pace that mankind masters nature, man seems to become enslaved to other men or to his own infamy. Even the pure light of science seems unable to shine but on the dark background of ignorance. All our invention and progress seem to result in endowing material forces with intellectual life, and in stultifying human life into a material force.[3]

Sociality is a nature in the real world and is the sense of belonging to a group. It is formed through the gathering or separation of different groups because of their differences. Karl Marx said, "Man is a Zoon politikon [political animal] in the most literal sense: he is not only a social animal, but an animal that can be individualized only within society."[4] A man is not isolated from others; rather, he is the sum total of his social relations in his attempt to realize himself. Belonging to groups and a collective are the essential content of the social nature of men.

Intellectuality is man's essential nature. It involves the inborn cognitive abilities of humans to discover, use and create knowledge. It is an objective nature that underpins science, technology, labor, productive forces and markets. Knowledge is mankind's systematic description of the world through our subjective cognitive abilities which are represented by the possession of intellect. Knowledge is made up of three systems – natural science, social science and mental science – which correspond to the three types of human nature. Natural science is man's understanding of laws that govern materials and is represented by the extension of the human body. It also determines the efficiency of the development of productive forces. Social science is man's understanding of laws that govern behaviors and is represented by the organization and management of groups. It determines the results of the development of productive forces. Mental science is man's understanding of laws that govern the mind and is represented by values and methodology. It decides whether the development of productive forces is positive or negative. Difference in knowledge structures dictates the differentiation and levels of actual labor. The "price scissors" that exist between urban and rural areas are determined by the average possession of knowledge, the environment for knowledge sharing and the difference in the realized value of knowledge. Institutional arrangements should be made to facilitate the flow, appreciation and spread of knowledge, thus breaking the multipolarity of knowledge ownership and reach a pattern-like equilibrium. This is the theoretical basis that makes common prosperity possible. The progress in intellectual nature would not only free men's individual characters but also shape independent minds. In the meantime, it would enhance man's sense of collectivism and overall awareness to make it easier to cooperate with each other and to balance altruism and egotism. Alexis de Tocqueville wrote in his book *Public Organizations in Civil Society* to the effect that "in democracies, knowledge about how to collaborate and invent is the mother of all knowledge. All other progress relies on its progress."

The materiality, sociality and intellectuality of mankind are united and belong to an integral whole. Together they form human nature. Individuals represent the unity of opposites between material and mental desires and are the beginning of subjective logic. Individuals in society embody the unity of opposites between men and the environment and are the start of objective logic. The former is the inner practice, or theoretical practice, and the latter the outer practice, or behavioral practice. From the perspective of the three natures of mankind, human labor is naturally divided into material labor, social labor and knowledge-oriented labor. The intellectual nature is something inherent, consistent and fundamental to labor. Therefore, labor is the comprehensive process of the knowledge nature being translated to services and results. It is the common application of theoretical practice and behavioral practice. The act of Indian elephants moving logs is called servitude, not labor. This shows that human labor should be the combination of the three types of labor, which genuinely manifests the greatness of men. Any attempt to separate the three united types of labor fall into the category of servitude and exploitation of men and could potentially undermine the coordinated development of productive forces and relations of production.

In the new era of reform and opening up, we keep attaching great importance to the issues surrounding agriculture, rural areas and farmers. For years, the annual No. 1 Central Document of the Chinese central government has been about rural issues, which shows that the government takes reforms in this area very seriously. Yet in reality, the results are not so satisfactory – developmental imbalances among regions and between the urban and rural areas are increasingly huge, leading to rising public concerns. Some say the unclear ownership of land hampered the flexibility in its use, including its capitalization. But in truth, land ownership is clear – it is a collective ownership at multiple levels. It's just that for a long time, we've been lacking a deep theoretical understanding of the explicit collective ownership. Owners' interests are eroded by proxy, an approach that is not based on the market, leading to an "incomplete ownership." Some scholars argue that it's because the in-demand financial services are not there and financial liberalization lags behind. They believe that the opening up of the financial industry and the involvement of private capital would address financing difficulties in the agricultural sector. But this is not the case. Financial institutions would only serve those with wealth and special privileges and would never do any good if they just "rob the poor to feed the rich," sacrificing the interests of most people in the process, rather than rethinking and reforming the country's socialist financial system with a view to achieve common prosperity and make up for the inherent defects of the current financial system – the inherent contradiction between the pursuit of profits and huge negative exogenous effects of finance and the natural habit of private capital to obtain surplus value. Those with radical views think that the privation of land would solve all the problems facing agriculture, rural areas and famers. But this suggestion is not conducive to the nation's development and reforms; it is challenging the logic of China's constitution and social system. The essence of radicalism is to turn the social system upside down and change it according to some predetermined "rational theory." The "ideal society" in the minds of its believers is not the product of combined human experience (common knowledge) but the "the result of the great way." Hence it's an illogical idea. Harsh realities show yet again that it's dangerous and ignorant to get simple, fragmented lessons from extremely complex development experiences which contain all kinds of twists and turns. The top issue facing reformation is whether the systems we choose could incorporate the three types of human nature comprehensively and systematically into the overall framework of development ideas. In particular, in facilitating the comprehensive development of man's intellectuality, practical measures, direct or indirect, should be taken to ensure that reforms relating to the agricultural sector are based on the sharing of knowledge and achievements of development.

History shows that numerous intellectual revolutions resulted in enriching material content in human society and transforming social relations. The shift from a feudal society to a capitalist one fully showcases the glory of progress in man's intellectual nature – the candlelight of industrial civilization shined in the dark tunnel of feudal society and brand-new relations of production broke the restrictions that feudalism placed on human nature. In the one hundred years that followed, wealth created under capitalism exceeded the total wealth created before its existence. However, financial instability – an inherent "tumor" in any capitalist economy – was then experienced frequently, and the exogenous effects of individualism led to many disadvantages. As a result, scientific socialism is created as a natural evolution.

History witnesses the continuing recognitions and improvements among mankind, society and nature through the division and integration of the identity or differentiation of human nature. The development of intellectual nature and its effects correspond to the development of productive forces, the progress in production relations and the improvement in mode of production. In a specific period, based on the conditions for the development of productive forces and relations of production, a certain human nature would become more pronounced, and other parts of human nature are deemed less important or even suppressed. In the real world, as productive forces grow, the relations between men and nature, society and men, undergo a process of evolution, from being imperfect to being perfect, from being one-sided to being comprehensive and from the realm of necessity to the realm of freedom.

Institutions create room for man to secure comprehensive development in the real world

Comprehensive development of man is needed for human nature to manifest itself. As Karl Marx said, "Man appropriates his comprehensive essence in a comprehensive manner, that is to say, as a whole man."[5] Individuals' comprehensive development is an ultimate goal of modern society. A combination of natural, social and intellectual factors, man's comprehensive development means the integration of activities and abilities, enriched social relations and the free development and flow of knowledge, ultimately leading to harmony among the three. However, men cannot be in an isolated existence, and individuals' comprehensive development and the manifestation of human nature have to be achieved under certain social systems. A man is "a citizen in institutions."[6] Institutions are set up and transformed according to men's activities, social relations and the way we exist. Clearly, men's development direction pertains to human nature. Men created institutions on the basis of human nature, and institutions in turn place constraints on men's development to a certain extent. Man's understanding of human nature constantly transforms institutions and in the end creates a perfect match between human nature and institutions.

In practice, institutions are manifestations of social relations. Man, a creature of social existence, is also in existence under institutions. Also, institutions come from the interactions among men, nature and society. They make social relations into law, restricting human existence itself and its way of development. Therefore, institutions constitute the reality in which men determine their development and how human nature manifests itself comprehensively.

Institutions are manifestations of human nature

Institutions are a product of human activities – they emerge through the interactions between man and nature and between society and man. Ludwig Feuerbach once saw men as an emotional existence and completely ignored the fact that the way men exist and develop is to be engaged in activities. The first time men took the initiative to address the contradictions between man and nature signified the distinction between man and other animals. And man's activities to transform nature are manifested in the dealings among men and their social relations. Karl Marx once said, "Only within these social connections and relations does their influence upon nature operate – i.e., does production take place."[7] Therefore, man's existence relies upon social relations, and "social relations mean the activities that many people are engaged in together."[8] This refers to cooperation among individuals, preconditioned by order, stability and consensus. Historical experience tells us that people often found themselves in conflicts due to reasons revolving around resources, values and interests which impede social progress and individuals' comprehensive development. Thus reasonable institutions are required to reduce conflict possibility and ensure unimpeded cooperation and the manifestation of human nature. If cooperation makes institutions possible, then conflicts make them necessary. During the long-term practice of the materiality, sociality and intellectuality of men, institutional arrangements are designed to regulate social relations and seek sensible ways of economic development. This conforms to what Karl Marx said as follows: "The reality which communism creates is precisely the true basis for rendering it impossible that anything should exist independently of individuals, insofar as reality is nevertheless only a product of the preceding intercourse of individuals."[9] The "reality" here refers to social institutions.

Therefore, human nature gives rise to institutions, which are manifestations of human nature. They are the way men cooperate with each other in the context of society, and they are stable, standardized social relationships. In turn, human activities and the interactions among men represent an institutionalized life.

Institutions restrict the manifestation of human nature

Institutions influence and restrict people's activities. They define the scope of these activities and regulate social relations among men. They also constitute the real world in which men live and develop. Based on the scope of institutions, men identify the boundaries of freedom and seek proper development directions. They safeguard justifiable freedom within these boundaries and bring about "incentives in human exchange, whether political, social, or economic."[10] Institutions, through incentives and punitive measures, specify directions for human behaviors and influence human preferences, thus encouraging or restricting the manifestations of human nature. What occurred in practice proves that incentives are different in different institutions. "The sole principle of dictatorship is to despise men, so that men are no longer men."[11] Dictatorship places constraints on the mind, hinders economic development and human nature and restricts the manifestation of man's intellectual nature and knowledge. The institutional arrangements under a socialist market economy, on the other hand, give play to human creativity and potential to a certain extent.

Institutions regulate social relations and provide the basis for their existence and development in the real world so that men genuinely become "the sum total of social relations. In the meantime, institutions ensure order and stability in social relations. However, we must understand clearly that social relations under different institutions display different characteristics – men's reliance under feudalism, men's independence based on materials under capitalism, and the comprehensive development of men under socialism. In terms of ownership, public ownership is based on people's mutual trust and the principle of "benefiting others first and oneself later." It embodies human nature and ultimately achieves common prosperity. Trust between people is an effective institutional arrangement under public ownership and meets its requirements. It makes good use of financial instruments and gives equal weight to equality and efficiency. By pooling knowledge, it ensures that capital is shared and the needs for men's comprehensive development are met.

Therefore, men construct institutions, and institutions serve them. Institutions are tangible manifestations of social relations, and they make human nature specific and real. Institutions also determine the direction of human development, regulate social development and manifest the power of human nature. Without institutional arrangements, human nature would lose its power and basis in the real world, which means it won't be translated into real human existence, let alone human development and the pursuit of freedom.

Reform and development relies on intellectuality

Ruins lie in the East, yet buildings are erected in the West. New ideas always emerge from the reorganization and summarization of old ones. For more than thirty years, China witnessed nonstop fast economic development thanks to the freeing of mind, reform and opening up. This is a remarkable achievement. In essence, the importance of mind emancipation lies in the fact that the constraints of a planned economy were broken, restraints for knowledge accumulation were removed and more channels for knowledge exchanges were created and that human creativity was unleashed and the enthusiasm of self-decision was ignited. Reform and opening up are processes to improve knowledge sharing, which not only shortens the path to acquire knowledge and reduces the cost for knowledge accumulation but also ensures the time to gain knowledge. During this period, a fundamental intellectual revolution took place at the levels of mind, instruments and institutions, one that involved everybody and made learning a task for every citizen. Endogenous and exogenous knowledge and intellectual nature met at the right time, creating prosperity in China for thirty years. If we were able to start another process where added values are constantly created and new knowledge is accumulated at an accelerated pace so that there is a strong basis for the development of natural, social and mental sciences, then we will create yet another miracle and greater glory in the next three decades.

Based on a deep understanding of man's intellectuality and collective knowledge, we will create a brand-new cognitive system and establish a new logical path to clarify and explain historical practice and to offer insights and predictions that make sense for issues in the real world. It must be pointed out that the research and development of man's intellectuality doesn't mean that we belittle materiality and sociality. We underscore the importance of the intellectuality and knowledge to human development precisely because it is a key factor in the coupling of the three dimensions of human nature.

Analysis of the real world through this new framework will inevitably lead to the integrated development of some important concepts, including – but not limited to – ownership, the market economy, commodities and their nature, egotism and altruism. To unleash the potential of man's intellectuality and the power to transform the future, we have to rely on our own human nature and the universal effects of expanding knowledge. All these depend on a sharp and fundamental understanding of cognition.

Thinking on ownership system based on common prosperity: common ownership

The basis of socialism is common prosperity, which seeks the greatest common ground of all issues in China. Therefore, to uphold high the banner of socialism with Chinese characteristics and develop our great cause, we need to explore the road to common prosperity in a scientific way and define future development with both theory and practice.

As Deng Xiaoping put it,

> How can we realize the prosperity of 1.2 billion Chinese people? Then, how to distribute wealth? Uneven distribution will inevitably cause polarization. In the past, we gave priority to economic growth. Now with all the achievements from growth, we still have problems no less than before. A society with few people being rich and the majority of people being poor is not a socialist society. The superiority of socialism lies in common prosperity. It reflects the nature of socialism.

Only the path of common prosperity can ensure political stability, social harmony, people's satisfaction, improving domestic demand, inclusive development and the rejuvenation of the Chinese nation. China's sustainable development depends on how we involve the majority of people in the multilevel community of common interests with capital sharing as the bond.

Thinking should be based on reality. The reality is that the gap between the rich and the poor is approaching qualitative change, with the outcry for equity permeating across all social classes. The imbalanced development and constraints of transition pose a threat to the future of the Chinese economy. With the "retrogress theory" at home and the "collapse theory" abroad, China is faced with grave challenges. The worst-case scenario for its future will be a decreasing value of the existing development mode and insufficiency of the newly built system, severely testing the macro decision-making ability. Despite the rapid gross domestic product (GDP) growth and remarkable improvement of people's livelihoods, China's socialist market economy is still questioned time and again; public resources are unfairly distributed; differential land rent is still the privilege of a few; and social benefits of natural resources are irrelevant to the majority of the population. All these reflect theoretical confusion and crippled action.

To make effective exploration of the dilemmas facing development, we endeavor to start from the uniformity and consistency among man's knowledge, decision-making and common ownership (a new form of ownership) and socialist market economy. It requires us to be bold in breaking from conventional ideas; if theory goes against reality, we are unable to explore the causes from the perspective of theory but to find them in the logical premises, that is, the ideas. Otherwise, we cannot build confidence in our actions.

Facts have proven that a social system, where few people create wealth by exploiting the majority or where the majority cannot benefit from constantly growing social wealth, cannot long survive. The social reality in China requires new political decisions and firm reform. We need to conform to the historical trend of ecological civilization and promptly and effectively refine and adjust the circular route of interests.

The logics of common ownership

The thirty-year-long "reform and opening up" has proven that innovation in ownership theory is an important source driving economic and social development.

Before the reform and opening up, the public ownership system gravely hindered the development of productive forces. The Third Plenary Session of Eleventh CPC Central Committee ushered in a new era of reform and opening up. Since then, the CPC constantly has made innovations in ownership theory based on the principle of freeing up mind, seeking truth from facts and keeping pace with the times; it first put forward that economic practices based on privatization are "a necessary and helpful complement" of the socialist economy; then it "encourages the development of individual and private economy and protects their legitimate rights and interests"; later it unequivocally put forward the basic economic system of "the public sector remaining dominant and diverse sectors of the economy developing side by side," to unswervingly cement and develop the public sector while encouraging, supporting and guiding the private sector and fostering "a new pattern featuring fair competition and mutual promotion." We can see that the CPC Central Committee has constantly made new explorations in ownership theory in accordance with the new circumstances. As a result, we have realized the historical change from a highly centralized, planned economy to a socialist market economy full of vigor and vitality, immensely freeing the social productive forces and contributing to long-term, rapid development of the economy and society, with China's economic aggregate ranking second in the world, foreign exchange reserves first and per-capita net income on a par with middle-income countries.

The basic economic system can arouse people's enthusiasm for innovation and entrepreneurial activities, free the productive forces and inject vitality into the reform and opening up along with socialist modernization. We must further improve our basic economic system to unleash people's entrepreneurial enthusiasm and vitality in labor, knowledge, technology, management and capital and give full play to all the sources of social wealth. China's economic development has proven that the connotations of an "economy with different types of ownership" has changed a lot with the emergence of a mixed economy and new economic organizations. The dichotomy between "public" and "private" enterprises no longer fits the new requirements for economic and social development. Thus, it is an integral requirement for us to improve the basic socialist economic system with Chinese characteristics.

The source of common ownership

"The realm of freedom actually begins only where labor which is determined by necessity and mundane considerations ceases; thus in the very nature of things it lies beyond the sphere of actual material production."[12]

> Freedom in this field can only consist in socialized man, the associated producers, rationally regulating their interchange with Nature, bringing it under their common control, instead of being ruled by it as by the blind forces of Nature; and achieving this with the least expenditure of energy and under conditions most favorable to, and worthy of, their human nature.[13]

The path of socialism with Chinese characteristics should be the gateway to the realm of freedom. Only when we understand the most basic nature of human beings which is "beyond the sphere of actual material production" and "under conditions most favorable to, and worthy of, their human nature" can we facilitate Chinese people's overall development and the comprehensive rejuvenation of the Chinese nation.

Man has three basic attributes – materiality, sociality and intellectuality – which have been mentioned before. Intellectuality is an essential attribute (nature) of man, which manifests itself in the ensemble of all social relations. With the development of society, material-based means of production can no longer dominate man's will, while knowledge-based means of production increasingly become the decisive factor in the development of productive forces. Less material resources and more knowledge-based resources are being used. Thus, we must make decisions in line with all the changes in modern times; that is, we must develop new interpretations of man's essential attributes, of possession and subsistence as well as revolutionary thinking on ownership forms.

The essence of ownership is possession, which manifests itself in the possession of material-based means of production and knowledge-based means of production. The former is obviously exclusive, "In this survival mode, the only rationale is the infinite right to take possession of things and preserve them."[14] Once a person takes possession of a certain thing, he excludes the possibility of its use by others or sharing it with others. The hereditability of material means of production determines "repossession" and the survival mode of "possession instead of sharing as the aim of life." On the other hand, the ownership of knowledge is the overall possession of natural sciences, social sciences and the science of thinking, which is not exclusive. One's knowledge possession does not exclude that of others, nor will the growth of one's knowledge result in the loss of others'. Knowledge cannot be inherited or presented as a gift; rather, to pass on and enrich an individual's knowledge requires teaching and education or the sharing of knowledge. The nature of knowledge possession is the possession of information, while the nature of information is relations, which are interactive and shared by people. Therefore, we can conclude that knowledge- and information-based means of production are shared by all human beings, and the possession of it by any individual shall be based on the socialization of knowledge. Thus, we can realize "the re-establishment of individual ownership based on common possession of the means of production," which is represented by the common possession of knowledge-based means of production, pushes forward the "collaboration of capital," and forms a new type of ownership system – common ownership. It is the knowledge of man that helps us build a connection with society. As this kind of ownership system derives from human nature, it forms the basis of the social system.

In all the social production systems, the factors of production embody human intelligence and subjective spirit. Non-material means of production represented by science and technology have become the decisive force of boosting productivity. Non-material means of production, which can neither be inherited nor

presented as a gift, reject the conventional concept of ownership as they participate in all kinds of creative activities.

The carriers of science and technology are humans who possess knowledge.
Man should be given full play of their role. If we study humans and how they
use their intelligence, we will discover that knowledge is the innate attribute of
work, which manifests itself in the form of science and technology, constituting the premise of increasing productivity. From a realistic and forward-looking
perspective, we can see that science and technology are no longer subordinate to
capital but have become the revolutionary force; the same is true with knowledge,
which is now the direct driving force of scientific and technological progress.

According to Marx and Engels, the common ownership of means of production
will replace private ownership after the latter's elimination. From the perspective of possession, we will find that private ownership is featured by a minority
of individuals' direct possession of the means of production; in a public ownership system, no individual takes possession of the means of production, yet in
a common ownership system, the means of production are possessed by united
individual workers. In this sense, common ownership is individual ownerships
united as one. Thus, it differs from private or public ownership in nature. From
this definition we can see that the concept of public ownership cannot reflect the
original intention of Marx and Engels, for the boundary of public ownership is
hard to define, and that of ownership subject is blurred. Meanwhile, public ownership often equals to state ownership, which sets itself against "individual ownership," severely weakening the rights of individuals. In fact, individual owners
"lose the property or that it becomes their indirect property."[15] Therefore, public
ownership can neither seek logical support nor reflect individual ownership or
workers' reasonable status. Different from public ownership, the "common ownership of united laborers" as an expression of socialist system's nature not only
reflects man's intellectuality but also the original intention of Marx and Engels
as put forward by them unequivocally on many occasions about the ownership
subjects –"united social individuals." In practice, common ownership is actually
"featured by socialized property, which is a new type of public ownership that can
accommodate the subjectification of multi-ownerships and stimulate the intellectual potential of the individuals."

The ethical logic of common ownership

The ethical logic of common ownership starts from the interpretation of goods,
which is first an external object then being a service to meet the demands of
man. The former is innate, which separates the attribute of being service from the
demanders, resulting in the emergence of exchanges and markets. It is the result
of man's intellectual development and social development, irrelevant with choosing a social system. The latter is the integration of man's materiality, sociality and
intellectuality, reflecting the intelligent, physical and aesthetic power of man. The
two attributes of external object and service constitute the duality of goods. The
attribute of external object is the sufficient condition of the existence of goods,

while the attribute of service an essential condition. Studying the two attributes as a whole, we reach the conclusion that the ethical attribute of goods is altruism. As an external object, goods determine the existence of exchanges and markets. The service attribute realizes the integration of altruism and self-interest. Whether the owner of goods starts from altruism or self-interest, it cannot change the ethical attribute of goods as being altruistic in nature. Therefore, the ethical logic of a socialist market economy with Chinese characteristics should be defined as based on altruism and aimed at the coordination between altruism and self-interest. In reality, it is manifested as putting altruism before self-interest. "Psychological study shows, when acting in altruism, people feel happier and seldom suffer depression. . . . A society with altruism as the standard of behavior will benefit all the social members."[16]

Thus, common ownership opposes both traditional molecular collectivism and atomic individualism. The former perceives an individual as a puppet of various social forces, a building block of the palace of historical contingency, or a walker crossing the river of destiny, with no respect or awe for humanity or intellectuality. It opposes atomic individualism which perceives man's solitude as real and believes that man can live independently with no need of sharing.

Characteristics of common ownership

The theoretical and behavioral practice of common ownership is featured by multiple forms, homomorphism, a clear boundary, multiple levels, randomness, restrictions, dynamism and stability. First, ownership combines multiple forms with homomorphism. Different forms of common ownership include state ownership, collective ownership, joint stocks, private ownership and "common-ownership trust." Whatever forms it may take, the common ownership is always featured by socialized personal property. On the premise that the nature of common ownership remains unchanged, the means of production are commonly owned, which combines common interests and personal interests, and overcomes the weakness of private or state ownership, thus forming a new type of public ownership with multiple property rights and clearly established ownership. Second, common ownership features a clear boundary and multilevels. It clarifies the equal status of the owner, user and beneficiary in law, and defines the responsibilities, rights and interests concerning the means of production. Meanwhile, many subsystems exist both in and out of the common ownership system. Third, common ownership features the unity of randomness and restrictions. The forms of common ownership change with economic development, from state and collective ownership models after the founding of the People's Republic of China to joint-stock and "common-ownership trust" systems after the implementation of reform and opening up. No matter how the forms change, it will always be restricted by the common ownership's goal of achieving common prosperity in China. Finally, common ownership features both dynamism and stability. As we constantly make progress, we must stay committed to the principles of common prosperity and reestablishment of individual ownership.

The connotation of common ownership

Common ownership means the combination of production factors. First, we need to recognize and establish the leading role of labor in production and management. At the same time, we need to recognize the role of capital and assets. Based on the diverse forms of social labor, production factors evolve into different forms, including intelligence, management, technology and labor force. As laborers are the subject of enterprise, society and wealth creation, they should also be the subject of entrepreneurs and business owners. These production factors cover every aspect of production and management, which are indispensable. Therefore, the common ownership based on factors of production is an all-dimensional one, which can no longer be called the ownership of the means of production or the property system but rather the ownership of the factors of production as the means of production cannot cover other productive factors except for capital and assets.

The subject of ownership takes different forms. Under the traditional model of public ownership, the owner is onefold, be it state ownership or collective ownership. For state ownership, the owner is the country in general; however, common ownership has multiple ownership subjects (at least two), which feature different forms and levels. For instance, the ownership subject can be a country, an organization (community) and an individual; it may also be a representative public entity and individual, or enterprises and individuals at home and abroad, or a legal person or natural person. Thus, the different forms and levels are attributed to the different subjects and ownership relations. In practice, common ownership effectively integrates different forms and removes the ideological barriers which hinder us from freeing people's minds.

The system of common ownership is an open and inclusive one. Under traditional public ownership, both state ownership and collective ownership are closed and exclusive systems, which to some extent, hurt reasonable personal interests and dampen laborers' enthusiasm. On the other hand, under a common ownership system, different types of ownership subjects and relations are mutually beneficial and develop side by side in one economic community, which makes them inclusive. Of course, public ownership as the main form is the precondition for this system, with the ultimate goal being the prosperity of a socialist economy.

Common ownership is flexible and widely applicable. Under traditional public ownership, the closed and exclusive forms of state ownership and collective ownership cause inertia and inflexibility in the system. If adjustments are made in accordance with changes in the market by making the transition from small public ownership to large public ownership, or from collective ownership to state ownership, then it will deviate from the country's reality, further centralize ownership and reduce the system's flexibility and adaptability. Common ownership, due to its diverse forms of ownership subjects and inclusiveness, demonstrates full flexibility and extensive applicability.

Based on this analysis about ownership, we see common ownership as an ownership system in which diverse sectors of the economy coexist; in terms of the common possession of the means of production, common ownership does not change the nature of public ownership; rather, the means of production is shared by all owners. In this system, everybody is a shareholder. As the corporate interests have a direct bearing on personal interests, the weaknesses of private or state ownership can be overcome.

Common ownership in line with the socialist theory and practice with Chinese characteristics

At different stages of freeing social productive forces and building socialism with Chinese characteristics, the CPC has put forward the guiding thoughts of "science and technology constitute as the primary productive force," "Three Represents" and "a comprehensive and sustainable Scientific Outlook on Development," which "meet the requirements of the development of [an] advanced productive force," which keep up with the times. I am convinced that the study of common ownership, which is in line with the socialist theory mention here, has great theoretical and realistic significance.

The meaning of the concepts of humanity, science, technology and productive forces are as follows: humans are the perfect combination of flesh and spirit, who have three basic attributes, materiality, sociality and intellectuality, as "the ensemble of the social relations" in reality; science is a complete and logically consistent knowledge system of human practice; technology is the sum of the means and measures to transfer science into material and mental products; and productive forces represent the ability of subjective entities in shaping the objective world through practice, which is the externalization of human knowledge.

Sprouts of the seeds of thought

Man has carried out complicated theoretical and practical explorations in understanding themselves and pushing forward the development of productive forces. As Marx said in the book *Das Kapital*,

> The development of labor productive forces – which can be partly combined with the progress in the field of mental production, especially the application of natural science – the development of productive forces is always reduced to the social character of labor in action; to the division of labor in society; and to the development of intellectual work, in particular to the natural sciences.[17]

This is a forward-looking conclusion drawn by Marx at a time of underdeveloped productivity. He fully recognized the high relevance and importance of intelligence, science and technology to the development of productive forces, sowing the seeds of realistic development for scientific socialism. Obviously, the development of social productive forces in modern society depends on the progress made in science and technology and other fields of mental production, indicating that knowledge-driven science and technology are becoming the decisive force of the development of social productive forces. As Engels put it, "As Marx believes, science is a revolutionary driving force of social progress in history."[18]

"In fact, the realm of freedom actually begins only where labor which is determined by necessity and mundane considerations ceases; thus in the very nature of things it lies beyond the sphere of actual material production."[19] The realm of freedom is established on the basis of the realm of necessity. It gives full play to the power of the mental world so that the power of man is fully unleashed in a way beyond the sphere of actual material production or in the field of mental production, reflecting the innate attributes of man in the form of knowledge. Actually, throughout the ages, every critical turn of the human society is accompanied by unleashing the power of knowledge.

Science and technology as the primary productive forces

"Science and technology as the primary productive forces" is an epoch-making theoretical judgment made by Deng Xiaoping by drawing on the lessons of scientific socialism in modern times, marking a breakthrough in the development of Marxism. It not only reveals the essence of social productive forces development in our time and the basic attributes of man, labor, goods and value creation but also paves the way for scientific socialism in China.

That "science and technology as the primary productive forces" tells us that we should not only be aware of the sociality of man but also have more comprehensive and accurate understanding of its innate attribute – intellectuality. Engels once said, "The further removed men are from animals, however, the more their effect on nature assumes the character of premeditated, planned action directed towards preconceived ends."[20] Science and technology are the fruits of human intelligence and wisdom as well as the most valuable source of material welfare. Scientific activities, which help humans gain new knowledge, form the fundamental basis of social progress. Ren Hongjun, the founder of the monthly journal *Science* (founded in 1915), talked about the functions of science, "Science should not only be utilized to make a country rich or build up its military power, or to augment material welfare, but more importantly, to manifest itself in its relations with the academic and metal world." The history of civilization is the history of the evolution of human knowledge. Man's power derives from his intellectuality, which enables science and technology to become the primary productive forces. Meanwhile, the superposing and amplifying effects of knowledge enable science and technology to create a multiplying effect in improving productive forces. The result is that the faster science and technology develop, the greater the multiplying effect has on the development of productivity.

"Representing the development trend of China's advanced productive forces"

The Three Represents theory is the fruit of the development of Marxism in China, which reflects history and reality, and globalization and Chinese characteristics, thus building a logical connection between Marxism and socialism with Chinese characteristics. The idea of "representing the development trend of China's advanced productive forces" especially marks a theoretical breakthrough in the development of Marxism-Leninism, Mao Zedong thought and Deng Xiaoping theory.

To understand the idea of "representing the development trend of China's advanced productive forces," we should be grounded in the development of China while taking economic globalization into perspective. We need a profound understanding of the nature of advanced productivity to face the emergence of a new world order and competition pattern.

The development of human society is a historical course of the replacement of older productive forces by advanced productive forces. China's modernization must be based on the development of advanced productivity, the major features of which are the vitality of society and the strongest force pushing forward human progress.

Advanced productive forces are an integration of all related factors, which not only plays a leading role in the development of human civilization but also drives higher productivity and the self-renewal of society. Advanced productive forces reflect the development of science and technology and are the results of human knowledge and originality. As people are the most dynamic productive factor, their knowledge and innovation are the engines driving the development of advanced productive forces, which determines the width and depth of their exploration of tangible resources as well as the progress of productive forces.

Comprehensive, sustainable and Scientific Outlook on Development

An idea is a reflection of an objective matter and is seen as the beginning of understanding an issue. The Scientific Outlook on Development contains the content, goal, subject and ideas of development, which ensure that our development keeps pace with the times, being innovative, coordinative and sustainable.

The essence of the Scientific Outlook on Development is to identify the rules governing the development of a thing with the Marxist world outlook and methodology – the rules governing the development of natural sciences, social sciences and people. It answers the questions concerning China's development from different aspects, including socialization, perspective, methodology and subjectivity.

The Scientific Outlook on Development is not an outlook on technological development but on the development of social patterns, which means a socialist development concept with Chinese characteristics. In this sense, the Scientific Outlook on Development is a Marxist social development theory grounded in the realities of China while keeping up with the times.

The Scientific Outlook on Development, as a conceptual system of rational social development, represents the scientific abstraction and generalization of complicated and confusing phenomena in social development, which has been proven by practices and serves as the principle guiding people's understanding of social development. From this perspective, we can say the Scientific Outlook on Development is based on one of man's innate attributes – intellectuality.

Giving people high priority is an essential idea of the Scientific Outlook on Development, which also reflects its nature and goal. Therefore, the Scientific Outlook on Development is a people-centered development concept that studies the knowledge and understanding of human beings.

People-centered concept

Man has three basic attributes: materiality, sociality and intellectuality (or knowledge as aforementioned). Man is "the ensemble of the social relations." Intellectuality exists in all the systems of social production. As a sign distinguishing man from other animals, intellectuality is shared by different production factors including the laborers, the object of labor and the means of labor, which determine the direction and efficiency of productive forces development. The major engine driving the development of modern science and technology and the productive forces is the externalization of human knowledge, which serves as the basis for "[dealing] with human nature as modified in each historical epoch."[21] Under the premise that "the free self-development of each would be the condition of the free self-development of all," we need to "respect knowledge, talents and science, so that the common nature of man is honored as it deserves." Robert Fogel, a Nobel laureate in economics and professor at the University of Chicago, said that China was far ahead of the developed countries in western Europe before 1750. Yet things changed in a short span of two hundred years. How did these countries exceed China? There are two reasons. One is that they invented a corporate structure called the "joint-stock company" that combined laborers, resources, technology and capital to serve production goals. The other reason is that these joint-stock companies created a sound environment that fostered their existence and development, that is, the market economy. The Chinese people who aspire for national rejuvenation must equip ourselves with knowledge and push for the coordination of socialist modernization and the market economic system to prove the incomparable advantages of the socialist system.

The latest biological research shows that the human brain is developing rapidly. Thus, human knowledge appears to be getting more powerful. Techno-globalism is gaining pace, while independent innovation is becoming the decisive force in competition among countries. Intellectual property is changing the traditional rules of games and balance of power, becoming the greatest and most uncertain factor influencing the modernization of developing countries. It is obvious that the driving force of independent innovation comes from technology or the enhancement of a nation's soft power. The key to building an innovation-oriented country is for the people to be innovative, which is based on their improvement of knowledge. Therefore, we need to give full play to people's knowledge in achieving all-around development.[22]

To give people top priority, we need to rectify the developmental imbalance between urban and rural areas through knowledge and to uphold scientific development as a priority. The people-oriented development is not only the basis of social equity but also the source of efficiency. It is imperative for us to tap people's knowledge potential and foster creativity on the basis of their knowledge, thoughts and intelligence. In this way, we can make breakthroughs in the development of productive forces, realize comprehensive and coordinated social development and eliminate the negative influence caused by the misuse of technology.

In conclusion, the concept of governing the country by giving the people top priority integrates the humanistic thoughts of Marxism with the Chinese cultural traditions. It prompts us to combine the power of knowledge with the guiding thoughts of "science and technology as the primary productive force," "representing the development trend of China's advanced productive forces" and the "Scientific Outlook on Development." As Marx said,

> Needless to say, man is not free to choose his productive forces – upon which his whole history is based – for every productive force is an acquired force, the product of previous activity. Thus the productive forces are the result of man's practical energy, but that energy is in turn circumscribed by the conditions in which man is placed by the productive forces already acquired, by the form of society which exists before him, which he does not create, which is the product of the preceding generation.[23]

Be it a political party, an organization or a country or a people, it must keep up with the times and develop productive forces; or in other words, as intellectuals are becoming a part of the working class, the latter needs modern technology to maintain its leadership. Be it a political party, an organization, a country or a people, without knowledge, it cannot fully implement people-oriented policies in building a harmonious society. A harmonious society is one based on the emancipation of humanity and human's free development to realize the free and common development of the whole nation. A harmonious society must serve the fundamental interests of all people. It should be in line with man's three innate attributes with the enrichment of our knowledge as the ultimate goal.

Interpretation of the logics of common ownership

Common ownership is consistent with the logic of human intellectuality and decision-making and the socialist market economy. It is also in line with the development of ecological civilization, which coordinates the interests of different aspects and offers an effective institutional model to achieve common prosperity. With common ownership as the logical starting point, we can re-examine economic planning and markets, the system of democratic centralism, ecological civilization, urbanization and the utilization of resources. It is clear that common ownership is not for the people to trust any particular person and treat him as the savior but to let people trust in themselves, in human rationality and in the power of knowledge, thus being their own maters. It is just as the saying goes, "[P]eople, and only people, are the power that creates the history of the world."[24]

Market

The common ownership model does not acknowledge the objective existence of market. It argues that market is a not a being for itself but rather the fruit of human intellectual development and a way of sharing and exchanging knowledge. The sharing of knowledge among people forms a "network of markets." Knowledge is invisible; the products, inventions and other things we see are the fruits of knowledge. As Douglass C. North said in the book *Understanding the Process of Economic Change*, "The world we build and try to understand is the architecture of human mind. It cannot independently exist outside of the mind."[25] Like in mathematics, the market is a function of human knowledge, except that it is more complex than any model of natural science. "The specialization and division of labor as put forward by Adam Smith – the prerequisite for the development of market – is actually the specialization of knowledge."[26] This also confirms the functional relations between knowledge and market. The "invisible hand" behind market is actually the hand of knowledge. As an innate attribute of nature, knowledge is omnipresent in human society as the wealth shared by all people. This directly proves that the market economy is not an exclusive right of any specific social system. Neither capitalism nor socialism can do without the market. Just as Deng Xiaoping wisely pointed out, "The market is the means not the end, and both capitalism and socialism can take advantage of it." Our confidence in socialist market economy just derives from it, which balances and coordinates the centralized decision-making of socialism with decentralized decision-making of capitalism. Instead, a planned socialist economy runs counter to dialectical materialism. The result is the overemphasis on equity at the cost of efficiency. Yet what we want is to fully unleash the power of human knowledge, which is the decisive force of social economic development.

Planning and the market

The common ownership model views plan and market as the externalization of human knowledge. Decision-making is the choices of action made by man based on cognitive competence. The decision-making ability is ultimately determined by human knowledge. As an important form of the manifestation of knowledge, planning is a kind of centralized decision-making based on the macro-intelligent structure of a tiny minority of people. The quality of such decision-making depends on the quality of the macro-intelligent structure.

Why does the centralized decision-making system exist? The goal of this system is to gather the knowledge scattered throughout the minds of different people to make them serve the general objective of social development. At the same time, legal protections of scattered knowledge – or laws that protect intellectual property – are needed to boost knowledge growth. Just as Engels said, "The further removed men are from animals, however, the more their effect on nature assumes the character of premeditated, planned action directed towards preconceived ends."[27] At the second preparatory meeting for the Eighth CPC National Congress, Mao Zedong pointed out, "There are a lot of engineers and scientists among the members of the Central Committee. Yet I still think the Central Committee is a political rather than scientific committee."[28] This is probably one of the earliest remarks on macro-intelligent structure. On the other hand, market represents decentralized decision-making based on the knowledge of the majority of people, the essence of which is a system of knowledge and rules formed by people in understating the development of things. The "invisible hand" behind the market is actually the hand of knowledge. Therefore, the argument that "a free market" exists outside of human knowledge is groundless. Market frees individuals from the relations of dependence on authorities and power. Therefore, centralized decision-making features coordination, coherence and optimization, while decentralized decision-making features freedom, autonomy and initiative. Thus, from the perspective of knowledge-based decision-making, there exists the unity of opposites between the planned economy and the free market. Their respective share is dependent on the balance between the macro-intelligent structure and the average knowledge of society. It proves the rationality, feasibility and effectiveness of the path of a socialist market economy, which guides the development of a socialist market economy with Chinese characteristics. "The achievements made by China over the past 20 years pose a legitimate challenge to us (the Western society) on the understanding of the relations between the government and the economy."[29] Therefore, human knowledge reminds us to make good use of planning and guard against market fundamentalism.

The future of the world economy and social development are decided by two forms of decision-making: planning and the market. In the United States, where decentralized decision-making plays a dominant role, its capitalist market economy scored remarkable achievements. Though it puts individual interests above collective interests, the United States cannot achieve growth without accommodating the interests of the majority of the people. In countries like China, where centralized decision-making dominates, the socialist market economy excels in pooling resources to solve major problems. While seeking common interests, it might encounter difficulties in independent innovation. The different social systems are faced with similar challenges, for example, the gaps between the rich and the poor and among different social classes. To tackle these challenges, we need to strike a balance between the visible hand of economic planning and the invisible hand of the market. Imbalance will result in ill health of a society or even collapse of the social system.

Common ownership and ownership by the whole people

The essence of both public ownership and ownership by the whole people is common ownership. The two are different expressions in different contexts. The word *communism* derives from the French word "commum," meaning common. The core of communism is that the means of production are owned by the whole people, with the aim of breaking up the vicious cycle of poverty. The content of traditional public ownership and ownership by the whole people is not clearly defined, which is manifested in the fact that no common people possess any means of production. The right of ownership is transferred to the rulers, who thus virtually take possession of the means of production. The result is that people scramble for the right to control the means of production. That accounts for the mania of civil

servants' examinations in China. The Chinese citizens, who are the actual owners of the state assets, have no say on them, nor can they benefit directly from the
assets. The separation of ownership and right of control leads to the absence of
guardians of state assets, which breeds power-for-money deals. When the right of
control is misused, it becomes a hotbed for corruption. That is why it is hard to
treat either the symptoms or the roots of corruption. Therefore, common ownership offers a feasible option to ensure that people who control state assets act in
public interests and to prevent misuse of rights.

Common prosperity

Common ownership views common prosperity as a joint action. To build a society featured by equality, fairness and common prosperity, we need to falsify the
argument that personal gains reflect only the value of individuals. Rather, we
should take into consideration the productive forces based on social coordination.
There is no simple causal relationship between individual knowledge and economic growth. It is the sharing and integration of knowledge by an organization
or a country that improves productivity and boosts the economy rather than any
individual's knowledge. In other words, it is when an organization or a country
possesses the capability to transfer individual entrepreneurial impetus into a collective one that common prosperity can be realized.

Democratic centralism

The philosophies about common ownership assert that the essence of democratic
centralism is the ability to make choices and decisions by the people independently, with the decision-making ability reflecting their knowledge. Centralism is
an active process of unifying scattered decision-making under a macro-intelligent
structure, while democracy gives full play to the independent decision-making of
each individual and his or her knowledge. Therefore, centralism and democracy
are the unity of opposites. The development of democracy depends on society's
average knowledge. With the improvement of the common person's education
and knowledge, the balance of democratic centralism will have tilted in favor of
the socialist cause with Chinese characteristics, people's common interests and the
progress of human knowledge. As Tocqueville said, "Two kinds of people hurt
the people the most, those who oppose democracy and those who uphold radical
democracy." Only when we realize this point can we build a genuine democratic
culture without sliding into populism or totalism. The governance of a state is by
no means a simple choice between democracy and autocracy but more of a balance between freedom and centralism.

Finance sector

Thought around common ownership holds that the correct developmental direction of the finance sector is to achieve "financial inclusion and capital sharing,"

which means ordinary people have access to the reform in the financial sector. To rectify the imbalance caused by the unceasing pursuit of profit of capitalism and the huge negative effects, it is imperative to make innovation on the basic finance theory of socialist market economies and answer the question of how to reform the financial sector so that financial products can better integrate with the common people and help them share the benefits of financial development. If the finance market is exploited as a tool to "rob the poor to feed the rich," it will be a short-sighted approach ultimately hurting the society's overall interests. The wealth snatched through excessive financial leveraging has already impaired social development. The absolute control of labor by capital, the disproportionally high distribution of wealth toward capital owners and the lack of equal opportunity to success can, to some extent, be attributed to the lack of "financial inclusion and capital sharing" in the current finance sector. In the future, the financial system should develop into an integral whole accommodating for people's diverse demands for interests and serve as the bank of social wealth shared by all people.

Ecological civilization

The common ownership model features a more comprehensive understanding of an ecological civilization. Being green, low carbon and environmentally friendly characterize an ecological civilization, and we cannot build it without educating people. Therefore, the core of building ecological civilization is to improve the average knowledge of society. As argued at the beginning of *Doctrine of the Mean*, "What Heaven has conferred is called The Nature; an accordance with this nature is called The Path of duty; the regulation of this path is called Instruction." Education, in the real sense, is to enlighten people and serve the development of knowledge.

Urbanization

According to common ownership, urbanization is more than the forced changes in the farmer's living place, lifestyle or occupation. The process should be accompanied by progress in farmers' knowledge, for the essence of the gap between urban and rural areas lies in education. In a large country like China, where farmers still lack modern technology and knowledge, the potential risks of social instability and political unrest caused by accelerated urbanization cannot be underestimated. Farmers' knowledge growth should be an essential part of the new-type urbanization. The urbanization process cannot be completed if we fail to improve and enrich farmers' knowledge, even if their income grows.

Resources

The common ownership model also argues that we should redefine resources. It refuses the economic hypothesis of "scarcity of resources." The value of visible or tangible resources is a reflection of the invisible resources of human knowledge. As W. R. Ashby put it, "The number of elements in one set is not an intrinsic attribute of the set; to decide the number we need to first decide the observer and his observational ability."[30] Therefore, to free the mind and carry out reform and opening up, we must foster the growth of human knowledge to create a new knowledge-based value of resources. For instance, the reason why rare Earth minerals become a strategic resource can be attributed to the progress in science and technology and the growth of human knowledge.

The power of knowledge lies in that it can break from the traditional constraints of economies of scale. Knowledge, like sunlight, wind, seawater and air, can be found everywhere. The conflicts of interests caused by the centralized control of resources can be resolved when knowledge levels are well advanced. Knowledge will be the solution to problems caused by uneven distribution and depletion of non-renewable resources. In the future, the GDP will be redefined in accordance with the increment of knowledge.

The most valuable resources in China are the people, their knowledge, intelligence and wisdom, which are inexhaustible with immense potential. The Chinese are brilliant, and their innovative ideas are the source of the country's strength, like a treasure house waiting to be explored. Our confidence in China's development path, theory and system as well as the biggest dividends of social and economic development all derive from this source. In practice, the new type of productive relations created by common ownership is in line with the inner demand of knowledge growth and offers a system of knowledge coordination at the minimum cost.

Land

Thoughts about common ownership also hold that land is the foundation of a country. It is owned by the whole people. The land theories of J. S. Mueller and H. George and Marxism as well as the current Chinese land ownership system are all developed in accordance with such beliefs. It is rational to free the land and industrial capital from individuals and small interest groups and enable all the owners to share the rental and the added value. "Higher land value is the result of social and industrial progress, which is made possible through the efforts of all the people. Therefore, the benefits should be reaped by the whole people, instead of a small part of them."[31] "The value of the land does not equal the payment for production. . . . It represents the exchange value of monopoly. In no case is such value created by the people who occupy the land, but by the development of the society. Thus, the society can take back all the value."[32] The current market value of land, including the part of unearned growth, belongs to society as a whole, especially in a socialist country like China. If individuals are compensated in accordance with the market value of land, it would deem the unearned growth as private property, which is a blatant infringement of other owners' rights and goes against the fundamental principles of China's socialist system. In addition, the administrative system in China leads to the centralization of administrative power. The result is that various factors of production, life, medical care, education, politics and culture are highly centralized. In some major cities, such concentration, combined with the saturation of population and industry, raises the value of surrounding land, most of which is the high added value caused by irrational costs and artificially rare resources. However, the huge added value has become the privilege of a minority of farmers, stakeholders and property developers, which is unfair and leads to the income gap between the rich and the poor. Whether the added value belongs to the public or private owners, or should the interests created from "land development" be shared by the land owners, are questions facing the future of land reform. In fact, theoretical and pragmatic debates on these issues never cease. Therefore, the starting point of this book is to find a solution to the issue of sharing land added value while accommodating different interests. In reality, labor is isolated and land capital is not liquid, thus making it impossible to inject vigor into capital. The land trust system can serve as the legal foundation to achieve this goal.

"Common-ownership trust"

In capital operation, it is increasingly clear that the collectively shared trust is a new common-ownership mechanism that effectively accomplishes public ownership. Allowing the capital to run with 100 percent autonomy under tri-party separation of rights and powers, the collectively shared trust, based its cornerstone on "managing the trustor's finance on behalf thereof," generates the "common-ownership trust" mechanism, where productive forces and relations of production are adapted to the socialist market economy. The "common-ownership trust" mechanism is built upon bi-party separation of powers under the shareholding system, taking trust as the medium and credit as the foundation and highlighting advantages of trust, where the right to earnings also gains autonomy thanks to trust's innate nature – tripartite power separation. In this way, it achieves what's described by Karl Marx – "rebuilding individual ownership based on the common ownership of the means of production."

Embodying features of common ownership, the "common-ownership trust" socializes personal property, enables ownership diversity, clearly defines the rights of "communities of free individuals," and ensures universal gains in benefit sharing, all within a new legal framework. In this sense, the mechanism assimilates traditional models under public ownership. This explains why the property rights system represented by this mechanism is richer in content and supports more inclusive goals. As an intermediate institutional arrangement, the mechanism reconciles the tension caused by labor force and means of production, being both individually and socially possessed, balances fairness with efficiency, and properly takes care of equality and freedom to perfectly combine common ownership with the market economy. Also, the mechanism facilitates the development of a socialist market economy, ultimately leading toward common prosperity.

"Common-ownership trust"

Currently, the state-owned sector, the private sector, the individual sector and foreign capital develop hand in hand to boost China's socialist market economy, resulting in multiple coexisting types of ownership. Among these, all-people's ownership is actually equivalent to state ownership, and collective ownership is part of the socialist public-ownership economy, where a group of people occupy means of production all together. In contrast, common ownership combines international, state-owned, community and individual stakeholders and transcends regional and industry-specific boundaries. Such ownership features socialized individual property and represents a new model to realize public ownership under diversified yet clearly defined property rights.

Compared with all-people's ownership or collective ownership, a "common-ownership trust" mechanism takes public ownership as the fundamental mainstay and absorbs forms of economic activity under other ownership models, embracing a more inclusive property-right design that supports new structures under diversified property rights. The mechanism is innately aligned with the socialist market economy, assimilates the capitalist production mode and allows multiple types of property rights to coexist with each other in harmony – a brand-new production relation indeed! Besides, it reconciles the contradictions between socialism and a market economy, balances fairness and efficiency and patches up loopholes in traditional models of financial service, presenting a boundless intermediary institutional arrangement. This is how the "common-ownership trust," an effective way to achieve common ownership, combines common ownership and market economy, and revolutionizes the ownership structure.

"Common-ownership trust" as a new production relation

"Common-ownership trust" covers the capital market, monetary market and industrial market. It assimilates private production and private capital while transforming production modes and forms of capital. On the basis of large-scale socialized production, social production and social capital come to the fore against the premise that the means of production and labor force are centralized at a certain scope. As a result, personal property is socialized, and elements of property rights become more diverse, leading to more inclusive property rights. The mechanism represents a new production relation along the path of common ownership.

First of all, "common-ownership trust" socializes personal property and diversifies elements of property rights. The mechanism uses trust to gather scattered social funds, which are then integrated and optimized before being invested into various sectors of China's economy and society. In this way, funds become capital. The capital gathering here is not simply the sum total of public funds. Rather, according to Karl Marx, it is "no longer as the private property of individual producers, but as the common property of associates, as social property outright." In essence, trust capital guarantees that trust is personally owned on the one hand while highlighting common ownership on the other, where individuals cannot occupy and control all the capital. It means that trust capital gets separated from private property to become a direct part of society's common property. This is what Karl Marx described as "the abolition of capital as private property within the boundaries of capitalist production itself," which socializes personal property and expands space for society to occupy means of production against the premise of socialized owners. Trust capital ultimately gets manifested as diversified property-right elements.

Under a "common-ownership trust" mechanism, diverse property-right holders, mainly including the state, the community and individuals, merge within the legal framework. According to the *Trust Law of the People's Republic of China*, to establish a trust, there must be certain trust properties lawfully owned by the trustor, where the trustor is willing to transfer his or her property rights. The trustee manages and disposes of the trust property in its own name with the aim to maximize the benefits of the beneficiary. Throughout the operations, trust relies upon credit and is based on laws with the respective rights and obligations of the trustor, the trustee and the beneficiary clearly defined. And trustors' isolated idle funds get gathered into highly efficient social capital that harvests added values via the agents' management and operations. People's investment demand gets satisfied, even if they might have little professional investment knowledge and capability. In this way, economic development benefits all stakeholders.

Second, "common-ownership trust" is based on tripartite power separation, resulting in more inclusive property rights. Such inclusive property rights under common ownership can be interpreted from two perspectives: first, property rights are separated from the title of possession, which means separation between the title of possession and the management right; second, property rights become more open, which means property can flow freely and be gathered and traded freely throughout society. Practice has proven a "common-ownership trust" mechanism has all the conditions to achieve inclusive property rights under common ownership. The mechanism realizes liquidity in the rights to use and usufruct (the right to use and derive profit from a piece of property belonging to another). Based on clearly defined property rights, it integrates the state-owned sector, the community collective sector, the private sector and foreign capital to develop the economy. The mechanism provides space, capacity and structures that are necessary for multiple layers of productivity to develop. It holds more potential and more inclusive space than a mono production relation, allowing multiple property-right holders to stay hand in hand in a new pattern of diversified property-right holders.

"Common-ownership trust" as an intermediary institutional arrangement

"All are connected into a whole via intermediaries; all are linked via transition."[33] The "common-ownership trust" mechanism, with its function to "manage the trustor's finance on behalf thereof," is quite flexible and efficient as a system. The mechanism is an effective form for corporate governance in China and effectively combines common ownership and the market economy while bridging the latter with socialism.

Years of practice have verified that it doesn't suffice to effectively combine common ownership and the market economy if we only rely upon state-owned enterprises, community enterprises, shareholding systems or other similar forms that recognize common ownership. There must be innovative forms of ownership where propriety rights of the means of production are clearly defined. Also, modern corporate systems shall be established and improved; relations between the state and companies in terms of property rights should be properly adjusted, while individuals should be entitled to property rights. On such a basis, means of production being personally and commonly occupied are further clarified, that is, while clearly defined as being subject to personal entitlement, means of production are highlighted as being social. The "common-ownership trust" mechanism takes trust as the means and revolutionizes corporate property-right structures, socializing personal property and diversifying elements of property rights. Modern corporate systems are established, through which enterprises are restructured into legal persons (companies and corporations). The mechanism is definitely an effective way to realize common ownership.

Take state-owned enterprises as an example. Shortly after the founding of the People's Republic of China in 1949, state-owned enterprises made historic contributions, propping up China's economic development, fostering social stability and laying the foundation for China's industrialization. As the socialist market economy keeps developing in China, the mono-ownership structure has lagged behind in productivity and could no longer stay aligned with China's social development. Shortcomings of state-owned enterprises have come to light. First, there are neither clearly defined personified holders of property rights nor clearly drawn boundaries concerning property rights; second, under the centralized management system, enterprises themselves are generally subject to state administrative control and intervention. As a result, enterprises and government authorities are hardly independent from each other in practice, and fairness and efficiency couldn't be properly balanced. Should the "common-ownership trust" mechanism be adopted in state-owned enterprises, loopholes in state-owned enterprises could be effectively addressed to present clearly drawn boundaries, ensuring well-defined property rights among players in the market, where ownership holders and corporate property hosts are unequivocally identified. On the other hand, corporate governance structures can be naturally adjusted to clearly identify the legal rights and obligations of state-owned enterprises' trustors, trustees and beneficiaries so that corporations and government authorities become independent from each other, while the corporations remain state owned. This reduces state-owned enterprises' loss in efficiency and lowers the possibility of irrational decision-making. Also, the "common-ownership trust" mechanism would effectively enhance justice and awareness for alignment with laws and disciplines in private enterprises and optimize their financial structures. Via transformations in both state-owned and private enterprises, the mechanism materializes contracted-based property relations to effectively allocate resources, such as capital, knowledge, technology and human resources.

Therefore, the "common-ownership trust" mechanism isn't just a financial tool but also an intermediary institutional arrangement, a means to facilitate social development. The mechanism, with its flexibility and effectiveness as a system, addresses the most fundamental problem in China's socialist market economy in a comparatively sound manner. Via indirect fairness and indirect efficiency, the mechanism eases vulnerable groups' confrontational moods against the government, increases social harmony and effectively integrates common ownership with the market economy.

Philosophy underlying "common-ownership trust": the intermediary theory

Tri-party power separation under trust is in line with universal laws governing intermediary existence, development and changes. Tri-party power separation in property rights is internally connected with intermediaries, endowing trust with powerful financial, economic and social functions besides its role to keep property alive.

Philosophy underlying the intermediary theory

Hegel and Marx presented often in their classic discussions on intermediary theory. A dialectic view is that internal components and links of contradictions are at two mutually opposite sides or poles and are mutually linked in both affirmation and negation. Such polarity represents relations where beings are interconnected, influence each other and contain each other. Chains or circles that connect two opposite sides are intermediaries. Approached from perspectives of contradiction theories, intermediaries present their own internal links and evolutionary connections. In terms of the links, intermediaries are media generating indirect contacts between things. When it comes to evolutionary connections, intermediaries represent transitional stages or interspace in transformations between things. According to Hegel, "Limit is the mediation through which something and other each as well *is, as is not.*"[34] Hegel's intermediary theory illustrates what's meant by the intermediary theory in unity of opposites: intermediaries are circles or boundaries between two opposite poles. This is to say that what are between two poles are intermediaries. Intermediaries are interspace and transitional stages of mutual transformation or mutual negation. Transformation of polarity is achieved via intermediaries. The intermediary issue is also much discussed by Engels, "[A]ll differences become merged in intermediate steps, and all opposites pass into one another through intermediate links." Dialectics knows no clear-cut or unchanged boundaries, nor does it know unconditionally universal "either this or that." In dialectics, metaphysically fixed differences transit to each other; besides "either this or that" and "both this and that" are also recognized whenever it's proper. Also, intermediaries link opposite things up. "All are connected into a whole via intermediaries; all are linked via transition."[35] Chinese cultural classics, be it *The Book of Changes*, *Tao Te Ching*, or traditional Chinese medical theories, all shine in the glory of the intermediary theory. As long as methodologies and world views are concerned, the Chinese culture advocates views for dialectical intermediaries. This requires that any analysis shall take into consideration differences and contradictions between two opposite sides as well as the opposite sides' nature to be transformed into each other so as not to ignore the intermediary circles and stages that connect and fuse two opposite sides. It means intermediaries or intermediate circles are how things exist, which is a ubiquitously applicable law. One must become adequately exposed to the objective existence and roles of intermediaries; otherwise, it's difficult to know things in an all-round and objective manner.

Intermediaries are what connect things and what integrate things' evolutionary processes. Intermediaries are connective circles linking up two opposite poles in contradiction. Such connectivity exists objectively, where the objectivity originates in intermediaries' being intermediately connective, universal and direct. These characters of intermediaries determine the fundamental role of evolutionary processes. First, the essence of intermediaries is connectivity. Intermediaries are open channels through which two things connect and exchange information, energy and substances, where at the same time, the two contain each other in constant disintegration, updating and assimilating. Second, universality here means that intermediaries exist between two beings; they belong to both sides in contradiction and are the two sides' shared joints, derivatives and affiliates. Intermediaries have features of both sides in contradiction and can communicate with both sides. The mutual penetration and containment between the two sides in contradiction have an impact on intermediaries. Last but not least, directness means that intermediaries directly link up two sides in contradiction, where the two are directly transited via the intermediary. Intermediaries are direct causes for two contradictory sides to transform into each other, where the two sides generate direct and indirect links in coexistence. Transformation between two contradictory sides is realized via intermediaries, which means that direct links also contain indirect links. The two sides, besides influencing and containing each other, also exist in direct unity. Directness is a basic condition between things being intermediary and the intermediaries.

Intermediaries are very important transitional circles during transformations of contradiction. The opposing poles in contradiction get interconnected, blended and transformed via intermediaries. A fundamental view of materialistic dialectics is that all things are transited and evolve via links by intermediaries. Through intermediary circles, materialistic dialectics reveal the position and roles of laws governing things' evolution and changes. It is of theoretical and methodological significance in analyzing functions and roles of trust intermediaries within the framework of the dialectical intermediary theory which brings about theoretical and institutional confidence in a new way to explore the socialist market economy based on the joint-ownership trust mechanism.

Logic ties between tripartite power-separation trust system and the intermediary theory

The intermediary theory provides new paradigms in studying the efficiency of trust systems. The tripartite separation of powers in trust, together with the property-independence system, is logically tied to functions of the intermediary theory as well as to laws governing development. Such logical ties are in line with trust-concerned legal systems, property-right theories in modern economics and common-ownership theories, all of which give birth to and develop trust mechanisms and their accompanying functions while endowing trust with vitality. The tripartite power-separation system of trust presents modern cognition toward wealth, capital and knowledge. Essential nature and functions of the system are, in essence, logically tied to the intermediary theory.

JURISPRUDENCE UNDERPINNING THE TRIPARTITE POWER-SEPARATION
TRUST SYSTEM

The *Trust Law* constitutes the foundation of China's legal system concerning trust. Major stipulations in the law include:

- Trust's being established with legitimate goals, against well-defined trust property, and in written forms, besides being registered in line with laws.
- Trust-property articles, which stipulate legal characters of trust property's autonomy.
- Trustee articles, which stipulate trustees' obligations concerning honesty, faithfulness and prudence, outlining professional, dutiful, honest and credible property managers.
- Beneficiary articles, where beneficiaries, as established by trust activities between the trustor and the trustee, adequately enjoy benefits brought about by the trust property.

Modern trust is such a universal system arrangement that is innovative in generating values in terms of property transfer and wealth management. Features of trust reflect basic legal rules related to modern trust, which include power-benefit separation, property autonomy, continuous existence and so on.

According to the *Trust Law*, under trust as a property management system, property rights are further divided into nominal title of possession, actual title of possession and management rights, which are allocated to the trustor, the beneficiary and the trustee. The trustee enjoys the nominal title of possession to the property and therefore could manage, use and dispose of the trust property. The beneficiary enjoys the actual title of possession to the property and therefore is entitled to economic benefits generated by the property rights. Via trust arrangement, the property witnesses separated nominal title of possession and the management rights. Properties could transfer from a trustor to a trustee who has professional management capabilities. The trustee gives play to its professional capabilities to gather together properties, which are then effectively managed and subject to professional financing or investment. In this way, scale effects incurred by pooling, and wealth effects generated by professionalized management, as discussed in institutional economics, are realized, while property potentials get maximally released.

LOGIC TIES BETWEEN TRIPARTITE POWER-SEPARATION TRUST SYSTEM AND THE NEW
SYSTEM PROPERTY RIGHT THEORY

According to property right theories in the West, it might not be the most effective way to acquire economic benefits if an individual or an institution holds all
attributes of certain property and owns 100 percent of such property. Separating
an individual's or an institution's property into different attributes and allocating
such attributes to different holders, for example, allocating the title of possession,
the usufruct and the right of supervision, and other rights and privileges, to different managers and operators via certain systems, would generate higher economic
efficiency. The premise, however, is that there must be perfect system designs to
ensure that the separated title of possession clearly identifies relevant rights and
obligations in all circles of capital operations, including containment and limitation toward property managers of different natures. Different economic operation
patterns can emerge as a result of choosing a property owner's exclusive occupation or proper arrangements between different stakeholders, which enables higher
efficiency in resource allocation and distribution. It is such advantages that trust
mechanisms make the most of to highlight advantages enjoyed by trust institutions and financial institutions in allocating and distributing financial resources.
And trust companies are major drivers behind such advantages. These companies
turn financial resources that are not liquid into resources that are both liquid and
safe so that idle financial resources are channeled to areas where they are urgently
needed, which in turn promotes economic development.

Property rights theories are the theoretical basis of effective economic operation and manifestations of economic operation rules. Meanwhile, property rights
theories believe that property rights are a core element in economic operation
because property rights enable their holders to allocate and distribute resources.
Additionally, changes with the property right holder also have an impact on
resource allocation and distribution, resulting in changes in the direction and
amount of resource flows and in distribution of resource uses. Besides, property
status might even have an impact on the modulating mechanisms that determine
resource allocation and distribution. Highly concentrated property rights mean
that resource allocation and distribution are subject to planning, while dispersed
property rights mean that resources are allocated and distributed by the market.
The function of property rights in resource allocation and distribution is innately
coordinated with that of trust functions to separate property rights and reconstruct
the rights and benefits.

According to modern property rights theories, "under property-right systems,
residual claim and residual control rights of property rights complement each
other, limiting the free allocation and distribution of many a property right. Thus,
human activities involving property rights are not flexible."[36] Reputation systems establish implicit incentive mechanisms which prevent trustees from taking
short-term action. In resource allocation and distribution involving trust property,
"more pay for more work" mechanisms raise both the trust's and the whole society's efficiency. Through systems comprising trustors, trustees and beneficiaries,

trust separates the title of possession, the management rights and the usufruct of financial resources, which form "checks and balances" among the three rights in line with the internal mechanism for effective resource allocation and distribution. Through special system arrangements, trust alters the nominal owner of entitlement to the trust property, reconstructing rights of financial resources holders while optimizing knowledge increments in capital activities. Also, certain laws are in place to regulate the rights and obligations of trust stakeholders, which ensures safety of the financial resources. Such system design improves the liquidity of financial resources as well as efficiency in allocating and distributing such resources. Configuration of trust stakeholders' rights separates the residual claim and residual control rights.[37] Separation between the residual claim and residual control rights makes it possible for owners of the trust assets to gain and maintain the property's residual incomes.

LOGIC TIES BETWEEN TRIPARTITE POWER-SEPARATION THEORY OF TRUST AND THE "COMMON-OWNERSHIP TRUST" MECHANISM

Institution is a tool for effective resource allocation and plays a critical role in ensuring efficiency in resource allocation and distribution. To some extent, without proper institutional arrangement, it might not be possible that social resources get allocated and distributed efficiently; nor could the accompanying goals be realized. Previous analysis mentioned that the intermediary theory advocates universality, which is ubiquitous in evolution and development of intermediaries. Universality is the relation through which things transform into and coexist with each other. It's the foundation for things to evolve. Common ownership originates from the universality of human knowledge. In essence, the ownership sets the least hindrance to knowledgeable application and allows minimum cost. The "common-ownership trust" theory is logically unified with the uniqueness of trust systems. Trust systems, which are bankruptcy proof and allow property autonomy as well as property-right separation, are theoretically consistent with common ownership. In this sense, common ownership is quite aligned with trust systems, which turn economic systems that vaguely define property rights into more feasible forms of common ownership. This is done by merging finance and trust as well as merging society and trust under common ownership theories. Such an arrangement presents flexible financial tools, which gather idle financial resources for social development. Meanwhile, under common ownership, without changing the state's status as a beneficiary, trust-based relations channel state-owned, monopolized resources to economic players at all levels to optimize resource distribution and allocation, which allows all the citizens to benefit from interests gained by the state. Trust, based on credit and trustworthiness, effectively combines finance with property management systems and legal systems and allocates financial resources more efficiently. Via financial operations, trust allows the means of production to be owned jointly as well as by individuals at the same time. Via socialized trust, a contribution-based, income-sharing mechanism will ultimately lead to a public ownership where all citizens share the state's interests.

Value of trust's intermediary function: boundless service

Trust vitalizes economy by promoting social well-being, public benefits and economic relations adjustment. The advantage of trust in financing and investment is mainly attributed to its intermediary functions and wide range of business patterns, including stock rights, creditor's rights, equity trust, and so on. Meanwhile, trust allocates resources across different cycles, covering the monetary market, capital market and industry market. Such effective and innovative functions optimize the arrangement of a large amount of social resources and channel such resources into promising industries that generate higher rates of earnings.

OPERATION MECHANISMS THROUGH WHICH TRUST INTERMEDIARIES FACILITATE
ECONOMIC GROWTH

Trust intermediaries function mainly by influencing internal mechanisms for economic growth. First, they create liquidity. In line with the intermediary theory, trust intermediaries transform ways to distribute and allocate resources via innate creativity. Such asset transformation embodies liquidity creation. Trust intermediaries provide services targeted at asset transformation to allow asset portfolio managers to select portfolios in line with risks and profitability in the market. Second, trust intermediaries hold functions that are endogenous (i.e., developing or originating internally). The trust intermediary theory and trust intermediaries are mainly based on analysis concerning information asymmetry and transaction costs. By introducing endogenous market transactions, trust intermediaries take advantage of economies of scale in its financial functions to improve efficiency in allocating and distributing financial resources. More importantly, trust intermediaries satisfy diverse demands in personal asset management and save the cost for individuals to make investment decisions. Plus, via special arrangements, costs for supervision during this process also decrease. Trust intermediaries enjoy advantages in the sense that effects of economies of scale can help lower costs that should have been shouldered by dispersed investors who search for investment opportunities. Trust intermediaries gather together financial needs and process them in a professional manner so that cost for processing information concerning financial demand is reduced, which in turn improves the efficiency for financial demand to transform deposits into investment. The trust intermediary theory expands the boundaries of financial functions to cover new trust businesses in its analysis.

THE COMPREHENSIVE-FUNCTION VIEW TOWARD TRUST INTERMEDIARIES:
EMBODYING VALUES OF BOUNDLESS SERVICES

Intermediary functions of trust dramatically expand the vision of economic theories and push forward research on trust intermediary theories to a new level. Trust intermediaries provide customer-tailored trust products in line with diversified demands in the market place, including products targeted at investors with special financial needs. Trust intermediaries create innovative products to explore new markets while increasing transactions of existing products. Trust companies enjoy professional advantages in property management that cannot be matched by other financial institutions. Moreover, the systematic structures of trust eliminate transaction costs that could have incurred by property-right separation, increasing efficiency of financial resource allocation and distribution. Property-right agency and management agency get separated, and public investors manifest their title of possession and their usufruct via them. Intermediary functions of trust in financial resource allocation can also be illustrated in the following two points:

First, we must consider risk management and participation cost in connection with trust intermediaries. Risk management has long been a core business of financial intermediaries. As financial business expands and derivative trust products emerge, trust intermediaries substantially strengthen their function in risk management. Risk management has become a key function that enables financial intermediaries, including trust institutions, to survive and develop. Trust institutions manage risks mainly through inter-temporal smoothing of risk. Since the market is volatile, customers of trust intermediaries, especially corporate customers, hold great demand for risk-management services, which trust intermediaries are called upon to provide. Trust institutions, as agents for asset transaction and risk management in the financial market, maintain and increase values of trust assets against the premise of safely managing the trust assets. Trust reduces the time market stakeholders need to take for risk management and the corresponding decision-making. Besides, since financial innovation, financial tools and financial transactions are increasingly complex, professionals from sectors other than finance find it more difficult to learn about risks in transactions or to manage such risks. Trust institutions help investors lower the research costs and enhance their ability to manage assets. More frequently, risks are managed via trust intermediaries in ways including:

1. Asset diversification for lowering risks, where asset collections are created via dynamic transaction strategies.
2. Businesses concentrate on risk trading as well as binding and separation of various risks involving financial contracts.

As the financial markets expand both in depth and width, trust intermediaries embrace increasingly powerful functions and play more significant roles. It's no exaggeration to think that modern trust intermediaries are service institutes for risk management and risk transition.

Second, let us examine value creation and customer orientation in connection with trust intermediaries. In essence, value creation refers to the initiative to save a certain kind of transaction fees to bring about a certain form of value. Trust intermediaries themselves gain profits via providing customers with comprehensive financial services. By innovating on financial products and transforming risks, time limits, scales, locations and liquidity, trust intermediaries provide customers with value-added financial services. Therefore, value creation is the driving force behind modern trust intermediaries' development. Value creation naturally occurs as a result of progressive increase in trust intermediaries' professional incomes in deepening labor division. At the same time, the intermediary theory of trust enhances dynamics in financial innovation and the accompanying market differentiation. Trust intermediaries act as agents (trustees) between the investors (the trustors) and the beneficiaries to reduce impact brought about by market uncertainties. They also enable value creation by providing a wide range of trust services to improve efficiency and to expand financial services. Customer orientation is a basic strategy of trust intermediaries. Reducing customers' transaction costs and information asymmetry is a key function of them.

Carrier of trust's intermediary function: comprehensive financial service supplier

Financial functions exist – in essence – to lower the transaction costs or to create values, which embody people's demand for higher efficiency in allocating financial resources. Trust systems feature autonomous assets, risk isolation, property right separation and right reconstruction, and so on. Such system design brings advantages not only in terms of property management but also in the sense that its derived financial functions, economic functions and social functions all facilitate sustainable economic development in China.

TRUST INTERMEDIARIES: COMBINING INDIRECT FINANCING AND
DIRECT FINANCING

Generally, there are two functions of trust in terms of direct financing. One is that trust intermediaries allow direct financing via financial businesses such as securities business. The other is the equity-financing pattern of trust. Both are innovative and extended functions of trust intermediaries. For higher efficiency in allocating financial resources, trust intermediaries naturally appear in areas calling for direct financing. As labor division deepens and systems evolve, transaction-cost structures and business models change accordingly. Trust, by playing roles in direct financing, develops functions of finance and allocates financial resources at a higher efficiency.

In the financial market, indirect financing exists because intermediaries exist. Indirect financing is a most basic activity by, and an innate feature of, trust institutions. As agencies for indirect financing and investment covering the monetary market, capital market and industrial market, trust institutions provide comprehensive finance services, including deposits agreements, credit agreements, reverse repurchase agreements, reverse repurchase agreements and other services. Trust also offers modern financial products such as pension funds or pension-fund contracts and so on. Traditionally, trust institutions fulfill three functions: temporal mediation, scale mediation and derived financial functions as institutions for indirect financing. They also enjoy advantages in terms of system design, human resources, technology and management. These institutions are not only intermediaries for indirect financing but also agencies for direct financing and non-finance activities. They have advantageous resources at their disposal. For example, commercial trust intermediary institutions effectively combine direct financing and indirect financing during transformations of financial products and deposits into investments, which transcends traditional categories of direct financing and indirect financing.

Trust intermediaries integrate indirect financing with direct financing. In the context of socialized production, social production and social deposits are transformed into investments which flow from where they are in excess to where they are in shortage to satisfy demand for financing. In indirect financing, trust intermediaries provide liability products such as trust loans, redemption for sale, fixed buying back and beneficial-right trusts and so on to channel funds from where they are in excess to the investors (i.e., to transform deposits into investment). In the financial market, trust companies make the most of the trust system's functions in isolating risks and reconstructing rights and implement stringently effective risk-control measures concerning trust products' investment strategies, portfolios, risk isolation and investment target area selection as well as the trading structure, credit-enhancement means and income structures. They transform deposits into investments by giving full play to trust's advantages in its flexibility, diverse tools and unique system design. Therefore, even defined narrowly, modern trust intermediaries are ubiquitous throughout the financial system, covering both direct financing and indirect financing. As implied in its definition, trust intermediaries can work as investment agents (for governments, investors and companies) to conclude transactions in direct financing and ensure effective allocation of resources in the financial market.

TRUST PRODUCT: MICRO CARRIERS OF TRUST INTERMEDIARIES

Economic functions are laws that enable a higher efficiency in resource distribution by lowering transaction costs. Innovative trust businesses fulfill the economic functions of finance. Trust is a set of economic functions and intermediary functions gathered through trust products, which meet requirements concerning fund safety, liquidity and profitability. Roles of trust intermediaries are not unchanged. As structures of trust products change and transaction costs rise or decline, trust products change their economic functions to stay aligned with the demand for financial products in different times. Intermediary functions of trust mainly include temporal mediation, scale mediation, fiduciary incentive and monitoring.

Temporal mediation means that trust intermediaries can modulate different preferences concerning expenditures and financing time spans between the financing stakeholders and the trustees. Suppose that the investor (the trustor) wants to do a short-term investment, but the trustee has a long-term investment plan. In such a case, trust institutions enable temporal mediation, where they borrow on short terms for long-term loans, so that both the investor and the trustee can be satisfied. Compared with direct transactions between borrowers and depositors, temporal mediation has more advantages regarding the system design, human resources, technology, managerial expertise, and so on. Trust intermediaries provide trust products of different time spans, such as trust loans, trade financing, equity investment and asset-backed securitization. They increase the efficiency for deposits to be transferred for investment and enable more efficient allocation of financial resources, both with their function in temporal mediation.

Scale mediation means that trust intermediaries can play a role in transforming fund resources of different scales before using them. This function can be illustrated as follows. On the one hand, trust intermediaries can provide trust products to gather idle small-scale financial resources from society and use these resources in line with specific financing demand. On the other hand, trust intermediaries gather and effectively allocate the funds in line with diversified financing demands in the market. Investment businesses collect scattered investment opportunities and adopt corresponding operation models by means of financial tools. Examples include fund-raising for small-amount loans issued to individuals and small or medium-sized enterprises. These intermediary agencies give play to their function of scale mediation. Temporal mediation and scale mediation are together known as asset transformation and configuration. What trust-intermediary theories emphasize is the function of trust for asset transformation.

Fiduciary incentive and monitoring means that trust intermediaries, as the fiduciary, work on behalf of trustors to monitor, and provide incentives to, the financing stakeholders. The function for information generation means that trust intermediaries play a role in addressing information asymmetry beforehand, while fiduciary monitoring means that trust intermediaries play a role in addressing information asymmetry afterward. From the perspective of contract economics, the trustor-agent relation between trust intermediaries and their clients are in fact a contract-based relationship, where faith and confidence play key parts. Financing stakeholders are key beneficiaries. Between the trust institutions and investors (trustors), trust institutions are the trustees. Aims of the beneficiaries and the trustors are not totally aligned. Trustors cannot directly monitor what's taking place. Yet they must supervise the beneficiaries to monitor them and provide incentives to make them act in line with the trustors' interests. Supervision by trust intermediaries are proven effective in reality. It is realized by trust institutions' monitoring over the financing stakeholders. Besides, trustors (the investors) also monitor the trust institutions, that is, the trustees. As they expand, trust institutions would pay the trustors as has been committed in the trust contracts, if they substantially supervise financing stakeholders that have made their commitments. Should they fail to conduct such substantial supervision, trust institutions would suffer from non-monetary punishment or even bankruptcy. It's believed that long-term commitment mechanisms can help reduce moral hazards among investors, managers and beneficiaries.

Trust intermediaries are the only sort of institution that simultaneously covers the monetary market, capital market and industrial market. Modern trust intermediaries enjoy unique advantages that facilitate transformation of deposits into investment, which cannot be paralleled by other financial institutions. In financial systems with separate operation, separate supervision or mixed operation, intermediary functions of trust are fulfilled by trust companies, which can invest in industries or purchase shares and commercial credit of other companies. By this way, trust intermediaries are enabled to function as companies that participate in deposit business. On such a ground, modern trust intermediaries are a comprehensive financial tool for both direct financing and indirect financing. As labor division, technology and systems evolve, modern trust intermediaries get more involved in direct financing, such as asset management or wealth management. Meanwhile, they get more engaged in intermediate businesses that are not directly linked with deposit-fund transformation, intermediary investment and so on, along with businesses that can be labeled as direct financing or self-investment. From another perspective, other financial institutions have also come to participate in activities involving trust intermediaries.

Institutional advantage of "common-ownership trust" mechanism: following the development path of common ownership

China adopts a developmental path of a socialist market economy on the premise of common ownership and takes common prosperity as the supreme goal, which is also regarded as the "greatest common ground" of socialist market economy. Therefore, we believe that common prosperity is the supreme and sole goal for common ownership, and achieving common prosperity is a must.

It is believed that a "common-ownership trust" mechanism is an effective form of achieving common ownership. A "common-ownership trust" helps clarify rights and grants shared and general benefits in communities of free individuals, which conforms to a socialist system and the principles of a market-oriented economy. With fairness and efficiency in hand, this mechanism reconciles contradictions between individual and common ownership in terms of labor forces and means of production. A "common-ownership trust" integrates common ownership with a market-oriented economy and defines the independence of the labor force and means of production ownership. With contribution rate-based capital sharing, financial inclusion and common prosperity will be achieved. This kind of institutional arrangement fully complies with the path of a socialist market economy and the principles of common ownership.

Clarify the attribution of trust ownership and achieve capital sharing by the people

Ownership is a legal concept and a legal expression of the possession of property. With the development of a market economy, ownership is gradually replaced by property rights, which means that ownership, as well as the right of possession, management, disposal, rights to earnings and other rights, constitutes a kind of property right with tradability and complexity through laws and contracts. Property rights lay a foundation for the development of a "common-ownership trust" mechanism. In the process of a market economy's development, it goes through three phases: product socialization, labor socialization and property socialization, among which the third one is a fundamental mark of a socialist market economy, the cornerstone of achieving common ownership and the beginning of common prosperity. A "common-ownership trust," based on property rights socialization, further defines attribution of ownership and optimizes distribution patterns to accomplish capital sharing by the people. It genuinely reflects a socialist market economy and follows the path of common ownership, which makes it "the primary form of social ownership system" that Karl Marx expected.

Defining the attribution of trust ownership which clarifies rights onto communities of free individuals. Trust is featured with separation between ownership and of management rights, between ownership and rights to earnings, and between management rights and rights to earnings. The trustor entrusts his money to the trustee by agency. The trustee then turns money into efficient social capital, and the trustor, through the trust products he holds, empowers the beneficiary to enjoy capital earnings based on laws. Ownership of trust comes from the trustor. As a trust relationship is built, the trustee "holds" trust, which means the trustor enjoys ultimate ownership, while the trustee has legal ownership. The trustor has no right to occupy, use, dispose of or get profits; instead, the trustor stimulates effective trust management and avoids abuse of rights through holding the trust, transferring and trading off. The trustee has management rights, while the trustor and beneficiary are not involved in any specific operation or management.

Attribution of trust ownership doesn't change as trust ownership is a kind of common property based on individual ownership. The trustor exercises his rights by "voting with feet" to ensure the mobility of trust assets and grasp open-ended property rights while beneficiaries share rights and interests of social capital investment. In the process of trust capital operation, the attribution of trust ownership doesn't change, which reflects separation between property rights and ownership. This mobilizes initiatives of different ownership and ensures coexistence of diverse ownerships.

Combining diverse distribution forms achieves capital sharing by the people. In trust relationships dominated by diversified property rights, the trustor possesses a double identity of labor and trust owner, while the trustee represents both labor and trust manager and the beneficiary both labor and trust beneficiary. The combination of distribution based on labor and distribution on the basis of means of production demonstrates that the trustor is a capital owner in a socialist market economy. This kind of combination protects the trustee's position as a capital user in this economy and clarifies the beneficiary's position of enjoying capital benefits in socialist market economies to provide necessary property guarantees for workers to achieve common prosperity and share economic gains.

The trustor gains income based on his ownership of the labor force that is consistent with his contribution. He also obtains earnings by ownership of trust assets. Thus, a unification of multiple distribution forms with distribution on the basis of labor as the principal means is reached in a trust. All these motivate the trustor's enthusiasm and encourage the public to invest more into trusts to increase asset mobility and enhance resource allocation efficiency. By taking advantage of efficient consulting systems and professional knowledge, the trustee has the right to use trust capital and share earnings to achieve distribution on the basis of labor. The beneficiary enjoys the right to earnings in accordance with laws. Trusts collect the scattered money of trustors to form an efficient trust asset to ensure capital appreciation, narrow the gap between the rich and the poor, ease social conflicts, balance fairness and efficiency, ensure social stability and security, realize shared interest and finally make people enjoy benefits from trusts.

Give full play to economic value of trusts to grasp financial inclusion

The economic value of a "common-ownership trust" mechanism is that as a new productive relation, "common-ownership trust" plays an important role in the socialist market economy. Through institutional arrangement, we can build a business operation platform of financial trust, reconstruct and optimize the investment system to enhance mutual trust, and improve management efficiency of capital use. It also helps strengthen vulnerable risk-prevention systems, raise funds from diversified channels to nurture rural development, and allow trusts to play a unique role in financial capital management and fund-raising as well as in taking full advantage of comprehensive finance service providers. It can also alleviate capital shortages that are caused by running off of agricultural capital and credit reluctance of mainstream financial institutions by introducing "common-ownership trusts" into agriculture. The CITIC Grassland Agricultural Fund is an exemplary case in this regard. This program is designed to serve agriculture, farmers and rural areas as well as animal husbandry, herdsmen and pasture areas. It uses trusts to design a comprehensive approach to address rural capital source and operation issues. The trust company, as the trustee, gathers idle money in rural areas to conduct process management. This program is beneficial to improve local financial systems. It makes the rural financial market more stable and well organized, helps herdsmen and small and medium-sized enterprises have better access to loans, channels capital into rural and less-developed regions and thus facilitates development of a new socialist countryside to achieve financial inclusion.

Rebuild individual ownership and balance fairness and efficiency
to reach common prosperity

Karl Marx proposed to "rebuild individual ownership" in the first volume of his book *Das Kapital*, which means to realize collective property rights based on individual ownership of the means of production. The essence of common ownership is to "rebuild individual ownership" and demonstrate an effective combination of a general property owner, socialized means of production and inclusive benefit sharing. It facilitates social harmony and balances fairness and efficiency in realizing both common prosperity and maximum economic benefits.

"Common-ownership trust," as a new mechanism in a socialist market economy, turns personal property into social property to accomplish capital sharing by the people based on social ownership of the means of production. It also rebuilds united individual ownership that is able to reconcile the contradictions between fairness and efficiency and finally reaches common prosperity. In terms of fairness, trusts working as a cushion can directly ease social conflicts with indirect fairness and efficiency. It's a better way to introduce trusts where conflicts are tense to address social problems in a proper manner, alleviate tension between the public and government and strengthen social trust and harmony.

In terms of efficiency, the trustor, trustee and beneficiary, on the basis of their contracts, constitute a property relationship that is protected by law. This kind of financial service relationship combines capital, knowledge, technology and human resources to maximize benefits. In terms of reaching common prosperity, trust turns a personal asset into a social one and rebuilds individual ownership to make people share capital based on social ownership of the means of production. In the process of production socialization, trust makes contracted and marketed capital. Ordinary people have access to investment and own trust capital. With this kind of socialization of property and capital ownership, they can enjoy the fruits of reform and opening up and finally reach common prosperity.

Common ownership of land

Human intellectual enlightenment comes from land in a broad sense. The observation of land and experience gained from it initiates human practices and knowledge accumulation. We start from here to analyze the concepts and connotations behind land, clarify land ownership structures and derive the objectives and innovative principles of land circulation.

Land

Land is the source of human production and survival as well as humanity's basic knowledge. It provides the basic condition for humans to survive and multiply and offers means of production and livelihood directly or indirectly. Land is connected with human life and survival closely. It is the most fundamental condition for different stakeholders to share interests with each other, so land has been the focus of research for economists throughout history into the present day. However, due to limitations of the times, knowledge and economic development levels, economists have different understandings of land in different times. This book, based on the natural and social logic of land, reviews the history of land study and explores the connotations of land and extension through the perspectives of philosophy and economics.

The basic properties of land include material, social and intellectual natures. Material nature is the basis of land, social nature is the state of land, and intellectual nature (i.e., to apply knowledge to land) is the integration of land and humanity, which is the essential property of land.

Material nature

Materiality is the way that land exists; simply put, materiality is the form of physical substance. The physical entity may be formed by the natural factors or by the power of knowledge or by the combination of the two factors. Currently, the word *land* generally refers to land surfaces, except oceans, in academic circles. The land surface here is the product of natural factors. In fact, land is formed and shaped by both natural factors and human knowledge. The land entity is composed by many natural elements of the land surface, such as climate, biology, soil, geology, landform, hydrology and other natural forces (all these elements are natural objects on the land), and economic and social elements, such as buildings, roads, bridges, underground pipelines, and other manmade structures (these elements are land improvements, land attachments or fixed objects, generally known as land capital). All these elements together combined make what we refer to as land. To put it simply, land is the integration of natural resources. Compared with air, water, living things and mineral resources, land is the most fundamental to human survival. Chrestim from Australia and others called land a "real resource." Being a resource is the main property of land because it can be used to meet human needs and improve living conditions. As a "real resource," land has the following basic characteristics:

INTEGRITY

Land is the synthesis of climate, soil, hydrology, geology, land formation, living things and human activities. All these elements are interdependent and related, forming a complete resource ecosystem. If human beings change one kind of resource or a part of the ecosystem, the surrounding environment will also be changed. At the same time, the ecosystem is not isolated, and the changes of one system will inevitably affect others.

PRODUCTIVITY

Land has productivity, which means it can produce animal and plant products that humans need. This is an essential characteristic of land. Land productivity can be divided into natural productivity and labor productivity. The former is its natural property. Land with different characteristics such as light, heat, water, gas and nutrients are adaptable to different plants and animals. The latter is a result of human influence, which has the following forms: to overcome land constraints, to change the land and to use it in an intensive way.

LIMITED AREA

Due to space restrictions of land surface, land area is limited. Although there may be small changes of land area because of natural disasters, the changes are usually small and hardly noticed. However, humanity only has one Earth, and the land surface is limited. As the world's population is increasing dramatically, there is fierce competition for land use, which poses tremendous pressure on land resources. Thus, we must cherish every inch of land and use it rationally. Besides, we must take effective measures to control population growth to reduce population pressure on land.

Land is distributed in different parts of the world, occupying particular geographic spaces. This feature is mainly reflected in the following aspects.

1. There is a fixed location of each piece of land (longitude and latitude), including land surface and underground space.
2. The distance between pieces of land is fixed. Of course, traffic conditions may change it to some extent. When traffic conditions are set, the distance between pieces of land is fixed.
3. Composed by environment and substance, each piece of land is fixed in general conditions. For example, it is impossible to change the environment and substance composition of arable land in different hydro and thermal circumstances.

The landform distribution has regional features. For example, the landforms, including mountains, hills, plateaus and plains, are distributed unevenly in China and the world. Thus we must understand the geographical features very well to use land according to its local conditions.

There is also the principle we could call "time variability." Land not only has regional differences but also changes as time goes by. For example, land changes in different seasons, in which plants and animals breed, grow and die; soil freezes and thaws; rivers flood in specific seasons. All of these affect the inherent properties of land and its production capacity. Time variability is closely related with land location as land in different locations has different changes in its energy and substance.

We must also consider renewable and non-renewable features of land resources. Resources are generally divided into two types – renewable and non-renewable. Renewable resources mainly refer to ecosystems composed by living things and nonliving things, and they can be constantly updated and used in a sustainable way if managed and maintained properly. Non-renewable resources such as minerals and fossil fuels will gradually deplete as human use of these resources increase.[38] As a complete ecosystem, land is renewable. In land systems, the living things on land continue to grow and die, and nutrition in the soil is constantly consumed and replenished. This is a replacement cycle. The replacement is relatively stable under certain conditions. Land also has the capacity to purify pollutants. It is just because land is renewable that human beings can multiply. Yet, it should be noted that renewable land doesn't mean that human beings can exploit it in a predatory way. Once the balance of the ecosystem is destroyed, land degradation will occur, resulting in soil erosion, swamping, salinization and/or desertification. As a result, land productivity and usage value decline. When the degradation reaches a certain level, the inherent properties of land may be completely destroyed and cannot recover any more. Especially in harsh natural environments, it's very difficult to renew the land, and it makes ecosystems very vulnerable.

Intellectual nature

Human beings change the natural properties of land. Land is increasingly becoming a product of human labor, evolving from a simple natural object to an economic and social synthesis. In this process, human beings manage the land effectively by applying knowledge, so the land becomes a type of capital. Therefore, we say "to apply knowledge to land." It can be reflected in two aspects: first, human beings exploit the land to gain economic benefits by applying knowledge; second, the land itself has economic benefits in the future.

In the early times, human beings were in the initial stages of applying knowledge to land, and their relationship with land was manifested in exploiting, depending upon and adapting to it. With the improvement of productivity, human beings are engaged in all kinds of social production and living and management activities, leaving the natural ecosystem with human wisdom. As a result, the original natural ecosystem gradually becomes an artificial one. Based on this, land evolves from a purely natural state into the integration of knowledge and natural resources. Relying on knowledge, human beings constantly develop and use land to produce land products (arable land, gardens, etc.). Because of its intellectual nature, land is no longer a simple natural object but becomes a labor product with the same sort of labor based on natural objects. Therefore, land has changed from worthless land into valuable land. Marx pointed out, "A cultivated field is worth more than an uncultivated one of the same natural quality."[39] It is because of the intellectual nature of land.

First, land can be reshaped. Although land is not renewable, its physical properties, chemical structures and landforms can be changed by using knowledge. For example, we can enhance the carrying capacity of a soft foundation through physical or chemical means and develop land into building lots by land formation, building roads and providing access to water and electricity. Thus land can be reshaped based on the intellectual nature of human beings. By applying knowledge to land, land can be developed and improved, increasing its use value. Humans' improper land development leaves great room to increase land value.

Second, we must examine the historical accumulation of the intellectual nature of land. Marx believed, "Proprietorship of land parcels by its very nature excludes the development of social productive forces of labor, social forms of labor, social concentration of capital, large-scale cattle-raising, and the progressive application of science."[40] Here, "the progressive application of science" contains knowledge accumulation. Land, by integrating knowledge and technology, can create new use value which is sustainable, renewable and cumulative. Long-time human work on the same piece of land can change it from wilderness into arable land and then expand the land's scope to use it for transportation, business and other functions. In the land development process, due to the negative impact of knowledge, human beings develop many land products that go against nature, destroy ecological balance and even impede economic and social development, such as land reclamation and deforestation. This phenomenon only implies the negative impacts caused by knowledge but does not deny the historical accumulation of knowledge.

Third is the increase of land value. After being a part that helps build human society, land becomes the synthesis of nature, society and economy. As more and more people apply knowledge to land, land gradually becomes a human labor product. Therefore, the land has intrinsic value. As Marx said, uncultivated land has no value because no human labor is materialized in it, and the nature of materialized labor is knowledge. The source of land value is human labor. Here human labor not only includes materialized labor in forms of tangible substance that the owner of the land inputs, such as the investment of fertilizer, agricultural goods, steel, cement and other building materials, but also includes the labor of participants. In the labor, besides the general sense of physical labor (such as land surveys, construction, etc.), the input of intellectual labor (such as land use planning, land development, design and management) also accounts for a certain proportion. With the development of productive forces, technology and management play an increasingly important role in economic activity. [41] We can see that knowledge affects land value, and land value has impact on knowledge input again. The two elements are complementary and present land value together.

Social nature

Social nature reflects social relations of land. That is the relationship between different parties in land use, circulation and protection. In reality, the social nature of land is demonstrated in four aspects: land history, externality, land ownership and asset attributes.

First is the historical feature of land. The history of land is the history of human society. As productivity rises, humans continue working. Thus land has changed from a wilderness into labor products such as arable land, land for transportation and other uses. Land, as a labor product, is different from other products because its value doesn't derive from one-time labor input but persistent labor inputs. Thus the land has a historical feature.

The land history theory can be put into practice. This means human beings can continue developing and using land based on knowledge. So we say land has a past, a present and a future. In this process, knowledge has negative and positive impacts.

Due to the negative impact of knowledge, human beings develop a large area of land that goes against nature and destroys ecological balance, such as land reclamation and deforestation. Therefore, the negative impact of knowledge makes human labor in vain, while correct knowledge makes human labor effective and ensures the sustainable development of land.

Second, there is externality of land. Land development is not an independent process but will be influenced by the surrounding land development. This is so-called land externality. Externality has positive and negative factors. Positive factors are conducive to increasing land value, such as road building and improving traffic conditions in some areas. It will increase the land value in this area. For example, a piece of commercial land will increase its value because of clustering economic benefits brought by the development of its surrounding land. The value of a piece of residential land will be increased because of the improvement of its surrounding environment. On the contrary, negative factors will reduce its value. For example, a residential area will reduce its value because of its surrounding environment deterioration caused by building a slaughterhouse or a pesticide field. Thus more cost and labor have to be invested to improve the living environment of this area.

The externality of land shows that humans should properly handle the external factors in land development to increase land value and eliminate the negative impacts that reduce land value.[42]

Third is land property rights. The core of land social relations is land ownership or land property rights. Land property rights are the rights for land owners or users to possess, use and dispose of land and get revenue from it according to laws and regulations. It is not limited to the land surface but includes space above the land and underground at a certain depth. Initially, land ownership has been conceptualized as a "pancakes technique," which means that land rights start from a centrosphere and extend outward boundlessly, through the land surface to outer space, until the end of the sky. Therefore, land owners have mineral rights, air rights and light rights.

In a commodity society, land, with dual connotation of resources and assets, cannot exist independently without ownership.[43] What we trade or circulate on land or property markets is not only physical land but also the right to use or ownership or other rights.

Land ownership in the world can be divided into fourteen types. (See Table 2.1.)

Table 2.1 Different forms of land ownership in different countries and regions in contemporary times[44]

Forms of land ownership	Main features	Countries and regions
Ownership by the whole people and the state	Land is owned by the whole people of the country, and the state is the representative of its people to own the land. The whole people, collectives, organizations, enterprises and individuals are entitled to land use.	Socialist countries: mainland China, North Korea, Vietnam, etc.
Ownership by the state and central government	Land is owned by the state, which is the central government, and administered and used by the central government. Local governments need to pay for land use.	Japan and New Zealand
Ownership by the state and governments at all levels	State ownership, which is ownership by a central government and local governments at all levels. The state has ownership, and provincial, municipal and county governments have usufruct.	Taiwan

(*Continued*)

Table 2.1 (Continued)

Forms of land ownership	Main features	Countries and regions
Ownership by governments at all levels separately	Governments at different levels have independent land ownership. Governments at different levels or at the same level cannot transfer land freely.	Federal states, such as the US
Ownership by the king and state	The king owns land, which means the state owns land.	The UK and Canada, etc. The land owned by the Mikado of Japan also belongs to the state.
Superior ownership by state and governments at all levels	Individuals have no absolute ownership. The state or government has superior ownership of land, which means the major part of land administration, rights of disposition and a small part of management earnings are held by the state, while individual land ownership is subordinate.	Taiwan
Collective ownership by cooperative organizations	All members of the cooperative organizations collectively hold the land.	Mainland China's rural areas
Ownership by public organizations or groups	Ownership held by groups such as schools, churches, welfare houses and kindergartens with purposes of public service, social relief and religious charity.	Capitalist countries, such as the US and Singapore, etc.
Ownership by tribe, clan, village community and churches, etc.	Remnants of primitive or feudal land ownership. It features collective ownership by tribe, clan, village community and church and land cultivation by group members.	Mainly in sub-Saharan Africa. It also can be found in other parts of Africa, some regions in Latin Africa and Native American reservations.
Co-ownership by several individuals	Owners share the right of survivorship, which means a co-owner is entitled to the rights and interests of another co-owner upon the latter's death. Each co-owner is regarded as the owner of the whole land and is not allowed to give his share of land to others freely.	The US, etc.

Forms of land ownership	Main features	Countries and regions
Joint ownership by several individuals	Each one is regarded as the owner of his share of land. However, each one's share has no clear boundary line in practice, only a proportional number.	The US, etc.
Ownership by limited liability company	Owned by all shareholders.	The US, etc.
Ownership by people of the apartment	The apartment is not directly connected with land. All people at each floor or unit hold rights of the land proportionally.	The US, etc.
Private ownership	Land is owned by individuals.	Exists widely

Fourth, land has attributes as an asset. The attributes of land as an asset have become increasingly significant with the development of human society. Land, as a type of asset, has the following attributes.

THE SCARCITY OF SUPPLY

The scarcity of land supply refers to the phenomenon that in some regions, land demand for specific purposes falls short of supply, making land a scarce economic resource that results in conflict between demand and supply. There are two reasons behind this phenomenon.

First, land with a desirable location or with good soil enjoys higher utilization rates and efficiency. Demand for these lands is enormous, while their area is limited, resulting in land scarcity. Second, scarcity is also closely related to the total amount of land which is fixed, while land demand keeps increasing along with population growth and economic development. This aggravates the imbalance between supply and demand and causes land monopolies.

FIXED LOCATION

Land features a fixed location, which determines its nature as immovable property. The location of land cannot be changed with the transfer of ownership. This is one of the major features that differentiate land from other business properties such as machines and facilities.

HETEROGENEITY OF LAND RESOURCE

Land property differs in quality, purpose and economic value due to different locations, geography, soil and geology. These factors make each land property unique.

SUSTAINABLE USE AND APPRECIATION

Land managers' investment in land, infrastructure improvements, changes of land purpose and increases in land demand all contribute to the result that land resources can be used repeatedly and sustainably with no depreciation. Land resources keep creating value along with continuous investment of human labor and may even appreciate with social and economic development. However, the sustainable use of land is not an excuse for inattention to land protection. Violation of the laws of nature and economics will cause land depreciate in value.

DUALITY OF LAND PRICE AND VALUE

Land possesses both utility value and exchange value and is a part of commodity circulation. Compared with general goods, land has its own distinctive features. General goods are products of labor for exchange, while land possesses dual properties of being a labor product when it is worked and a non-labor product due to its existence. Fundamentally, land is created by nature instead of human labor, but at the same time it accumulates heavy human labor, which adds to it the property of a labor product. For general products, price is the monetary expression of value, but land price also possesses dual properties – the price of a natural product and the price reflecting value of the land for development. These two aspects are combined together, which is different from the prices of general products.

SPECIAL FEATURE OF CIRCULATION

The most important part of land as an asset is not the substance itself but the power of owning and using it or, in other words, property rights. Therefore, it's necessary for the state to enact laws and regulations to protect the validity of land transfer and transaction. Another distinctive feature of land circulation is the separation of ownership and use rights. In countries and regions where land is state owned and use rights are allowed to circulate, leasing is the most common means of land circulation; in countries and regions where land transaction is unrestricted, leasing practices are also very common, which leads to the separation of ownership and use rights.[45]

Common ownership of land

Theoretically speaking, common ownership originates from one of the essential properties of human beings – intellectuality. Practically speaking, common ownership is the combination of man's materiality, intellectuality and sociality. This combination refers to the phenomenon where a group of people directly or indirectly owns the land and its attached rights and interests.

Land is owned by all, justification of which can be found in a number of theories and practices, such as the rent theory by John Stuart Mill and Henry George, who are natural law theory supporters, and within theories of Marxism and China' s current practice of land ownership. In practice, land ownership by the state or the whole people is known as common ownership in large scale, and ownership by collectives or a group of people is defined as common ownership in small scale. Customarily, we refer to ownership by the whole people as public ownership, but collective ownership also reflects the essential properties of public ownership. By borrowing the concept of property rights, many scholars divide joint ownership into common ownership and co-ownership by shares: the former is non-concrete and non-quantitative ownership, while the latter is concrete and quantitative. Common ownership and individual ownership are a unity of opposites (a philosophical concept meaning "opposites coincide"), and everything else is the deduction around this unity of opposites. The primary aim of land reform is to transform the non-concrete and non-quantitative common ownership into a concrete and quantitative one. However, the process of this reform is not as simple as what some scholars say. It is not true that all conflicts and problems will be resolved as long as land ownership is privatized or divided into shares. No real achievements or progress will be made before any innovative institution comes out, which is effective enough to break down any obstacle against making rigid capital an active asset. The final goal of land reform is to deliver capital to farmers instead of issuing some red-head (official) documents, adopting some Western acts, or summarizing some empirical modes in an anxious way. Reform theorists and leaders with decision-making power should be acutely aware of the significance of this point. Only by establishing a set of legal processes to make non-concrete and non-quantitative public ownership a concrete and quantitative one will hidden economic potential come into play and create surplus value. As Margaret A. Boden says,

> Some of the most important human creations have been new representational systems. These include formal notations, such as Arabic numerals (not forgetting zero), chemical formulae, or the staves, minims, and crotchets used by musicians. Programming languages are a more recent example.[46]

Land trust uses principles of collecting and sharing and separation of the three rights and relies on a system of legal representations such as trust registration, contract and People's Congress to indirectly deliver land to each farmer in a concrete and quantitative way. Moreover, the financial functions of a trust transform rigid land assets into portable fortunes and tradable objects, which is a fundamental difference from creating value merely from the natural resources of land. Land, by nature, is not an asset, but rather its asset is the activation energy hidden in it, which is able to add new value to the land. Land trust makes the hidden value transform and show its worth and allows farmers to share it.

Originally, the word *capital* shared the same meaning with *brain*, indicating the inseparable, subtle and profound relationship between the two. It's not possible to let capital create surplus value without applying knowledge. Only knowledge is able to feel the existence and uncover the secrets of capital. The implementation of land trust is about infusing knowledge into land.

The implementation of land trust helps realize the concrete and quantitative public ownership of land, which means an innovation on ownership and the establishment of a legal order. The process of land trust is not so much being designed as being found out. Whether land trust is able to win farmers' trust will judge its efficacy. Accordingly, land trust must be based on three points.

First, reformers should put themselves in the farmers' position. Second, the interests of stakeholders should also be taken into consideration. The reform of public ownership of land will help unleash the economic potential and benefit for not only farmers but also the rest of society. Third, reform also involves evolution of philosophy and methodology and imposes challenges on the legal order. It is a political obligation and assignment and needs corresponding legal order and supervision. In other words, the reform requires legal protection.

Common ownership of land realizes diversified ownership subjects

The nature of the household responsibility system adopted in rural China in 1978 is to divide rural land property rights into land ownership and land management rights. The ownership of rural collective land belongs to rural collectives, and land management rights are held by farmers. The contract responsibility system has been implemented for several decades and undergone improvements, under which farmers are entitled to not only land management rights but also usufruct and the right of disposal. This rural land system has been equipped with features of a modern property rights system.

Common ownership of land is a desirable choice for the new pattern of current socialist market demands. It allows the coexistence of diverse ownership subjects and resolves problems such as void ownership of rural collective land, decreased efficiency and unequal distribution of interests on the theoretical level. During the ongoing reform of the household responsibility system, rural collective properties have left none in many localities, making rural collectives no longer an effective economic unit. They are no longer able to assume the corresponding responsibility in the two-tiered land management system. However, common ownership of land clarifies duties and rights of rural areas, rural collectives and farmers. It transforms the current land management system and confirms the legal status of farmer collectives as land owners. In this way, it protects farmers' rights of possession, use, earnings and disposal and ensures the proper use of rural collective land. It further confirms farmers' ownership and protects their land management rights. On the basis of common ownership, individual ownership of land will be reestablished, and fairness, efficiency, rights and liberty will be ensured during this process.

Common ownership of land realizes diversified subjects of ownership

China's land system consists of state-owned land[47] and collectively owned land[48] featuring diverse subjects. Common ownership of land possesses characteristics of inclusiveness and ideally fits in with the current environment. On the basis of not changing state ownership and collective ownership, common ownership of land makes the subject of ownership clear and accomplishes efficient circulation of land management rights. It will ensure both equity and efficiency and protect rights of earnings of land owners and land managers. Common ownership of land achieves socialization of ownership and realizes separation between ownership and usufruct, a move that promotes appropriate land use. Common ownership of land, while not changing the current land ownership, realizes circulation of usufruct. On the basis of distinct ownership, common ownership of land makes coexistence of diversified subjects of ownership come true and fits in with the development of a socialist market economy.

Common ownership of land further diversifies ownership subject, combines state ownership and collective ownership, and integrates common ownership and a socialist market economy on the basis of distinct ownership. Land management rights show the inclusiveness and openness of ownership and allow for free circulation and combination of ownership.

Common land ownership makes ownership subject clear, balances
equity and efficiency and reestablishes private ownership

Common land ownership properly divides property right into ownership, management rights and usufruct. Rights to land have been made clear with an effective system involving duties, rights and interests. Take rural collective ownership as an example. Common land ownership changes the strange phenomenon where "ownership belongs to everybody but nobody owns it; everyone seems to be master of land but no one actually is." It can solve problems of obscure ownership subjects and blurred duties, rights and interests. According to Article 10 of the *Land Management Law of People's Republic of China*, rural collectives endowed with land ownership consist of three levels: township, administrative village and villagers' group. It confirms the diversified ownership subject legally. Common land ownership takes both collective ownership and private ownership into consideration and shows the inclusiveness of property rights. Collective ownership refers to township, administrative village and villagers' group, while private ownership clarifies each villager's rights. Thus, farmers possess part of the ownership and benefit from collective earnings, which effectively protects private ownership and individual interests.

Under a socialist market economy, common ownership of land is able to balance equity and efficiency and help achieve common prosperity. Regarding equity, common ownership of land clearly draws boundaries of ownership and arouses enthusiasm for land management. It protects legal rights and interests of beneficiaries and avoids violation of land rights and interests. In terms of efficiency, common ownership helps achieve effective circulation of land management rights, contributes to scale management and intensive management of rural land and achieves efficient allocation of means of production. The land-society relationship under common ownership of land reflects the arrangement of capital, knowledge, skill and human resources in the process of pursing profit maximization. In respect to achieving common prosperity, common ownership of land takes advantage of private ownership and collective ownership and reestablishes private ownership on the basis that means of production is held by the whole society. During the socialization process of the means of production, common ownership of land realizes contract-based marketization. Common citizens have temporary land management rights in the forms of tenancy and subcontracting. With usufruct, they could share the fruits of reform and opening up and achieve common prosperity.

Features of common ownership of land

Theories and practices of common ownership have proven that it possesses the following eight features.

Polysemy

The existence of any substance is a unity of opposites (abstract nature and concrete form). "The feature of concrete integrates many rules and thus is the unity of diverse aspects."[49] Thus, polysemy is a fundamental feature of development. The nature of polysemy can be analyzed from two aspects: objectively speaking, any development is possible to move towards multiple orientations; subjectively speaking, people's understanding of a concrete form differs due to their different view angles.

Objective polysemy determines diversity of common ownership of land, which can be seen from the multiple forms of common ownership of land. These multiple forms are largely due to different social circumstances and are reflected through creative practices correspondingly. After the victory of the New Democratic Revolution (1919–1949), land reform was implemented across China to abolish the feudal land system. The land reforms confiscated land from feudal landlords and rich farmers and reallocated it to the majority of peasants with no or very little land. It enabled peasants to have land, abolished the landlord class and established individual possession of land. In the later Socialist Transformation, a transition to socialist public ownership and collective ownership was completed through three phases: mutual aid groups, elementary agricultural cooperatives and senior agricultural cooperatives. It is stipulated by Article 10 of the *Constitution of the People's Republic of China*, that urban land is state owned; rural land and land in the suburbs are collectively held unless otherwise specified as being owned by the state; homesteads, private plots and private hilly lands are also owned collectively. Article 9 stipulates that natural resources including mineral reserves, rivers, forests, mountains, grassland, wasteland and shoal are owned by the state, which means the whole people, unless prescribed by law as being held collectively.

Homogeneity

Homogeneity refers to the fact that different things are essentially connected and possess a unified form. Homogeneity is an abstract concept, an objective basis of rational thinking, which is represented by the argument – "any form has its nature while nature is represented by a form. In any condition, the change of a form follows the change of its nature."[50] Homogeneity of common ownership is the generalization, summarization and abstraction of the generality behind the very different forms of common ownership, or in other words, it is the reflection of the nature of common ownership through its appearance and provides theoretical foundation for manifestations of common ownership. Common ownership of land possesses two forms, state ownership and collective ownership, both of which feature socialization of personal property. Common ownership of land balances public interests and individual interests and overcomes defects of private ownership. It is a form of ownership with diversified and clear property rights.

Boundary

The unity of opposites is an essential attribute to any matter, which means each matter has a boundary. Boundaries can be seen from the fact that one side of a substance is separate from the other side, and together they constitute an independent entirety. We hold that "boundary" is the objective expression of the independent entirety.

Common ownership of land carries out border demarcation according to the unity of personal possession and common possession, clarifies the equal status of the owner, user and beneficiary, and defines duties, rights and interests concerning land. Take rural land collective ownership as an example. Rural land collective ownership covers the shortage of ownership by the whole people and makes ownership borderlines clear. Under rural land collective ownership, land owners possess land and regulate land management rights. Land is divided into small plots, and each plot is assigned to a manager who is also the owner of the land.

Level

Any matter has boundaries, is located at a certain level and contains several levels. Level and boundary are a unity of opposites. Both common ownership and its forms can be divided into two parts or two aspects of a contradiction. Meanwhile, with the synergy between boundary and level, common ownership possesses a number of internal and external subsystems, which also reflects the philosophical viewpoint that "the universe is infinite and everything is infinitely divisible."

In terms of common ownership of land, we can divide it into three levels. First, from the perspective of land ownership structure, private ownership and common ownership form a level. Second, in terms of common ownership of land itself, state ownership and collective ownership form a level. They assume different forms according to different degrees of common ownership. For instance, land owners of state-owned and collectively owned land are, respectively, the whole people and collectives. Third, regarding each concrete form of common ownership, state ownership is achieved through private and common possessions of means of production, which constitutes another level.

Randomness

Randomness is a reflection of motility. Along with varied external circumstances, each matter experiences movement, change and development. A number of possibilities may occur during the process from nonexistence to existence, which is polysemy as already mentioned. It exists in both the objective world and the subjective cognitive domain. The process of movement contains invariance, which is implied in a mass of contingencies. The origin of invariance discussed here comes from constraint, while the origin of constraint comes from randomness. Accordingly, invariance and randomness form the unity of opposites. The existence of one element is the precondition for another as there won't be any randomness if there is no invariance. In this way, randomness and restraint are two opposites, changing and developing under the dialectical contradiction.

In terms of common ownership of land, it contains state ownership and collective ownership, the development of which has undergone a very long history. Characteristics of land make it possible that land tenure assumes different forms at different historical periods. They also show that land possesses both natural property, as a means of production, and socio-economic property, as the object that forms social land relationships. The socio-economic property refers to the relations among people during the process of possessing, developing and using land. The most important part in this relationship is land tenure and the land use system. Due to the socio-economic property of land, land tenure and land use systems at home and abroad at different historical periods are different from each other. Different social systems have produced different land ownership types during the process of human development, such as communal ownership of land in primitive society, ownership by slave masters, feudal land ownership, capitalist land ownership and socialist land ownership. Practice has proven that collective land ownership is the form of achieving common land ownership with creative exploration and has revealed four features: the limitation of ownership scope, humanity of ownership subject, clarity of property right relationship and autonomy of joint property rights. Collective land ownership shows randomness of common ownership; however, randomness does not mean irregularity as science is to seek regularity.

Restraint

Restraint involves invariance. Invariance originates from regularity, which is the nature and universality of phenomenon. It can be seen from orderliness and is something that remains stable and unchanged. The nature, universality and orderliness mentioned here refer to the invariance in the movement of any matter, which is also called restraint. The objective world and subjective world are all in a condition of restraint. The contradiction of any matter is shown by constraint. The same principle also applies to common ownership.

The manifestation of restraint in common ownership can be seen from its goal of achieving common prosperity. We should be clear that common prosperity is a final goal as well as a process. During the whole process of achieving this goal, all forms of common ownership of land should center on and reflect this goal. The nature of prosperity is giving consideration to both the spiritual world and material world. Deng Xiaoping once said that "while building up high-level material civilization, we should also improve scientific and cultural levels of the whole nation and develop honorable and rich cultural life for the construction of a high-level socialist spiritual civilization."[51] Common prosperity attaches importance to both material and spiritual life, not merely material prosperity. Prosperity of material life only meets people's material demands but neglects people's need for knowledge. Especially in this knowledge economy era, rapidly developing scientific technology, cultural education and knowledge are increasingly becoming people's common needs. Thus, common prosperity is the dynamic integration of material and knowledge. Stress on material need but neglect of knowledge will hinder social progress and vice versa.

Evolvement

Evolvement is a general term for movement and change. Movement is the form of any existence and the essential attribute of common ownership. Our society won't achieve sustainable development without moving common ownership forward. Change refers to the changes of state, features or the nature of common ownership caused by the movement of its nature. In reality, changes of common ownership are not visible to us, while we only perceive the changes of forms of common ownership, which are caused by movements.

Evolvement of common ownership of land means common ownership forms are not fixed or permanent. Development of any ownership type takes development and retroversion of another one as a premise. Land tenure has gone through communal ownership in primitive societies, ownership by slave masters, feudal land ownership, capitalist land ownership and common ownership, which is currently implemented. Common ownership features independent operation of capital and separation of the three rights, which are ownership, use rights and rights to earnings. It realizes what Marx proposed as "distribution according to ones' performance" and offers an effective mechanism to arouse the enthusiasm of laborers and operators to the hilt.

Stability

Stability accounts for the conservation of a substance. Specifically speaking, any object in the objective world and reflection of the object in people's minds has essential features that differentiate themselves from others. These essential features correlate to both polysemy and homogeneity possessed by any substance. Due to eternal forces, a substance moves, changes and develops towards different orientations. The movement, change and development have two possibilities: the nature of the substance does not change during the motion, which shows its stability; the nature of the substance changes during motion, and it becomes something else. Stability of a substance has three forms. The first one is anti-interference, which is shown by the stability of nature during motion. Second, circularity is shown by the stability of double denial. The third is concertedness, which means the stability of the entirety during the exchange between the substance and external world.

In terms of common ownership, its stability can be seen from the fact that it reflects the nature of social ownership, which is "rebuilding the individual ownership," proposed by Marx. In *Das Kapital* (volume 1), Marx talked about the historical trend of capital accumulation and mentioned denial and double denial of three types of ownership. Private ownership of capitalism denies private ownership of small-scale producers. The development of capitalist means of production leads to the denial of capitalist private ownership and makes it clear that the denial doesn't mean rebuilding of private ownership but "rebuilding of individual ownership." "Rebuilding of individual ownership" is an important scientific thesis on social ownership under communism by Marx. It is proposed on the basis of scientific analysis of the contradictory movement between social form and means of production under capitalist production. Practice has shown that common ownership of land adequately realizes "reestablishment of personal ownership," which can be seen from the following aspects:

• Common ownership of land makes the laborer the subject of ownership and allows for the unification of laborer and land. Laborers become the master of land and land management and occupy their own products and surplus labor. In this way, the alienation between means of production and labor is eliminated.

• Common ownership of land realizes personal occupation of means of production as well as private ownership based on association of labors, which means the form of exercising land use rights by all labors is common ownership based on joint labor. As it is stated by Marx in *The German Ideology*, "Private ownership will end as the associated individuals occupy all means of production." From the angle of direct occupation, common ownership of land is common occupation by joint labors; from the angle of the eventual owner, common ownership of land is individual occupation based on social association.

• Common ownership of land ensures each laborer's ownership, which conforms to communism proposed by Marx, a social form with everyone's liberty and comprehensive development as fundamental principles. It is not a community with individual subject status as a basis and fully recognizing individual rights as its content but a community that unites all laborers to occupy land together and realizes individuals' ownership. Ownership mentioned here contains two aspects: first, every laborer has joint control right during the process of land use and production; second, each laborer has rights of possession, rights of distribution and rights to surplus value.

To sum up, the content of common ownership is the combination of the means of production. It acknowledges and recognizes the principal status of labor in production and management and also recognizes the role and status of capital and assets. The diversity of labor forms and types produces multiple forms of production factors. Intelligence, management, technology and labor forces are different forms of labor. Labors are the main body of companies, society and wealth creation. Thus, labors are naturally the main body of business owners. These production factors cover all parts of production and management. It won't work with the loss of any part, and no one can be replaced by another. In this way, common ownership based on production factor theory is an all-round one which cannot be regarded as ownership of the means of production or property systems but ownership of factors of production because the means of production include only part of asset and capital, not the whole of production factors.

3 Breakthrough point of China's rural land system reform

Cesar Pelli once said, "I am a strong believer that as one moves toward the future, the strongest and clearest way to do it is if you have a good sense of your past. You cannot have a very tall tree without deep roots." Now we first scrutinize China's rural land system and then analyze cases of rural land transfer to provide a theoretical basis for management model innovation and policy formulation of land circulation.

China's rural land system transition in history

China's rural land system transition before 1949

China's rural land system had experienced three periods before 1949. During the first period, it was the well-field system in Xia (c. 2070–1600 BCE), Shang (c.1600–1046 BCE) and Zhou (1046–256 BCE) Dynasties, which retained heavy traces of village community or tribe ownership. Private ownership of land was just sprouting. The second period started from the collapse of the well-field system and ended with the breakdown of the equal-field system in the mid-Tang Dynasty (AD 618–907). This period witnessed the *tuntian* system (a state-owned land system), the *zhantian* system (a system of quota) and the equal-field system. It was also a process of establishing private ownership, during which time the state exerted strong intervention on private land. The third period was from the adoption of the Two-tax Law in the Tang Dynasty to modern times prior to 1949. "No control on land occupation and land annexation," which was first implemented in Northern Song Dynasty (AD 960–1127), gradually became a national policy afterwards, and during this period, the feudal land tenure underwent stages of development, maturity and decline.

Land tenure during the slavery period

Land tenure in China's slavery period was the well-field system. The well-field system correlated to natural conditions of the Yellow River basin and took well-field as a division basis. It was related to taxes and the corvée system, military service system and urban and rural planning.

CONTENT OF THE WELL-FIELD SYSTEM

In ancient China, "well" （jing,"井"） had three meanings. First, it was an area unit larger than mu (fifteen mu = one hectare). Second, dividing land according to the shape of the Chinese character jing ("井").[1] Third, it meant the well itself. Well-field indicates equal land division as neat and square as the Chinese character "jing."[2]

OWNERSHIP OF THE WELL-FIELD SYSTEM

It was recorded in "Overseer of Public Affairs" in *Rites of Zhou*:

> The land given to dukes is subject to regulation on its boundary. Land boundary is made by digging trenches. Land regulation is made according to the number of household. For fertile land where crops can grow continuously, each household will receive 100 mu; for land where crops can grow every two years, each household will receive 200 mu; for land where crops can grow every three years, each household will receive 300 mu.

From this we can see that the well-field system adopted equal land distribution and tied laborers and land together. Land transaction was forbidden. The system carried out "joint farming" by means of village communities and collective force. It was a kind of state ownership of land in the slavery period.

LAND LAWS AND RULES OF THE WELL-FIELD SYSTEM

Land was owned by the "Son of Heaven" during the slavery period; "all land under the Heaven belongs to the Emperor and all people in the world are subject to the Emperor."[3] At the same time, King Zhou adopted the system of enfeoffment.[4] The king distributed land and the affiliated slaves to dukes and exploited the slaves and collected taxes from impoverished peasants by means of tribute, land rent and tax.

Land tenure in China's feudal era

Land tenure in China's feudal era had witnessed swings among feudal state ownership, ownership by feudal landlord and ownership by farmers, thanks to the trilateral game among the state, landlord and farmers. Eventually, ownership by feudal landlord took the dominant position. Detailed information about land tenure during feudal China can be seen in Table 3.1.

Land tenure in a semifeudal and semi-colonial society

During this period, land ownership by feudal landlords still dominated in land tenure. In the meantime, warlords and bureaucrats swarmed to plunder land and

Table 3.1 Transitions of the land system in feudal China[5]

Dynasty	Land tenure	Key features
Qin and Han Dynasties (221–206 BC and 206 BC – 220 AD)	Coexistence of state-owned land, large-scale private land and small-scale farmers' land	1. Qin Dynasty: land ownership by landlord, farmer and state. The group of "farmer" was the simplest, most scientific and most efficient organization for agricultural production. Taxes and labor from farmers were the main source of national finance and army construction. 2. In the Western Han Dynasty (206 BC–24 AD), Emperor Liu Bang issued a statute tying farmers to land and returning agricultural production to normal. Farmers were the dominant force in this period for agricultural production; however, due to limited economic strength, scale of production was not large with manpower and small-scale instruments. 3. Emperor Wu of Han adopted Dong Zhongshu's proposal "limiting land occupation," where landlord's ownership of land was recognized on some certain conditions, while land annexation was limited to protect farmers. The central government had control over strong landlords, an attempt to prevent land annexation and ease social conflicts. 4. In the Eastern Han Dynasty (25–220 AD), Emperor Liu Xiu announced, "I prefer a tender approach in governing my country," which meant a favorable change of policy for strong landlords. Scale management by a strong landlord was a main feature of agricultural production, but the strengthening of personal dependent relationship during this time was the most severe regression about relations of production since the Qin and Han Dynasties.
Cao Wei Dynasty (220–265 AD)	Tuntian system (a state-owned land system)	The tuntian system in the Cao Wei Dynasty was developed on the basis of tuntian practices (agricultural land reclamation made by military and peasants) in the Han Dynasty. It was a state-owned land system. 1. Differences: Tuntian in the Han Dynasty was done by frontier military units, purely an economic form of state apparatus; tuntian in the Cao Wei Dynasty was done by peasants, where peasants were organized by the state, as landlords, to do land reclamation and agricultural production. 2. Drawbacks of tuntian by peasants: It blurred the boundary between state administration and landlord management and hindered the process of land privatization, which exerted bad influence on state administrative functions and effective management of agricultural production.

w

Western Jin Dynasty (265–316 AD)	Zhantian system (a system of quota)	The zhantian system was the first land tenure system that allocated land according to political power. It allowed farmers to own land according to their farming ability, but it had limitations on the area of land and taxes. For officials, the area of land and number of *Yinke* (farmers owned by landlords) occupied by them were regulated according to their positions to prevent excessive occupation of land by strong landlords. This system attempted to protect the interests of bureaucrats as well as to restore and protect farmers' agricultural production. It featured compromise.
Southern and Northern Dynasties (420–589 AD)	Large-scale land ownership in the north	In this period, the state recognized the legality of personal occupation of mountains and rivers, which changed the previous phenomenon where only the state had the authority of occupying mountains and rivers. All people were allowed to exploit the unprotected mountains and rivers. Ownership of land in large areas entered a new phase.
Northern Wei Dynasty (386–534 AD), Sui Dynasty (581–618 AD) and Tang Dynasty (618–907 AD)	Equal-field system	1. In the ninth year of the Taihe reign period (485 AD), Emperor Xiaowen of Northern Wei issued an order to adopt an equal-field system, under which the state allocated the land to farmers according to the strength of the labor force, and farmers paid taxes to the state. When owners of land grew into old age or died, the state would reallocate the land to others. The equal-field system was adopted for the reason that rulers in the Northern Wei Dynasty were of Xianbei nationality. Xianbei people were experiencing the disruption of clan communes and the establishment of villages. The Xianbei people combined their own land policy with the zhantian system of the Western Jin Dynasty.
		2. The equal-field system in the Sui and Tang Dynasties: First, the land managed by farmers was allocated by the state. Land allocation was done according to population, and permanent land distribution according to official positions also existed. Second, farmers became tenant farmers. Tenant farmers didn't have land ownership, although their power over land was close to ownership. Third, land transaction was strictly limited with humane land policies. For example, when someone was too poor to afford a funeral, or moved from a place with a large population and a small area of land to a place with a small population and a large area of land, he was allowed to sell permanent land; bureaucrats and aristocrats were also allowed to sell permanent land. Thus, under the equal-field system, the management and control over land by the state was similar to macro-control on agriculture, postponing and limiting the process of land annexation.

(*Continued*)

Table 3.1 (Continued)

Dynasty	Land tenure	Key features
Song (960–1279), Yuan (1271–1368), Ming (1368–1644) and Qing (1644–1912) Dynasties	Land ownership by feudal landlords, the dominant form of land tenure	1. Northern Song Dynasty (960–1127): The state encouraged farmers to reclaim the wasteland and acknowledged their land ownership. The state allocated the land previously owned by officials and governments to tenant farmers and enlarged the class of farmers. Oppressive policy on land annexation by influential officials was adopted. There were also reforms on tax, such as easing farmers' burden of paying tax and corvée and preventing landlords from evading tax and corvée. With the transfer of land ownership to individuals, the main body of agricultural investment shifted from the state to individuals. A large number of small landlords emerged with the number of powerful landlords reduced. The proportion of tenant farmers was enlarged, while the number of tenant farmers declined. Correspondingly, hierarchical relationships were weakened, and farmers had higher social status.[6] Yuan Dynasty: The group of all kinds of privileged landlords grew, and feudal privilege of the landlord class rose to a peak. The social status of farmers was degraded rapidly with increasingly concentrated land. 3. Ming and Qing Dynasties: First, land transactions became freer with the state encouraging land transactions and giving support for market prices of land. A land market developed. For example, with fewer limitations on land transactions, the rule "priority to relatives and neighbors" on land transactions became invalid. Second, the land system conformed to economic and social development. Land ownership was separated from management rights. Land ownership was brought to market through some policies such as "paying deposit for land rent" and "permanent land use right." Third, through reform of tax and corvée, new tax and corvée policies were adopted in the Ming and Qing Dynasties. It played a positive role in easing farmers' burdens, preventing land annexation and promoting economic development.

business assets. Land annexation prevailed, and "opportunists" represented by the four big families of the Republic of China (the four big families begin with the Chinese surnames Chiang, Soong, Kung and Chen) bought land in large scales. (Please see detailed information from Table 3.2.)

Land tenure in modern rural China after 1949

After the establishment of the People's Republic of China in 1949, the rural land system had undergone a winding development process. Land ownership by farmers was established to ensure farmer collective land ownership. Land management models were transformed from collective management to family management. This book is going to analyze the land tenure reform in modern rural China and the reasons behind the reform and summarize achievements and lessons from the reform to offer guidance on ongoing and future rounds of rural land reform.

Rural land system reform before the establishment of the People's Republic of China

The phases of rural land tenure before the establishment of the People's Republic of China will be redrawn according to the revolutionary process – the First Civil War, the Second Civil War, Chinese People's War of Resistance against Japanese Aggression and the Third Civil War. (See Table 3.3.)

Land reform in rural China in the early years of the People's Republic of China

The People's Republic of China published the *Land Reform Law* in June 1950. It has forty articles in six chapters:

*   Chapter I "General Principles"
*   Chapter II "Land Confiscation and Expropriation"
*   Chapter III "Land Allocation"
*   Chapter IV "Handling of Special Land Issues"
*   Chapter V "Executive Organ and Executive Method"
*   Chapter VI "Supplementary Articles"

The *Land Reform Law* specifies the objectives and processes of this reform.

OBJECTIVES OF THE 1950S LAND REFORM

It abolished the feudal land tenure featuring exploitation of farmers by landlords and established a land tenure system featuring land ownership by farmers. Policies were put into place to free the forces of production in rural China, develop agricultural production and pave the way for China's industrialization. The mission of the

Table 3.2 Land tenure in semifeudal and semi-colonial society[7]

Period	Key features
Taiping Heavenly Kingdom in the late Qing Dynasty	A new land system was adopted by the Taiping Heavenly Kingdom. It was announced that all land was owned by God, and each person was allowed to get a piece of land from God. It was stipulated that the principle of land distribution was according to population and quality of land. However, due to historical limitations, the new land system was more like a fantasy and finally failed in practice.
1912–1949	From the Republic of China founded in 1912 to the People's Republic of China founded in 1949, the government had done great work about land management.
	1. Establishing a land management department: As the government established its capital in Nanjing in 1927, it set up a bureau of land. In July 1936, the Bureau of Land was changed to the Bureau of Land Administration. In 1942, the central government established an independent land administration organization and land administration office, with departments of cadaster, land price and land rights. The Department of Cadaster was in charge of land surveys, land registration, land atlas storing, land investigation, clearing public land and land replotting. The Department of Land Price was in charge of stipulating land prices, proposing land prices and compiling land price books. The Department of Land Rights was in charge of planning land rights, handling appeals about land rights, land acquisition, governing land use and land finance. In 1947, the Land Administration Office was enlarged to the Land Administration Ministry with four departments of cadaster, land price, land rights and land use.
	2. In terms of land management regulations, the government of the Republic of China enacted *Land Law* in 1930 and *Implementation of Land Law* in 1935, which were put into practice in March 1936. Amendments of them were put into practice in 1946. In addition, the government also published the *Land Registration Rule*, *Land Re-plotting Method*, *Public Land Management* to strengthen management on public and private land. In the name of protecting private assets, the government of Republic of China acknowledged ownership of land by landlords who therefore exploited farmers without violating the law.
	As the Republic of China founded its capital in Nanjing, all provinces and cities carried out cadaster regulation. However, no significant achievement was made due to the lack of unified methods. Land cadaster management didn't have any regulated process before the *Land Law* and *Implementation of Land Law* were put into practice in 1936. However, the Chinese People's War of Resistance against Japanese Aggression broke out in the following year. During the war, land administration departments only carried out work on cadaster management in urban areas in the form of choosing some pilot counties.[8]

Table 3.3 Rural land system reform before the establishment of the People's Republic of China[9]

Period	Key features
The First Civil War (January 1924 to July 1927)	There was the land policy to reduce rent and interest rates, but a land revolution of confiscating landlords' land did not happen. Fundamental reasons: There was an irresolvable contradiction between a thorough land revolution and the strategy of carrying out cooperation with the Nationalist Party. It was impossible to lead the farmers and carry out land revolution with the premise of cooperating with the Nationalist Party.[10]
The Second Civil War (1927 to 1937)	1. Land policy: "Rely on the impoverished farmers, unite the middle-level farmers and limit the rich farmers. Protect small and medium-sized businessmen and eliminate the landlord class. Change the semi-feudal and semi-colonial land tenure to land ownership by farmers. Take the village as a unit, and distribute land according to population." 2. Related laws: In December 1928, the *Jinggangshan Mountains Land Law* was enacted and issued. Land policy assumed legal power for the first time. It mainly included the following content: Confiscate all land, and the Soviet government takes charge of the land. The land will be distributed to farmer individuals, farmer collectives and farms organized by the Soviet government for farming. No land transaction is allowed. Land allocation is done with the village as a unit. Special circumstances are allowed. For example, several villages or regions are allowed to form a unit. Land allocation is done according to population. Male, female, the old and the young receive equal share in land allocation. In special circumstances, land allocation can also be done according to labor force. Distribution of tea-growing and firewood-growing mountain areas is done with similar principles of land distribution, taking the village as the unit and implementing equal distribution. Bamboo mountain is owned by the Soviet government. With permission from the Soviet government, people are allowed to use bamboo. In April 1929, after the Communist Party of China (CPC) entered South Jiangxi, it issued a new land law in Xingguo County where "confiscating all land" was changed to "confiscating public land and landlord's land." In June 1929, it was stipulated in the notice made by the Red Fourth Army Headquarters that "land is owned by farmers and farmers do not have to pay rent to landlords." Prohibition on land transactions was canceled in the land law issued by the CPC in the Central Soviet Area in 1930.
Chinese People's War of Resistance against Japanese Aggression (1937–1945)	1. Background: During the Chinese People's War of Resistance against Japanese Aggression, Chinese–Japanese conflict became the main conflict in China. The CPC united all forces and established a wide unified battle line. To meet demands of the national war and stimulate production initiative of farmers, the CPC changed the land policy of confiscating landlords' land to reducing rents and interest rates.

(*Continued*)

Table 3.3 (Continued)

Period	Key features
	2. Land policy: In August 1937, the CPC held enlarged meeting of the Political Bureau of the CPC Central Committee, at which *Ten Principles for National Salvation* was passed. It first came up with the proposal to make "reducing rent and interest rate" the basic policy to resolve farmers' problems. In January 1942, Political Bureau of the CPC Central Committee passed *Decision on Land Policy in Anti-Japanese Base* and put forward with three fundamental principles. First, it acknowledged the fact that farmers are the fundamental strength in resistance war and production. The CPC's policy was to help farmers by easing exploitation from landlords, reducing rents and interest rates and protecting farmers' rights, which would improve farmers' living conditions and boost their initiative of resistance war and production. Second, most landlords had the wish for a resistance war against Japanese invasion, and some of them were in favor of democratic reform. At this stage, the CPC's policy was to put aside the idea of eliminating feudal exploitation. With the reduction of rents and interest rates, farmers still had to pay rent and interest. Third, it acknowledged that capitalist production means were the relatively advanced production means in China. The bourgeoisie class, especially national bourgeoisie and small bourgeoisie, were the relatively enlightened social element and political power in China. To ensure that land policy was implemented in practice, a number of land regulations were passed in liberation areas during this period. For example, *Regulations on Reducing Rents and Interest Rates* was issued by the government in the Shanxi-Chahaer-Hebei border region in February 1938. The *Regulations on Reducing Rents and Interest Rates* was issued by the administrative office in the Jin-Sui border area in April 1940. *Interim Regulations on Land Use in Shanxi-Hebei-Shandong-Henan Border Area* was issued in November 1941. *Land Tenant Regulations in Shaanxi-Gansu-Ningxia Border Region (draft)* was enacted by local government committee in 1942. *Land Rights Regulations in Shaanxi-Gansu-Ningxia Border Region (draft)* was passed on the Fourth Meeting of Border Region Government Committee. 3. Significance: The policy of reducing rents and interest rates didn't bring any immediate reform to feudal land tenure in China. It was a policy proposed under the special environment of Chinese People's War of Resistance against Japanese Aggression. It was an effective policy under the unified national battle lines to solve farmers' land problems and boost production. The implementation of this policy not only improved farmers' living conditions and boosted their initiative for war and production but also eased the tension among different social classes in rural areas and consolidated the unified national battle lines. It accumulated experiences and created advantageous conditions for eliminating feudal power and carrying out land reform. It was of great significance for the final victory of the Chinese People's War of Resistance against Japanese Aggression.

Period	Key features
The Third Civil War (1946–1949)	On May 4, 1946, the central government issued *Instructions on Clearance of Reduced Rent and Land Problems*, which was also known as *May 4th Instructions*. The policy of reducing rents and interest rates was changed to confiscating landlords' land and distributing land to farmers. There were some important effects of the *May 4th Instructions*: confirming farmers' land ownership proved to be a right policy. It satisfied farmers' demand for land in a timely and firm manner, which helped the Communist Party gain initiative at the turning point of revolution and leadership over farmers. It also stipulated a series of concrete policies very clearly. It learned from the historical experience and lessons of the Agrarian Revolution and avoided the wrong tendency of the "left route." Different treatments were given to different social classes, and different policies had clear boundaries. It was stipulated that solving land problems needed insistence on the mass line. Commandism and monopolies were precluded. The issue of the *May 4th Instructions* marked a change of the CPC's land policy and the deepening of the democratic revolution.[11] At the time when the *May 4th Instructions* were issued, although the risk of civil war was severe, full-scale civil war hadn't broken out, so the hope of peace still existed. In this situation, efforts to unite people from all classes were needed, so it was disadvantageous and impossible for the CPC to carry out thorough land reform.
The Third Civil War (1946–1949)	In September 1947, the CPC Central Committee held a national land conference and officially came up with the proposal *Outline Land Law of China* to eradicate semifeudal and semi-colonial land tenure, which featured exploitation of farmers, and to implement land tenure that enabled farmers to own land. It contained sixteen items and mainly included the following content: eradicate land ownership held by landlords, ancestral temple, monastery, schools, institutions and offices. All debts before the rural land tenure reform are to be cleared. All land previously owned by landlords and public land is taken by a farmers' association that would then distribute the land to villagers according to population. Male, female, the old and the young would receive equal share in land allocation. There would be adjustment regarding land area and land quality to ensure equal land distribution. The land allocation would make all villagers receive the same amount of land and let farmers have land ownership. Large forests, hydraulic engineering projects, mines, ranches, wasteland, lakes and deserts would be governed by government. Land allocated to individuals would receive certificates of land ownership which acknowledged the rights of land management, transactions and renting under some certain conditions.

(Continued)

Table 3.3 (Continued)

Period	Key features
	According to the *Outline Land Law of China*, the CPC Central Committee successively issued a series of important instructions and decisions from late 1947, which not only rectified wrongdoings during the land reform but also made improvement of the *Outline Land Law of China*.[12] For example, in November 1947, the CPC Central Committee issued *Instructions on Reissuing "How to Analyze Social Class" and "Decisions on Some Issues Occurred During Land Reform" First Issued by the Central Government in 1933*; in January 1948, the CPC Central Committee issued *Instructions on Some Major Issues about Communist Party's Current Policies*; in February 1948, the CPC Central Committee issued *Instructions on Land Reform in New Liberation Areas* within the party. In April 1948, Mao Zedong made a speech at the Shanxi-Suiyuan Cadre Meeting and put forward the CPC's general route of land reform during the New Democratic Revolution (1919–1949). The general route relied on impoverished farmers and uniting middle-level farmers to eradicate feudal land tenure step by step and boost agricultural production.[13]

1950s land reform was to confiscate lands, livestock, farm tools, surplus grains and houses which would be taken over by farmers' associations at the township level, and allocated, under the principle of being reasonable and fair and square, to landless or land-poor peasants and impoverished farmers who suffered from lack of other means of production.

STANDARD PROCESS OF THE 1950S LAND REFORM

First, farmers' congress at all levels elected a committee of the farmers' association; second, they divided farmers into corresponding social classes according to the *Decision on Identifying Different Class Structures in Rural China* issued by the Government Administration Council of the Central People's Government in August 1950; third, they made a thorough investigation on land area and yield to allocate land; fourth, they issued land certificates for farmers; fifth, they handled the special problems that occurred during land reform.

At the end of 1952, this round of land reform was generally done across the country. Farmers who economically benefited from land reform accounted for 60 to 70 percent of the agricultural population. About 700 million mu (fifteen mu = one hectare) was allocated to 300 million farmers across the country. The 1950s land reform freed the forces of production and facilitated the rapid growth of agricultural production. For example, compared with 1949, the national grain production in 1951 increased by 28 percent, while that in 1952 increased by 40 percent.[14]

Agricultural cooperative

The agricultural cooperative movement in the 1950s was another land tenure revolution.

The movement went through three stages: agricultural production mutual aid groups, preliminary agricultural production cooperatives and senior agricultural production cooperatives.

(1) Stage of agricultural production mutual aid group   At this stage, individual farmers had land ownership and formed agricultural production mutual aid groups in accordance with the principles of voluntariness and mutual benefit. The CPC Central Committee issued the *Decision on Agricultural Cooperative Mutual Aid Group* in December 1951, which noted that forms of agricultural production mutual aid included temporary mutual aid groups, long-term mutual aid groups and agricultural production cooperatives. Statistics showed that the number of mutual aid groups nationwide was 2.724 million in 1950, 4.675 million in 1951, 8.026 million in 1952, 7.45 million in 1953, and 9.931 million in 1954. The number of mutual aid group members increased from 11.313 million in 1950 to 68.478 million in 1954.

(2) Stage of preliminary agricultural production cooperative   The CPC Central Committee issued the *Decision on Promoting Agricultural Production Cooperative* in December 1953, which marked the start of preliminary agricultural production cooperatives. According to the *Decision*, on the basis of agricultural production mutual aid groups, some mutual aid groups and other unorganized farmers united together to from preliminary agricultural production cooperatives. Means of production, including land, were handed over to cooperatives under unified management, and then farmers worked together. Farmers could "quit a cooperative freely" and took back the means of production which was handed over when they joined the cooperative. The number of preliminary agricultural production cooperatives across the country was 15,000 at the end of 1953 and 480,000 at the end of 1954.

In October 1955, the *Decision on Agricultural Cooperative Issues* was passed at the Sixth Plenary Session of the Seventh CPC Central Committee, which formulated a plan with details about the scale and progress pace of the agricultural cooperative movement. The number of preliminary agricultural production cooperatives was more than 600,000 at the beginning of 1955 and more than 1.9 million at the end of 1955, with 63 percent of farmer households involved.

(3) Stage of senior agricultural production cooperatives   In January 1956, the Political Bureau of the CPC Central Committee issued *Guidelines for National Agricultural Development from 1956 to 1957 (draft)* and demanded all provinces,

municipalities and autonomous regions to finish establishing preliminary agricultural cooperative in 1956 and senior agricultural cooperative in 1958. On June 30, 1956, the CPC Central Committee passed the *Senior Agricultural Cooperative Regulations*, after which a wave of senior agricultural cooperatives swept the country. At the end of the year, the number of senior agricultural production cooperatives nationwide reached 764,000, with 88 percent of farmer households involved. This marked that the agricultural cooperative movement or socialist transformation of agriculture was done on the whole. The land was collectively held under unified management and organized distribution according to one's performance. Governments at all levels facilitated preliminary agricultural production cooperatives and unorganized farmers to establish senior agricultural production cooperatives.

EFFECT OF IMPLEMENTATION

At the stage of the agricultural production mutual aid groups, the agricultural cooperative movement abided by Marx's economic theory on agricultural cooperatives and expanded the collective economy, which ensured farmers' rights and encouraged their participation. The combination of free entry and exit and farmers' cooperation formed a contract structure featuring self-supervision. However, along with the movement's progress, particularly at the stage of senior agricultural production cooperative, the movement increasingly deviated from the right track as it began to copy the model of Stalin's collective farming in the Soviet Union. This wrong track increasingly reinforced state compulsion and betrayed principles of voluntariness, mutual benefit and sharing profits according to contribution, which eventually became a compulsory system reform designed and implemented solely by the state.

People's commune movement

DEVELOPMENT PROGRESS

In March 1958, the Chengdu Meeting of the Political Bureau of the CPC Central Committee passed *Opinion on Properly Merging Small-scale Agricultural Cooperatives to Form Large Ones*, which said, "To meet the demands of agricultural production and cultural revolution, it is necessary to merge small-scale agricultural cooperatives to form large ones systematically and properly where practicable." After the meeting, the movement that small cooperatives merged into large ones began to prevail in rural China; communist communes, collective farming and people's communes appeared in different regions.

On July 1, 1958, the "people's commune" was first proposed in the article "A New Society and New People" (*Red Flag* magazine, third issue), which clearly said, "[T]he nature of turning a cooperative into a basic organizational unit combining agricultural cooperation and industrial cooperation is people's commune with combination of agriculture and industry."

In August 1958, at the Enlarged Meeting of the Political Bureau of the CPC central committee, *Decision on Establishing People's Commune in Rural China* (hereafter referred to as "*Decision*") was passed. According to the *Decision*, the people's commune, which involved farmers, workers, businessmen, students and soldiers, was an inevitable trend of rural economic development, a facilitator for socialization of rural China and a bridge for transition to Communism. As the *Decision* came into effect, an upsurge in the people's commune movement appeared. At the end of October, more than 740,000 agricultural production cooperatives were transformed into more than 26,000 people's communes. The number of farmer households involved reached 120 million, accounting for more than 99 percent of farmer households across China, which meant that people's communes covered almost every corner of rural China. Accordingly, land tenure in rural China entered a special period up to twenty years.[15]

EFFECT OF IMPLEMENTATION

The model of the people's commune system featuring "three-tiered ownership structure, production team at the bottom, collective management" had severe institutional flaws as important means of production, including that land was held collectively, property rights inside each organization were blurred, rights of land disposition and transfer were limited and opportunism prevailed. Moreover, the blurred property rights would definitely lead to a high cost of supervision and unsatisfactory labor incentives.[16] During the 20 years of the people's commune system, China's rural economy almost stagnated, with a mere 1.48 percent annual growth rate of agricultural production and a 2.13 percent average growth rate of grain production. Grain possession level per capita was equivalent to that of 1957, with nearly 23 percent of farmers having less than 180 kilograms and more than 100 million farmers still suffering from a subsistence problem. The people's commune system also decreased agricultural productivity as the net value of agricultural output per laborer lowered from 806.8 yuan in 1957 to 508.2 yuan in 1978, falling by 37 percent. Farmers' annual per capita income from distribution was as low as 88.53 yuan in 1978.[17] It proved that the people's commune had dampened farmers' enthusiasm, lowered supervision effectiveness and caused low efficiency of the land management system.

Household responsibility system

A movement of "fixing the output quota to individual households" prevailed at Xiaogang Village, Anhui Province, in 1978, unveiled a new round of rural reform and triggered a revolution of rural land tenure from the bottom up.

DEVELOPMENT PROGRESS

The household responsibility system in rural China went through four stages for improvement (see Table 3.4 for details).

Table 3.4 Household responsibility system[18]

Time	Events
1978	The agricultural management model featuring "unified management combined with centralized and independent management, and two-layer management" was adopted in 1978 with the allocation principle that "after turning over the part of grain to the state and keeping the part for the community, farmer individuals were entitled to the rest." In this way, collective ownership of rural land was ensured, while farmer individuals gained independent management, so the relationship between management and income distribution was optimized. This system enabled farmer households to become the basic unit of land management once again and farmers to have the right to land use, right of independent management and right of surplus product earnings, which repaired the defect of the high cost of supervision and lack of incentive under the people's commune system and largely improved efficiency of labor.
1984	*Notice on 1984 Agricultural Work from Central Committee of CPC* specified that "contract responsibility system normally should work over 15 years" and "encourage farmers with good farming skills to take more land" to ensure farmer households' land contracting relationship and give farmers fixed terms for land contracts. It was also required to make innovations on land use systems and encourage the circulation of land use rights under the fundamental framework that land was held collectively and managed by households.
1993	*Amendment to Constitution of the People's Republic of China* published in 1993 officially confirmed the legal status of the household responsibility system. The *Agriculture Law of the People's Republic of China*, revised in the same year, specified the rights of land subcontracting, transferring, priority contracts and inheritance with details. Starting from the second round land contract, the contract term would be prolonged for another thirty years following the first contract. Given the land was owned collectively and the land use for agricultural purpose didn't change, after having permission from contract-issuing party, farmer households were allowed to transfer, sublease and exchange their lands according to the law.
2003	*Law of the People's Republic of China on Land Contract in Rural Areas* officially came into effect from March 1, 2003, which meant that the household responsibility system have entered a new historical period and land contracting relationships have been stabilized. From the rural household responsibility system to the land use rights circulation system, China's rural land system reform has been progressing, and collective ownership has undergone fundamental changes. Land use rights, land ownership and land management rights have been separated from each other.

EFFECT OF IMPLEMENTATION

The successful implementation of the household responsibility system at the early period of reform and opening up established a direct connection between farmers and land resources, avoided the "free rider" phenomenon under collective production and solved the problems regarding supervision and incentive. The system largely improved agricultural production and farmers' living standards. From 1979 to 1984, the annual growth rate of gross agricultural production was 8.98 percent, among which the growth rate of crop farming was 6.61 percent, while that of gross agricultural production from 1952 to 1978 was 3.25 percent and crop farming 2.59 percent. From 1978 to 1984, the annual increase of crop was 34 billion jin (a unit of weight equivalent to half a kilogram) and that of cotton 13 million dan (a unit of weight equivalent to fifty kilograms); per capita grain possession increased from 637 to 790 jin and that of cotton from 4.5 to 11.8 jin. From 1979 to 1984, the total purchase price of agricultural byproduct grew by 1.58 times, with 7.1 percent average annual growth. The income from selling products by rural productive forces and members across the country grew from 58 billion yuan in 1978 to 150.1 billion yuan in 1984, up 17.2 percent annually. Farmers' net income increased from 38.1 billion to 146.1 billion yuan, up 25.1 percent annually.[19] But the progress could not conceal the accompanying negative effects of this rural land tenure reform: great changes on the main body and time limit of land use rights, little clear legal assurance and severe short-term predatory management. Meanwhile, agricultural development was faced with potential dangers in correlation to the unsound product supply system in rural areas and inappropriate water conservation planning.

Current circumstances and problems of land tenure in rural China

Current circumstances of land tenure in rural China

Corresponding to the requirements of rural land tenure reform, China has issued rural land management laws and rules and established a rural land law system with Chinese characteristics since 1978.

Legal and regulatory system of rural land system

Laws and regulations on rural land management can be split into four levels (see Table 3.5 for details).

Rural land ownership system

It is stipulated by the *Constitution of the People's Republic of China* and the *Land Management Law of the People's Republic of China* that rural land and land in the suburbs are collectively held unless otherwise specified as being owned by the state; homestead, private plot and private hilly land are also owned collectively.

Rural land use system

REGULATIONS ON RURAL LAND USE

It is stipulated by the *Land Management Law of the People's Republic of China* that

> [s]tate-owned land and collectively-held land (by farmers) can be used by organization and individual according to law; contracted management of the

Table 3.5 Legal and regulatory system of rural land system in China[20]

Level	Laws and regulations
Enacted and issued by the state	1. *Constitution of the People's Republic of China* (March 14, 2004) on fundamental economic systems including rural land tenure; 2. *General Principles of Civil Law of the People's Republic of China* on property rights (April 12, 1986); 3. Core elements and main framework of rural land management laws and regulations: *Land Management Law of the People's Republic of China* (Aug. 28, 2004) and *Law of the People's Republic of China on Land Contract in Rural Areas* (Aug. 29, 2002); 4. Other laws that have close connection with rural land management: *The Agriculture Law of the People's Republic of China* (Dec. 28, 2002), *Forestry Law of the People's Republic of China* (April 29, 1998), *Grassland Law of the People's Republic of China* (Dec. 28, 2002), *Auction Law of the People's Republic of China* (July 5, 1996), *Organic Law of the Villagers Committees of the People's Republic of China* (Nov. 4, 1998). These laws have laid down specific rules on rural land ownership, right of use, state control on land use, transfer of land contract and management right, transfer of right to rural land contractual management, land exploitation and utilization, cadastral management, land resource and environment protection.
Enacted by the State Council	1. Rules and regulations for the enforcement of laws, such as *Enforcement Regulations of Land Management Law of the People's Republic of China*; 2. Notices, measures, regulations and stipulations for some specific management goals such as *Emergency Notice from the State Council on Preventing Use of Agricultural Land for House Building* (1983), *Agricultural Land Occupation Tax Interim Regulation* (1988), *Land Reclamation Regulations* (1989), *Interim Measures for the Administration of Foreign-invested Development and Management of Tracts of Land* (1990), *Hydropower Development and Resettlement Interim Policy on Large and Medium Scale Water Resource & Hydro Power Engineering Construction* (1991), *Notice of State Council Approving and Forwarding the Document from State Land Management Bureau on Strengthening Rural Homestead Management* (1990) and *Regulation on the Primary farmland Protection* (1998).
Enacted by ministries and commissions under the State Council	1. Laws and regulations on regulating state control on rural land use and routine cadaster management: *Interim Regulations from State Planning Commission and State Land Management Bureau on Construction Land Planning and Management* (1987), *Notice of General Office of the State Council Forwarding Work Report from State Land Management Bureau on Land Utilization Planning* (1987), *Notice of State Land Management Bureau Issuing Routine Cadaster Management Measures (for rural areas) (for trial implementation)* (1992), and *Notice of State Land Management Bureau Issuing Handling Suggestion on Some Cadaster Management Problems* (1992);

Level	Laws and regulations
	2. Laws and regulations on land ownership: *Opinions from State Land Management Bureau on Determining Land Ownership Issues* (1989) and *Response Letter from State Land Management Bureau on Land Ownership Dispute Handling Problems* (1991).
Enacted by provinces, municipalities and autonomous regions	*Contract Management Measures on Beijing Rural Land Household Responsibility System* (1988), *Jiangsu Province Rural Land Resource Management Measures* (1992), *Hainan Province Regulations on Second Round Land Contract* (1996) and *Hebei Province Regulations on Rural Land Contract Management* (Sept. 1999).

collectively-held land should be done by farmers belonging to the collective economic organization in the fields of crop farming, forestry, animal husbandry and fishery production. . . . The collectively-held land that are collectively held by farmers according to law should be operated and managed by rural collective economic organization or villagers' committee; the collectively-held land that belong to more than two rural collective economic organizations should be operated and managed by rural economic organizations or villager groups; the collectively-held land that are collectively owned by village and town farmers should be operated and managed by village (town) collective economic organizations.

REGULATIONS ON OBTAINING RURAL LAND USE RIGHT

It is stipulated by the *Law of the People's Republic of China on Land Contract in Rural Areas* that

> [r]ural land contract adopt household responsibility system; for barren mountains, gullies, mounds and desolate beaches where household responsibility system doesn't fit, invitation of tender, auction and public investment promotion can be adopted; the collectively-held land that are collectively held by farmers according to law should be operated and managed by rural collective economic organization or villagers' committee; the collectively-held land that belong to more than two rural collective economic organizations should be operated and managed by rural economic organizations or villager groups.

Besides, the *Land Management Law of the People's Republic of China*, *Law of the People's Republic of China on Land Contract in Rural Areas*, the *Agriculture Law of the People's Republic of China* and the *Guaranty Law of the People's Republic of China* also lay down detailed regulations on how to obtain land use rights by farmers.

Rural land management system

The rural land management system mainly includes management of cadaster[21], land use, land transaction and land transfer by the state.

LEGAL BASIS FOR RURAL LAND MANAGEMENT SYSTEM

The legal basis for the rural land management system includes: *Land Management Law of the People's Republic of China, Regulation on the Primary Farmland Protection, Organic Law of the Villagers Committees of the People's Republic of China* (November 4, 1998), *Law of the People's Republic of China on Land Contract in Rural Areas*, and *Notice of State Land Management Bureau Strengthening Cadaster Management* (October 1987).

RURAL LAND MANAGEMENT SYSTEM IN CHINA

China had not developed a complete land management system from the establishment of the People's Republic of China to 1979, and only some preliminary and temporary land management work had been done at different phases. After 1979, a series of policies and measures were issued, and land management work was gradually standardized.

In 1982, the Land Management Bureau (under the Ministry of Agriculture, Animal Industry and Fisheries) was established. In 1986, the State Land Management Bureau, directly subordinate to the State Council, was established for national land management and rural and urban land administration affairs, which realized the unified management of national land resources. In March 1998, the State Council formed the Ministry of Land and Resources of the People's Republic of China to manage national land recourses and rural and urban land administration affairs. Since 1998, a five-level (central government, province, city, county and town/township) land management system, featuring "unified management of rural and urban land administration affairs"[22] and a "combination of regional and central systems while giving priority to regional,"[23] has been gradually established.

Problems of the rural land system

Fragmented land management restricts rural commodity economy development

The current rural land system is based on the principle of equal distribution, which results in land fragmentation, small land management scale and fragmented rural land management. According to an investigation by the Ministry of Agriculture of the People's Republic of China, the average land area operated by each farmer household decreased from 0.53 hectares in 1990 to 0.49 hectares (7.34 mu) in

2000 in 5.86 pieces, among which 4.16 pieces (accounting for 71 percent of arable land) have arable land less than 0.07 hectare each.[24] In practice, fragmented land management has the disadvantages of poor market adaptability, high cost and low efficiency, which hinders productivity growth and the use of modern management methods and techniques and restrains the development of the rural commodity market.

Blurred land ownership results in disordered allocation of land property rights

As the rural land system has no regulated legal protection, a series of problems remain unsolved, such as unclear rural land ownership, low marketization of the rural land use system and transfer system, and low income from land management. Laws such as *General Principles of Civil Law of the People's Republic of China*, *Land Management Law of the People's Republic of China* and *Agriculture Law of the People's Republic of China* have clear provisions that state rural land is collectively owned. But the definition of "collective" is neither clear nor definite. For instance, the *General Principles of Civil Law of the People's Republic of China* refers to town/township and village levels, while the *Land Management Law* and the *Agriculture Law* refer to town/township, village and agricultural collective economic organization. Different legal definitions make rural land ownership very confusing. Moreover, the legal definition of contracted management rights is neither clear nor sufficient. Management rights, by nature, fall into the category of use rights, which derives other rights, including the right to transfer, sublease, buy shares and mortgage and rights to earnings. However, contracted management rights, although by nature being use rights, is limited to cultivation rights, incomplete rights of earnings and a tiny part of disposing rights. There are neither certain legal norms of land use rights nor clear stipulation on legal processes, legal forms and legal protection methods of the main body, status, limit, acquisition and transfer of land use rights.

Limited land circulation methods limit the effectiveness of economies of scale

The nature of land circulation is land disposing rights (of land use rights) derived from land contracted management rights. According to related laws and regulations, rural land circulation is not allowed to change the purpose of land use. There are also limitations on two circulation models – "mortgage" and "inheritance." The right to mortgage is only limited to "barren mountains, gullies, mounds and desolate beaches," but the right of collectively held land, such as farmland, private plots, private hilly lands and homesteads, is not allowed to be used for mortgage. Only "forest land" is allowed to be inherited but with restrictions on inheriting contracted management rights. These restrictions deny the property rights endowed by contracted management rights. The restrictions on mortgages are derived from a dearth of social insurance in rural China and are supposed to protect farmers' subsistence. Logically speaking, the right to mortgage merely presents a possibility that farmers may lose land, but legislation allows land transfer, which means farmers can lose land in practice. From this perspective, limitations on the right to mortgage are confusing. Inheriting land contracted management rights is based on its asset attributes. Now that land circulation is limited to villages or communities, it is not proper to deny someone's right to inheritance with the reason that the person is a village or community member. Limitations on these two circulation models increase destabilizing factors of contracted management rights and decrease contractors' future investment expectations, which is detrimental to the development of scale land management.

Land management system "giving priority to regional" does no good for farmland protection

China's current land management system – "combination of regional and central systems while giving priority to regional" – can hardly fulfill the overall and long-term interest requirements for rational land use and farmland protection. In practice, assignment of personnel of land management authority is subject to the local government, while the land management authority at a higher level only has the power of personal proposal and the duty of filing, not the decision-making power. Such a system makes grassroots land resource authority (at prefecture-city level or under) only enforce policies and decisions from the local government at the same level. This leads to a phenomenon that higher-level land resource authority actually has little policy supervision or professional guidance on lower-level ones, and land resource policies are severely twisted when implemented. In this situation, a land management authority is marginalized to be only a will enforcer of local government at the same level, so it exerts no influence on illegal land action by the government.

Farmers' interest demand can't be fully satisfied

According to the *Decision of the Central Committee of the Communist Party of China on Some Major Issues Concerning Promoting Rural Reform Development*, issued at the third plenary session of the 17th CPC Central Committee, transferring rural land contracted management rights should not change its nature of being collectively owned, should not change rural land's purpose for agricultural use and should not jeopardize farmers' legitimate interests. However, in practice, due to farmers' limited knowledge, their interest demand is hardly met, and infringement prevails, which can be seen from the following aspects:

LAND TRANSFER IS AGAINST FARMERS' WILL

Some land transfer contracts, dominated by the government, neither have signatures of farmers nor letters of their authorization, which shows no respect to farmers as the main bodies of land transfer. The government adopts disguised administrative means to intervene with land transfers, making both sides of land transfers illegal. This means that the farmers' will and legal interests are being infringed upon.

INAPPROPRIATE LAND PRICES

Rural land circulation should protect farmers' economic interests and let farmers enjoy the corresponding economic benefits. In practice, however, land circulation normally features low rent (four hundred to six hundred yuan per mu each year) and long tenancy terms. Farmers can only get the immediate benefits but have no rights to future land value-added profit or long-term benefits. What's worse, in some areas, subcontracting prevails; whereby someone rents a piece of land from farmers for a low price and then lends it for a higher price to exploit the price difference.

INSECURE BENEFITS FROM LAND CIRCULATION

Some agricultural enterprises or contractors don't pay the rent or demand a lower one when they fail to generate as much revenue as expected. Some even abscond with money. Farmers' earnings cannot be secured.

LAND CIRCULATION CHANGES THE PURPOSE OF LAND USE, THREATENING FARMERS' SUBSISTENCE

After gaining land management rights, some contractors construct buildings on the farmland, which destroys farmland. After a land contract expires, the farmland can no longer be used for agricultural purposes. Farmers' subsistence and interests are damaged.

Thinking on the puzzling issue: establishing common ownership of land

Opinions on rural land ownership never reach an agreement among academic circles. There are mainly two opinions that call for privatization and nationalization of rural collectively owned land. Practice has proven that the quality of rural land being collectively held conforms to the law of socialist market economic development and China's national conditions. But it also presents a number of problems, such as the main body of property rights having no real power, land ownership being blurred and farmers' rights not being well protected. All these provide us with theoretical and practical orientations, for example, how to improve land ownership based on the principle of land being state owned and rural land collectively owned. Common ownership of land comes into being against this background.

Why is nationalization of rural collectively held land not applicable?

Opinions for nationalization of rural collectively held land

THOUGH NOMINALLY RURAL LAND IS HELD COLLECTIVELY, IT IS OWNED BY THE
STATE BY NATURE

Xiang Guohui (an associate professor of agricultural economy at Zunyi Medical University) holds that although rural land is collectively held nominally, it is owned by the state in nature. The legally blurred ownership and incoherent internal logic results in a lack of clear boundaries of rural land rights. This severe defect causes the nullity of rural land ownership and insufficient protection for farmers' rights of land use, earnings and disposing. Conflicts concerning land rights emerge and deteriorate. Farmers have no principal status in the market and thus are at a disadvantage. In reality, governments at different levels exercise authority on behalf of the state. While farmers' rights of land use, earnings and disposing are not ensured, land added value keeps increasing, leaving an institutional gap for monopolies of land markets by the government and land rent seeking by corrupt officers. Abolishing collective rural land ownership is to cut off the institutional basis for illegal occupation of farmland and illegal collection of fees and taxes from farmers by organizations at the village level. Nationalization of rural land makes land state owned. This move coheres with the property of land being state owned (owned by citizens) and a socialist nature. Land nationalization should be carried out on the principles of market rules and add no burden to farmers to avoid a problem under the background of the household responsibility system that farmers carry heavy burdens but receive little assurance for their rights. According to these principles, the plan for rural land nationalization is as follows: the state "purchases" the collective land ownership, the collective distributes the "earnings" to farmers and farmers purchase the eternal land use rights (privatization) with the "earnings."[25]

SUBJECT OF COLLECTIVE LAND OWNERSHIP POSSESSES NO REAL POWER

Yan Yunqiu (a law professor at Central South University) also holds that the subject of collective rural land ownership has no real legal significance. According to the law, collective rural land is owned by the farmer collectives at three levels: administrative village, town/township and over two collective economic organizations in the village. This means the legal subject of collective rural land ownership is "farmer collectives" of three levels, but there is no precise legal definition for "farmer collectives." Only when the right is combined with its clear subject can it be of significance. "Farmer collective" is not a legal definition. By legal definition, none of the towns/townships, villages or villager groups is a collective economic organization, so none of them is the subject of collective land ownership. China's current law only admits collective land use rights, while collective land ownership has become an appendant of state ownership and lost its actual function. Problematic issues such as nullity of collective land ownership, insufficient functions and unclear relationships with state ownership are manifestations of the absence of functions. As a result, no one is actually responsible for the land. In practice, a number of problems come up and hamper productivity growth, so reform on rural land ownership becomes imperative. The most desirable choice for the reform is rural land nationalization.[26]

Liu Fengqin (an associate professor at the School of Social Development and Public Policy at Beijing Normal University) also maintains that collective rural land ownership is based on no sound reasoning, and even worse, it could easily slip into ownership of village committees, a defect in the current rural land system. Rural land nationalization is to take back land ownership held by village committees and make the state the owner of land. Accordingly, the state will possess some macro-control power, such as approval of changing the purpose of farmland and rights of interference to prevent farmland destruction. The land use rights and rights to earnings will be granted to farmers. Farmers won't have to sign land contracts with their local village committees anymore, but with the state, and the village committee will only function as the deputy of the state with no right to change the contract terms, quantity or contractor of a land contract. This move will fundamentally stop illegal actions of a village committee based on its land ownership, such as forcibly changing land contracts and collecting rent.[27]

NATIONALIZATION OF LAND IS A REQUIREMENT OF FOOD SECURITY AND
AGRICULTURAL SUSTAINABLE DEVELOPMENT

Yan Yunqiu gives two reasons for land nationalization. First, food security is an important goal of any government's macro-control. Food production is seen as top priority in any society with any social system. Food security is a public undertaking, and the government should assume the responsibility of ensuring food security and preventing any tragedy concerning it. The state should provide safeguards for the food demands and needs of all citizens, which makes land nationalization necessary as the state is able to enhance macro-control and centralized management of farmland in this way. Second, it is necessary for agricultural sustainable development. Under the rural land collective ownership, the original "farmer collective" falls into the property right bearer. The household contractual management of farmland leads to land fragmentation, and an individual household is not able to do much about agricultural infrastructure construction, maintenance and management, and ecological environment construction and protection. Ecological environment construction needs considerable investment and has a strong external effect. Thus, this work can only be done by the state.[28]

Opinions against nationalization of collectively held rural land

First, the current economic and social relationships in rural China feature the rural community as a social organization unit and the household as a benefit distribution unit. Breaking down the current situation brings no good to rural stability. Furthermore, one has to solve the following problems before taking any measure: how will a rural social organization be run? How will the state exercise its ownership effectively facing the scattered and huge farmer population? In reality, the state is an abstract subject, the exercise of whose ownership must be realized by grassroots administrative organizations and personnel, which show no big difference with the current collective land ownership.

Second, rural China features a low degree of agricultural mechanization and productivity, and the imbalance between the large population and limited land is severe. The less-developed secondary and tertiary industries there makes non-agricultural employment very difficult. For farmers, land remains their subsistent resource, and it will take a considerably long time before changing farmland from pure living resource to wealth. Against this background, land nationalization, no matter by tenancy system or permanent lease system, it is hard to achieve scale management or improve agricultural efficiency. What's worse, high rent will become a heavy burden for farmers.

Third, farmland nationalization brings a considerably high cost. There are two ways to achieve land nationalization: land expropriation and confiscation. The state won't be able to afford the costs of buying land, while the latter choice, confiscating the collectively owned land for free, will clearly worsen the relationship between the state and farmers, which will endanger rural stability and trigger political risks.[29]

Fourth, unforeseeable costs and policy risks exist. The implementation of rural land collective ownership is the result of China's long-term practice. Both privatization and nationalization of land entails institutional change to land ownership. The cost of such revolution and the accompanying shock to agriculture and the whole society cannot be overlooked. After more than ten years' practice of reform and a market-oriented economy, land ownership is no longer the biggest motivation for farmers, while their real concern has turned to profits from land and land management costs. Thus, sticking to rural land collective ownership is undoubtedly the best institutional choice. It conforms to China's current national conditions, saves large costs for institutional reform and shows the future orientation of China's rural land system development. It is mostly applicable.

Fifth, there are unknown consequences of land nationalization. Land nationalization promises state land ownership, promotes land commercialization and scale management, and accelerates rural surplus laborer transfer. However, it is still unknown what means the state will adopt for land nationalization and whether it will actually improve land allocation efficiency. What's worse, land nationalization may lead to more serious illegal land requisition, and farmers' rights and interests unguaranteed, which is very likely to cause social turbulence.[30]

Why is privatization of collectively held rural land not applicable?

Opinions for privatization of collectively held rural land

PROPERTY RIGHTS OF COLLECTIVELY HELD RURAL LAND IS NOT CLEAR

The majority of scholars for privatization of collectively held rural land holds that the current rural land collective ownership and the household responsibility system haven't solved the problem of blurred land ownership and resulted in the nullity of rural land ownership, a historical problem left from the people's commune system. Rural land used to be owned by a production team, a production brigade and a people's commune before the reform, but who received the ownership was not clear. Nowadays, collectives are represented by organizations at three levels: villager groups, village committees and village and town governments. The relationship between farmers and collectives sees no fundamental change from that before the reform. It is merely a change of label. The blurred land ownership is not able to meet demands of market economy development, which can only be solved by thorough land privatization, specifying the ownership to farmer individuals.[31]

THE CURRENT RURAL LAND SYSTEM PUTS FARMERS AT AN UNFAVORABLE SITUATION AND RURAL REFORM AT A THEORETICAL TRAP

Scholars such as Zhang Xinguang (a professor at the Research Center of Comprehensive Rural Reforms, Xinyang Normal University) hold that China's current rural land system is unfavorable to farmers in the following ways. First, the current farmland ownership system results from the struggle between urban and rural interest groups. As farmers have little political power and lack legal protection of land rights and interests, any obstruction of farmland ownership marketization is actually to preserve the interests of urban interest groups. Those obstructive behaviors are a fight against giving up low-cost rural land resources and making deprivation of farmers' farmland easier. Second, the core of China's farmland equal distribution system is "farmer collective membership rights," which leads to rapid rural population growth and, in return, lowers the rural man-land ratio. It results in fragmented farmland management and decreased rates of return for land and marginal benefits. Third, equal distribution of farmland makes the functions of farmland as means of welfare and social security more obvious. In nature, this is to confuse farmland ownership with a social security system, the real intention behind which is to let the state assume the responsibility of providing social security for total population (mainly referring to 900 million farmers). However, it actually sets up a theoretical trap for deepening rural reform (the core is farmland ownership innovation). Due to this analysis of drawbacks in the current system, rural land privatization is the best choice for deepening rural land reform.

THE CURRENT TWO-TIER MANAGEMENT SYSTEM DOES NOT PROTECT FARMERS' INTERESTS AT THE ROOT

Zhang Xinguang believes that the so-called two-tier management system, which is expected to have advantages of both superiorities of a rural collective economy and the production initiative of the household responsibility system, is merely the "official language" of experts involved in rural policy making but cannot fundamentally solve problems related to scale management and economic development. Farmers' interests won't receive effective protection until farmers' land property rights become clear. Only in this way can the binding effect of legal systems and farmers' self-protection of land rights be combined together. It is proposed to take widespread privatization of farmers' homesteads as the beginning of solutions to the fundamental reform of farmland ownership marketization.[32]

Opinions against privatization of collectively held rural land

First, land privatization does not conform to the fundamental principles of socialism. Public ownership of means of production is the essential economic system of socialism. As China is a socialist country, land privatization runs counter to socialism. Neither socialist ideology nor the *Constitution* allows it.

Second, land grabbing would be the result of land privatization. There won't be any limitation on land transaction and transfer under land privatization, which is bound to cause land grabbing. A consequence will be the enlargement of the wealth gap and the increase of landless farmers, bringing a series of social problems concerning employment, residence, public security and so on.

Third, rural land privatization will damage farmland. Land owners or farmers will enjoy full liberty under rural land privatization and private ownership. Land owners will be more likely to invest their land in non-agricultural industries for higher earnings instead of agriculture with low efficiency. It will result in more unregulated land use and a decrease in farmland size and possibly lead to agricultural recession.[33]

Fourth, land privatization will not necessarily motivate farmers' enthusiasm for agricultural production and investment in land. From analysis on the land situation in Russia after the dissolution of the Soviet Union, some scholars found that although people had attributed the backward agricultural development to public ownership, the land ownership reforms in Russia haven't made any significant achievements, and its agriculture continued to slump even after privatization. Thus, they came to a conclusion that theoretically speaking, whether land system will generate motivation is not all decided by the fact of whether the land operator owns the land or not. Instead, it depends on whether the system can ensure a high productivity ratio. Thus, privatization of collectively held rural land in China is not applicable.

Fifth, land privatization is not necessarily meant to improve farmers' income. Some scholars argue against the opinion of improving farmers' income by means of land privatization. Scholars such as Sun Xiaojun (a lecturer at the School of Economics at Fujian Normal University) hold that the proposition of collectively held rural land privatization comes from the worship of land privatization; however, land privatization itself does not have functions of improving agricultural productivity or increasing farmers' income by nature. The practices in Chinese history and in most developing countries which implement land privatization now (such as India and Bangladesh) have proven that land privatization cannot increase farmers' income and rural productivity fundamentally but will cause land grabbing and destruction on productivity. Farm management, by means of land privatization in developed countries, such as the United States, Canada and Australia, conform to their national situations, small populations on large land areas and highly developed industrialization and urbanization, which is very different from China's situation. Under this consideration, privatization of collectively held rural land is merely a concept with no practical significance and is not applicable.[34]

Sixth, currently China has no institutional environment for rural land privatization. In rural China, there is no corresponding institutional environment for land privatization. It's hard to ensure justice during this process. Moreover, most

Chinese farmers have no demand for land privatization. The current rural land system does not hinder the transfer of land use rights. Land privatization deviates from the pursuit and choice of China's revolution and it's a historical regression.[35]

Insist on collective ownership of rural land, and implement common land ownership

Under the current rural land collective ownership, every farmer has an equal share of public ownership, but in principle, they assume no responsibility of public ownership in economic activities. Farmers enjoy owners' rights (such as land contractual management and homestead construction) on many specific issues but don't have to bother themselves as land owners. They will only remind themselves of their being owners to harvest interests of owners, meanwhile refusing to take responsibility as owners. From the perspective of an individual, in many circumstances, it is reasonable to disclaim the responsibility of owners. For example, to stop land misuse and ensure effective land use, a farmer may make attempts to exert pressure on the village collective in some way. As a result, the farmer will receive no increase of personal interest, even if his interests in rural and are protected. It illustrates why, from a personal perspective, most farmers won't bother themselves with collective land. Consequently, the larger scale the public ownership is, the larger population will get involved, and the less balance there will be between the costs and return of a certain action taken by an individual farmer as a land owner. "Free riders" will see more chances, and rural land collective ownership will be more likely to become an abstract concept. There come the problems of how to insist on rural land collective ownership, protect farmers' legal interests and motivate their initiative together. Common ownership of land arises naturally.

Common ownership of land achieves the combination of collective ownership and individual ownership of rural land. On the basis of upholding the institutional foundation of the three-level ownership with production teams at the bottom, common ownership of land will further ensure farmers' individual rural land management rights and effectively separate ownership and rights to land use and earnings from rural land. It protects farmers' legal interests, conforms to the development rules of China's socialist market economy and is a historical inevitability. At the same time, rural land collective ownership has functions of social security and unemployment insurance. Land remains the main source of living and income for farmers. Giving up rural land collective ownership will cause social instability. Land is a scarce and non-renewable resource. It provides a place for farmers to set their foot on and makes room for farmers' labor. It is also the platform where everything goes on, so land ownership has direct influence on farmers' living conditions. Apparently, land ownership and fair land distribution are two significant factors for popular support. Rural land common ownership ensures clear ownership, protects the legal interests of the state, collectives and individuals, and accomplishes sustainable agricultural development.

4   An unique opportunity for China's rural land circulation

The nature and principle of rural land circulation

Nature of land circulation: population movement and wealth movement

The nature of land circulation should be understood as a movement of wealth and a necessity for achieving the public's integrated development. The visible side of this process is the transfer of land, while the invisible side is the flow of knowledge and information and the movement of wealth.

The circulation of rural land arises from the wealth effect. The nature and source of wealth is shifted to land when farmers are decreasingly dependent on it and have increased liberty. As the famous quote by William Petty goes, "[L]abor is the Father and active principle of wealth, as lands are the Mother."[1] Land reflects the nature of wealth, records human work and accumulates human wisdom. It connects productivity with relations of production, the history of social development, the integrated development of human beings and comprehensive social reforms. Land witnesses the replacement and development of social patterns.

The transfer of land is the movement of wealth, which is a population movement and a process of realizing people's integrated development. As Karl Marx said,

> In fact, however, when the limited bourgeois form is stripped away, what is wealth other than the universality of individual needs, capacities, pleasures, productive forces, etc., created through universal exchange? The full development of human mastery over the forces of nature, those of so-called nature as well as of humanity's own nature? The absolute working-out of his creative potentialities, with no presupposition other than the previous historic development, which makes this totality of development, i.e. the development of all human powers as such the end in itself, not as measured on a predetermined yardstick? Where he does not reproduce himself in one specificity, but produces his totality? Strives not to remain something he has become, but is in the absolute movement of becoming.[2]

This paragraph demonstrates the relationship between wealth and people's integrated development and provides the theoretical basis for our analysis on how land carries wealth and realizes integrated development.

To sum up, rural land circulation equates to population movement, reflecting people's liberty and emancipation. It also illustrates knowledge integration and information flow. Rural land circulation makes knowledge and information flow come true and infuses land with intellectual value, which covers the shortage of farmers' limited knowledge.

Principle of land circulation

According to the third plenary session of the 16th CPC Central Committee,

> the household responsibility system for contracting land is at the heart of the basic rural management system. In the long term, we must maintain and improve the two-tier management system of household responsibility and overall coordination, and safeguard farmers' land use rights in accordance with the law. Within the land contractual period, farmers can voluntarily transfer their land use rights and get compensation in return according to the law. Measures for land transfer shall be improved, and large-scale agriculture shall be gradually developed.

In 2013, it was highlighted in the No.1 Central Document (the first policy document of the year issued by the State Council) that China must stick to the rural management system in building a new socialist countryside. Indeed, it is the cornerstone underpinning the development of agriculture and rural areas in China. It has been proven that this institutional arrangement is of great potential. We should follow government policy, improve the rural management system and ensure that farmers enjoy more comprehensive and secure land use rights. While the nature of contracted land under the household responsibility system shall remain unchanged in the long run, a system for the transfer of land use rights can be put in place and further improved on a legal, voluntary and compensatory basis. This is in line with the way the relations of production evolve in rural areas.

Achieving common prosperity

The household responsibility system, adopted in 1978 against a special historical background, had greatly unleashed an initiative for agricultural production among rural households. The long-term shortage of major agricultural products in China was quickly addressed. Food and clothing, an issue Chinese people had grappled with for thousands of years, miraculously became sufficient. However, with the development of agricultural productivity, a large number of rural residents left their hometowns to find work or do business in cities, leaving farmland idle or unattended in a number of regions. Today, the major concern of rural communities is no longer "food on the table"; rather, it's about the "wallet." In others words, it's about how to achieve prosperity after sufficient food and clothing is provided. Thus developing agriculture, maintaining stability in rural areas, and increasing farmers' incomes have become relevant issues in China's economic and social development. Under the household responsibility system, farmland is separately managed by households, seeing no advantage to large-scale production. Both crop yield and economic efficiency are low. And any major breakthrough can hardly be made in the attempt to realize common prosperity in the countryside. The household responsibility system, once an incentive for farmers to increase income and become well-off, is gradually losing steam. Thus a new land system reform is essential if China wants to address the institutional defects of the household responsibility system, to boost its rural economy and to solve problems relating to agriculture, rural areas and farmers. The top priority now is to design a system that is conducive to the transfer of land management rights in rural areas. Large-scale, intensive farming is the most important way to increase incomes. China has been home to individual farmland ownership, collective ownership and separate management based on collective ownership. Now it's shifting to large-scale management on the basis of collective ownership. A commercialized production and marketing system that meets the needs of modern agriculture is taking shape and the transformation of traditional agriculture in the process, which can help avoid production and management risks faced by individual farmers. Moreover, large-scale, intensive farming will boost competitiveness and increase incomes. This shift could help identify a method of agricultural development that suits China's national conditions, one that could bring common prosperity to the new socialist countryside.

Incremental land reform

Land circulation reform will be an incremental process. The transfer of land management rights on the basis of collective ownership is in line with the historical trend of shifting away from a radical rural reform to an incremental one. The land reform, the agricultural collectivization and the people's commune movement in the 1950s were all radical reforms. However, the transfer of land management rights is developed on the basis of the household responsibility system, and it shows a steady and incremental change. It has been proven that incremental reform has less resistance and can reduce reform risks and that it better fits the realities of rural areas in China. Therefore, it's more conducive to the reform in relations of production in rural areas. And in exploring ways for rural land system reform, we must choose a prudent, incremental, least risky and phased approach. Comprehensive reforms are needed to facilitate rural development, and the key is to coordinate and balance all aspects of the reforms. Only by doing so could it be possible for reforms to be undertaken. Yet comprehensive reforms aren't equal to the sum of work in all areas. Something of great significance shall take the lead in the process. And that is innovative change to the relations of production concerning farmland.

Self-improvement under the socialist relations of production

Land circulation is aligned with the overall shift from fundamental changes of relations of production to self-improvement of the socialist relations of production. In terms of the nature of changes to relations of production, the four previous reforms were very different from each other. The 1950s land reform changed land ownership from the hands of feudal landlords to those of individual farmers. The agricultural collectivization and people's commune movement transformed private land ownership by farmers to a socialist collective ownership. Ownership is the basis of relations of production, and the focus of the first three reforms was precisely on land ownership. These were all fundamental changes. The household responsibility system introduced in early 1980s separated land ownership and land use rights and changed the way land was used, while the commitment to collective land ownership remained unchanged. Therefore, progress was made in handling the relations of production, and socialist production relations in rural areas were improved. And so was land circulation. While collective land ownership, the land use rights of farmers and the nature of farmland are unaltered and the land-related rights and interests of farmers are protected, land management rights have now become transferable, and farmland can be used more efficiently. This boosts economic returns, increases farmers' income and stimulates the initiative and creativity of rural residents, demonstrating the great vitality of rural reforms.

Positive interactions between the government and the people

Land circulation is yet another example for the transition from "farmers accepting reforms driven by the government" to "the government actively guiding new changes initiated by farmers." In the early days of the People's Republic of China, the 1950s land reform, the agricultural collectivization and the people's commune movement were all forcibly pushed through by the CPC and the government. Back then, under the country's industrialization strategy, agriculture, rural areas and farmers were supposed to provide resources for industrialization and urbanization. Institutional arrangements like the people's commune, the unified procurement and sales system for certain agricultural products and the dual urban-rural structure were imposed by the state. However, since 1978, farmers started to play an active part in reforming the relations of production in rural areas, which proved highly successful. And it began with an experiment conducted at Xiaogang Village, Anhui Province, where farmers carried out production by household. Most noticeably, the roles of the government and the farmers were reversed in the process. Farmers began to drive new reforms, and the government provided guidance. Currently, many regions in the country are trying out new methods of land transfer, during which local governments are more proactive in offering guidance and services, and a market-based approach is used. Effective models suited to different places have been developed – land shares, land cooperatives, land banks, land circulation service centers and so on.

These models conform to the economic realities of rural areas and help accumulate valuable experience. They have made a difference in rural reforms and development and injected fresh impetus into the development of agricultural and rural communities.

The practices of land circulation

It is pointed out explicitly in the report of the 18th National Congress of the CPC that we should uphold and improve the basic system for rural management and set up a new system for the intensive, specialized, well-organized and commercialized management of agriculture. Based on this, models of rural land circulation will be discussed, and existing financial practices will be reviewed in a bid to identify reasonable approaches to develop a new agricultural management system for China.

After the adoption of the household responsibility system, the No.1 Central Document issued for the first time in 1984 stated that rural households were allowed to subcontract their farmland to more capable farmers with the permission of the village collective. And the policy concerning the transfer of land management rights was legislated in the *Rural Land Contracting Law*, which was passed in 2002. As the government stated in the *Decision on Several Major Issues on Promoting the Reform and Development of Rural Areas* adopted at the third plenary session of the 17th CPC Central Committee, "[W]e must strengthen the regulation of and provide better services to the circulation of land management rights, and establish markets for it. We encourage such ways of circulation as subcontracting, leasing, swaps, transfers, and shareholding cooperatives. And we support large-scale farming."[3] These are the policies concerning land circulation in rural areas.

As the rural economy grows, rural land circulation will occur in a number of ways, with increasingly diversified subjects participating in the process. At present, land circulation has three main features: (1) there is a rapid increase in the acreage of land transferred, yet the percentage of farmland transferred varies greatly among different regions. Statistics show that more than 30 percent of farmland was transferred in six provinces, and less than 10 percent in three other provinces. (2) Subcontracting and leasing are major components of land transfers, while land swaps and land shares are quickly gaining momentum. By late 2012, 49.3 percent of land circulated was subcontracted, 28.9 percent leased, 6.5 percent swapped, 5.9 percent converted into land shares, 4 percent transferred, and 5.5 percent circulated in other ways, like temporarily tilling by other farmers. There were surges in the acreage of land circulated through land shares, lease and shareholding cooperatives, up 30.2 percent and 29.1 percent over 2011, respectively. (3) There is a clear trend of land being circulated to people engaged in specialized farming, cooperatives and companies. By late 2012, 64.7 percent of land circulated went to rural households, 2.9 percent lower than that of 2011; 15.8 percent went to specialized cooperatives, and 9.2 percent to companies, an increase of 2.3 percent and 0.8 percent year on year, respectively. By late 2012, more than 200 million mu of arable land was managed by entities other than the owner of land use rights, accounting for 15.9 percent of the total contracted land in the country.[4]

In actual practice, quite a few types of trials have been conducted to circulate land management rights in rural areas and develop large-scale management. A variety of models have been developed in the process, and some typical ones are as follows.[5]

Rural land swap: the Shawan model in Xinjiang

Rural land swap refers to the act of owners of contracted land in village economies swapping their farmland and accordingly land management rights to make farming more convenient or to conduct large-scale farming. The most representative case is the Shawan model in Xinjiang.

In 2004, Xiabahu Village in Shawan County in Xinjiang Uygur Autonomous Region was the first to swap farmland. The three or four plots of land previously owned by each household were consolidated to two pieces so that land was less scattered, making it easier for cultivation and laying irrigation pipelines. In 2005, to promote drip irrigation, cut costs, improve efficiency and conduct large-scale farming, all the arable land of the village –10, 368 mu in total – was swapped. This brought the coverage of advanced water-saving technologies like drip irrigation and micro-irrigation to 100 percent. After that, annual net income per capita in the village reached RMB eight thousand yuan, and the land utilization ratio increased by 3 to 5 percent. There was even a four hundred mu net increase of arable land, bringing an extra 347 yuan of income per person per year. Because of the considerable returns from land swaps, six villages in Sidaohezi Township, including Xiazhuangzi village and Zhongxin village, followed the practice, with 42,700 mu of land swapped. It realized relatively concentrated, standardized and intensive agricultural production. As a result, the cotton production base at Shawan Village saw higher coverage of the same strain, better quality and higher yield per unit area. This greatly facilitated large-scale and intensive farming, accelerated industrialization of agriculture, increased both efficiency and farmers' incomes and sped up the development of rural economy.

Lease of rural land: the Xiaogang model in Anhui

The lease of rural farmland refers to the practice of farmers leasing all or part of their contracted land through lease agreements to large producers, leading businesses engaged in agricultural industrialization or cooperatives for the purpose of agricultural production. This doesn't change the nature of contracted land under the household responsibility system – leasers continue to enjoy their rights and assume their obligations related to their contracted land. The lessee makes rental payments regularly to the leaser according to the lease agreement and is not allowed to change the nature of the farmland. The rent can be paid annually in cash or in kind. Those who rent land include agricultural companies, large producers and the village collective itself. The Xiaogang model of Anhui is a typical case in point.

Land circulation in Xiaogang Village, Anhui Province, began with the village itself renting land from farmers and then leasing it to other farmers or large producers. This encourages land transfers to large producers and more capable farmers so that they can do large-scale farming. It changes the way land is used through coordination by the village collective, tapping the potential of land and generating more profits. Xiaogang Village has about two thousand mu of arable land, of which 60 percent has been rented out and consolidated for cultivating mushrooms, flowers, grapes as well as poultry farming. This new model, featuring concentrated use of farmland, development of large-scale agriculture and increased productivity, has brought huge economic benefits to local farmers. In 2009, per-capita income in the village hit 6,600 yuan, 1,446.8 yuan higher than the national average of 5153.2 yuan in rural areas in the same year.[6]

Rural land shareholding cooperatives: the Nanhai model in Guangdong

Land shareholding cooperatives enable households to become land shareholders when they transfer their land use rights on a legal, voluntary and compensatory basis. This way, land use rights become equity stakes, and land is transferred to enterprises to be used efficiently. The Nanhai model of Guangdong Province is the most typical case. In the 1990s, the Nanhai District of Foshan City, Guangdong Province (previously known as Nanhai City, Guangdong Province), implemented the Rural Land Shareholding Cooperatives system. Different zones were clearly defined first and the number of land shares and their coverage determined. Land Shareholding Cooperatives were set up, and everyone in the collective participated and was given shares. The age distribution of farmers, method of land share distribution and population changes were also taken into account. The transferred land was either leased directly or had factories built on it and leased. Farmers get returns from their land shares as the non-agricultural use of farmland generates added value.

Rural land share-based farming: the Fengxian model in Shanghai

Rural land share-based farming refers to the practice where households contribute their land use rights to get land shares, and the pooled farmland is used for industrialized agriculture. Shareholding companies or rural production cooperatives are formed in the process to facilitate agricultural industrialization. The Fengxian model in Shanghai is the most representative one.

In Fengxian District, the minimum return of land per mu was set at four hundred yuan and the minimum dividend per mu two hundred yuan; the order and way of distributing profits within the cooperative was also stipulated. Statistics show that by late 2011, the total number of specialized cooperatives in Fengxian District had reached 350, with 65,000 household participants. Agricultural products sold by these cooperatives were worth 2.2 billion yuan, an increase of 7.3 percent over the previous year, generating a profit of 112 million yuan. The value of the cooperatives' unified procurement and sales stood at 1.68 billion yuan, about 76 percent of the total, up 8.4 percent from the previous year. These cooperatives have three characteristics. First, they cover a wide range of industries. Apart from the traditional cooperatives for food production, vegetables, fruits, flowers, twenty-nine new rural tourism and marketing cooperatives, accounting for 8 percent of the district's total, are developing rapidly. Second, they are organized in diversified ways, including "cooperative + base + rural households," "cooperative+ rural households," and "established companies + cooperative + households." Eighty percent of them are organized in the first two ways. Third, their performance is improving year after year. More than two hundred cooperatives are doing fine or good. Democratic management is in practice, and information about internal affairs is disclosed. The entity that uses the land is obligated to hire workers from the cooperative, and favorable considerations are given to nearby households when job opportunities come up. This boosts the development of industrial agriculture.

Rural land subcontracting: the Wenzhou model in Zhejiang

Rural land subcontracting means farmers in a village subcontract all or part of their contracted land to other farmers in the same village for agricultural production. This doesn't change the nature of the land as the original owner continues to enjoy his rights and has obligations under the household responsibility system. Subcontracting is the most common way of land circulation in China in terms of the acreage and percentage of farmland it covers. And the Wenzhou model in Zhejiang Province is a good example, where subcontracting takes place either via the village economic cooperative by large producers in the village or by entities from outside the village.[7]

Homestead for an apartment and contracted farmland for social security: the Jiulong model in Chongqing

Under this model, farmers give up their homesteads and get an urban apartment in return. The homestead is then used for urbanization and industrialization. At the same time, farmers voluntarily give up their contracted land and then enjoy urban services like health care and pensions. Gradually, a unified urban-rural public services system will be set up. The most representative case is the Jiulong model in Chongqing.

Basically, two things were done in Jiulong, Chongqing. First, homesteads were exchanged for apartments. The government built new residential communities on about 20 percent of the original homestead area. The remaining 80 percent was either reclaimed as farmland or for urban use. Every villager got twenty square meters of floor space in return for the homesteads they surrendered, and an additional five square meters for free. They needed to pay 580 yuan per square meter for extra floor space. Second, contracted land was exchanged for social security. In this aspect, first, the Jiulongpo District introduced a policy that stipulates rural residents are allowed to apply for urban household registration on a voluntary basis if they have no stable source of income and voluntarily surrender their homestead and farmland use rights. They will enjoy the same rights as urban residents in terms of education for their children, reemployment training, health care and pensions. Meanwhile, a new rural cooperative health-care scheme has been rolled out to ensure that rural residents get proper health-care services. Second, land-management rights are leased and rent is collected on the assumption that annual yield of rice per mu of land is worth about a thousand yuan on average. The transfer of land is done on a voluntary basis so that farmers no longer have to work on their land but could instead seek employment in agricultural parks or urban companies. By doing so, their employers provide them with social security, and they receive stable earnings from the transferred farmland, leading to a continued rise in income.

5   Land trust

The new system for rural land circulation

Why a trust?

A trust is an effective form of practicing common ownership as it conforms to the rules of a socialist market economy. It achieves a socialization of personal property and diversification of property rights, while ensuring clear rights among the unity of free individuals and shared interests. It holds onto merits and gets rid of drawbacks of traditional public ownership. A "common-ownership trust" is a property rights system of richer content, less restricted in form and more inclusive of goals. Based on common governance, sharing and joint possession, a "common-ownership trust" takes trust as its basis and entrustment as its means. Taking the separation of three rights as a principle, it gives consideration to both individual possession and joint possession of productive forces and the means of production. It stresses fairness and efficiency and combines socialism and a market economy in an ideal way. Thus, to explore effective solutions for rural land circulation, we study the history of trusts to re-add the functions of land management and land exploitation to trusts and let "common-ownership trusts" play to its institutional advantage.

The origin of trusts

The history of trusts can be dated back to before the Norman Conquest in 1066. "Use" was then the form of a trust and prevailed at a time when land owners left their homes to join the Crusades. The land owners entrusted their land to their friends who clearly knew that they managed the land not for their own interests but to allow the land owners to reap revenue. When the original owners returned, they would regain land ownership.[1] When the land transferee kept his promise to make the land transferor beneficiary of any land revenue, land ownership was transferred concerning a legal relationship, but the usufructuary still received revenue from the land. In this way, land was regarded as the origin of a trust.

Advantages of a "common-ownership trust"

A trust has been given a new mode of life with socio-economic development. Its innovation has penetrated through all fields, and it is an important institution in the current economic society. As an integrated financial platform, a trust takes full advantage of the institutional advantages of the capital market, currency markets and industry markets. With diversified means such as stock rights and creditor's rights, a trust is able to broaden financing channels and offer comprehensive financial services. The trust industry adopts active measures to cooperate with other financial industries and provides systematic financial services to satisfy diversified and multilayered capital needs. The industry has allowed flexibility in financial innovation and set up an example for the entire financial industry to follow, all in a bid to perfect China's financial system. Trust development will help build a balanced, flexible and vigorous financial system, offering service and support for the development of a substantial economy. By giving financial support to the transformation of the country's mode of economic development, trust development will upgrade China's economy and boost common prosperity.

Transform the country's development mode and ensure steady growth of the private economy

While financial development becomes a fundamental element of China's economy, trusts will play an important role in the country's financial development. Since 2013, China's then newly formed government signaled a reorientation of China's policy stance as Premier Li Keqiang confirmed a willingness to "support substantial economic development by stimulating the current capital stock." Credit growth has been increasing rapidly over time, but the money has not been invested into the market, either being absorbed by the real estate market or "circulating" inside the bank system. Under this condition, stimulating the current capital stock shows great significance, which is also a necessity for regulating a monetary transmission mechanism. Against this background, the trust industry will fully play its role in bettering the allocation of financial resources, making good use of increased capital and stimulating the current capital stock to make the existing financial resources a key point in the transformation of the country's development mode; all this means "a good use of money." Trust development follows marketization, diversification and globalization and provides China's economic development with better and more efficient financial services.

TRUST INDUSTRY ATTACHES IMPORTANCE TO THE VALUE OF CULTURE AND
PROMOTES ITS DEVELOPMENT

Currently, the culture industry is faced with a tremendous amount of opportunities. In September 2009, the executive meeting of the State Council approved the *Plan for Promoting the Culture Industry*, which indicated that the industry's development was raised to a level worthy of a national strategy. With a large market and vast development space, the culture industry was an integral part of China's Twelfth Five-Year Plan, which ended in 2015. Against this background, the industry has witnessed rapid development and has grown faster than a number of other industries. The culture industry has become a new economic growth point, among which film and television, animation and other forms of art have witnessed tremendous growth. Considerable capital needs grow under this rapid growth, but special features of the industry make it hard to meet capital needs through traditional financing channels. Thus, a culture industry of trusts has sprung up. A trust serves as an important means for financial services to back up cultural development. It is a financial tool with features such as asset management, fund circulation and a combination of financing and leasing goods. Trust products for culture, film and television, and artwork have gradually been launched, and these products have encouraged the trend of artwork financialization and promoted the prosperity of diversified cultures. A culture trust encourages commodification of the culture industry and gets access to financing through a cultural product trust plan. It relieves the capital shortage in the development of the culture industry, turns cultural products into future earnings and brings investors continuous earnings.

As a creative industry, the culture industry features intangible assets and services. Its profit generation is quite different due to its long project cycle with no cash flow during the process, and projects are all subject to risks. Take filmmaking as an example. Unpredictable factors exist at all stages, including seeking permission to film, filming progress, marketing, the box office and copyright selling. A culture industry trust is usually an asset-light business. As pledged real assets are insufficient, risk control should give more importance to cultural brands, influence, teams and successful cases as well as add intangible cultural assets and other pledged goods to set credit levels and firewalls. The trust industry is developing financial products that are fit for the culture industry and that are able to improve the chain of financial services. It has been strengthening regulation for asset use and project management, offering financing help for medium and small-scale enterprises and accelerating the development of medium- and small-scale and creative cultural enterprises. The culture industry usually takes a project-by-project business model, especially in film and television production. It conforms to a trust model where a project is in place first and then targeted financing follows. Most cultural enterprises are not capable of capital management, but financing from traditional banking channels is difficult. Newly emerged financing means such as cultural industry funds and trusts are undoubtedly becoming an important supplement for financing. Earnings from the culture industry trust mainly come from box office revenues, sales revenues, copyrights, advertisements and transfer income. However, investors are faced with market risks as volatility and uncertainty exist in the market of cultural products. Thus, trust companies attach more importance to credit enhancement measures such as cultural brands and other intangible cultural assets like a security and a third party's guarantee. Trust companies are involved in projects and have control of accounting and cash flow to achieve optimized management and risk control.

A TRUST ERASES CAPITAL BOTTLENECKS AND SUPPORTS DEVELOPMENT OF THE
PRIVATE ECONOMY

Small and medium-sized enterprises play an irreplaceable role in China's economic development; however, financing has long been a headache for them due to narrow financing channels. There are a number of cases about enterprises with very promising market potential getting into trouble due to financing difficulties. "The loan growth rate of small and micro business is not lower than the rate of the average considering any category and the increased load amount is not lower than that of the corresponding period last year." Had the capital needs of small and micro business been met, the enterprise "cell" would have been stimulated, and consequently structural adjustments would gain a micro foundation. Because of some inherent factors in China's financial system, loan on credit widely exists in the financial market, although indirect financing dominates. Financing of small and medium-sized enterprises mainly comes from self-owned capital and private lending. An effective solution to financing problems requires broadening financing channels of nonbank financial institutions. A small and medium-sized enterprise trust is a practical choice. A trust is able to find a distinctive solution to financing problems as it helps break down institutional barriers and structural deviations. Trust companies have institutional advantages such as intensive integration and compatibility, which is also a distinctive feature of such companies. Thus, a trust is able to become the main model of innovation for the financing needs of small and medium-sized enterprises.

The trust industry, bank industry, security industry and insurance industry are four major financial pillars. As the market environment, policy system and legal parameters of the trust industry make progress, trust products will have a larger development space and become a realistic and important choice regarding the financing for small and medium-sized enterprises. A combined trust refers to the practice that a trustee manages, uses and disposes property (personal property, immovable property or intellectual property) from a number of trust settlers collectively. By combining the strengths and credit of multi-enterprises, a trustee is able to enhance the strength and credit of enterprises and free up private capital. In this way, a trust combines a loan on credit from financial institutions and government resources together and solves financing difficulty. Through a combined trust, a number of small and medium-sized enterprises are integrated. A trust company issues a trust plan for financing and allocates funds to different enterprises. As direct financing, a combined trust is relatively flexible considering scale, terms and interest. It has more self-control on capital flow and fewer limitations. A combined trust gathers a number of small and medium-sized enterprises and makes a package, making up their shortage of limited financing capacity. Financial institutions like banks and securities have complicated evaluation and approval procedures and a high time cost, while for a trust, detailed matters fall under the responsibility of the trust settler and trustee, with high efficiency, a less complicated assessment and approval procedure and easy operation. Directed at the characteristics and financing needs of small and medium-sized enterprises, the trust industry has designed a number of innovative financial products and given support to their financing needs. These products concentrate on the "innovation of the financing model of small and medium-sized enterprises" and take advantage of a trust such as multifunction and good ductility, which forms a complete new financing platform with high efficiency, wide application and low risk and where government policy and resources take the lead, social capital gives support, and trust, guarantee, and commercial companies interact with each other. A trust constructs a new financing channel for small and medium-sized enterprises, ensures a win-win structure between it and the government, banks and enterprises, and is an effective trial for addressing the financing problems of small and medium businesses. To sum up, with advantages such as simplified and convenient procedures and lowered financing costs, the trust industry optimizes government structures and breaks through restraints of high costs and risks faced by small and medium-sized enterprises, thus showing a strong capability for financial innovation.

TRUSTS PROMOTE ECONOMIC TRANSITION, UPGRADE AND DEVELOPMENT

At the Eighteenth CPC National Congress in November 2012, the CPC Central Committee changed the term of office, and so did the central government at the National People's Congress (NPC) and the Chinese Political Consultative Conference (CPPCC) in March 2013. Premier Li Keqiang then put forward the idea of building an upgraded version of the Chinese economy when meeting the press from home and abroad. The idea is a realistic one. With thirty years of rapid development since the reform and opening up, the country's economic aggregate has reached a considerable size. Both the productive forces and a comprehensive national power have witnessed great development. However, the previous economic growth model featuring high investment and considerable pollution has not fundamentally changed. The impact of the international financial crisis has made China's long-accumulated problems even more severe, and institutional and structural contradictions have worked to worsen each other, making the problems more severe and pressing. Currently, China's economy is at the critical restructuring stage with enormous capital demand. The current financial system with the banking industry at the center has limited financing channels. Choices are either high-risk stock investments or low-risk and low-interest bank deposits. There is a lack of financial products that feature good investment returns. As private capital is limited, the trust industry has launched a combined trust fund to provide a long-term stable capital source and financing mechanism for economic restructuring and upgrading. It both satisfies the realistic needs for investment and opens up a reliable capital channel for economic development. Drawing on international experience, the long-term financing function of the trust is able to integrate the large amount of development funds and to promote long-term development of the national economy. Through a wide range of trust products, China is able to flexibly raise and regulate development funds, which is conducive to long-term, stable economic growth as well as the development of the trust industry itself.

Finance supports economic restructuring and promotes economic upgrading, the essence of which drives the real economy. As a financial integration platform, the trust industry fully utilizes its distinctive advantage of being "cross-market, cross-industry and cross-product" and absorbs capital from diversified sources into industries related to national welfare and people's livelihoods, including the culture industry, transportation, science and technology, water conservation, electric power, logistics, agriculture and so on. It provides comprehensive, systematic and matching financial services for the real economy and satisfies diversified and multilayered demands. The development of trust is in line with the country's national development strategy and policy orientation. With favorable opportunities, trusts effectively play the role of being highly innovative, flexible and diversified to meet market needs. New trust products are coming out, such as for agricultural investment, culture and artwork, low carbon and loans for small and medium-sized enterprises. Engaged in the vast capital market, the trust industry is active in all industries dedicated to nation building. Trusts have broken down previous institutional restraints, shown extraordinary vitality and illustrated their ability to be innovative in the process of economic restructuring. While promoting a coordinated and robust economic society, China's trust industry also witnesses its upgrading and stronger growth. In line with national policy, the trust industry gives consideration to "addition" as well as "reduction." To enhance regional coordinated development, the trust industry strengthens financial support for "issues of agriculture, farmers and rural areas," small and micro enterprises, strategic emerging industries, the modern service industry, independent sci-tech innovation and so on. At the same time, the trust tightens credit granting and loans to high-pollution and energy-intensive enterprises and projects to push for technical changes, the upgrading of business and the promotion of low-carbon economic development.

Support agriculture, farmer and rural areas; develop the real economy and realize financial inclusion

Changing the country's economic development model and promoting a strategic adjustment of its economic structure is inevitable to turn China's large economy into a strong one. The report to the Eighteenth CPC National Congress took the strategic restructuring of the country's economy as the orientation to change the country's development mode. Finance is the core of a modern economy. China's economic upgrade requires the structuring of its real economy as a basis, which is impossible without financial support. As the second largest financial pillar, the trust industry ensures key industry adjustment and boosts reasonable capital needs. By weeding out outdated capacity, it accelerates the transformation of economic growth and improves the quality and efficiency of economic development. Relying on its functional advantage of "being a financial mall," trusts give full play to the diversity, flexibility and innovativeness of financial products and contribute a lot to the aforementioned restructuring and mode transformation through financial support. As a financial management system, where trust property is managed and disposed by other people, trusts exert highly effective efforts for better industry coordination and asset allocation and play a growing role in China's economic restructuring, being a backbone for the rejuvenation of the Chinese nation.

TRUST SUPPORTS THE DEVELOPMENT OF THE REAL ECONOMY AND IMPROVES INTERNATIONAL COMPETITIVENESS

Along with the development of a socialist market economy and the advancement of the reform and opening up, China has entered a key stage of economic restructuring, industrial transformation and upgrading. The real economy is an important carrier for upgrading the Chinese economy, while capital is a crucial factor for developing the real economy. As a critical innovative financial means, trusts are committed to supporting the real economy and promoting industry growth. They have given tremendous support to improving China's international competitiveness. Currently, China is at a critical period of its development mode transformation and economic restructuring. At this stage, higher requirements for capital markets are in demand for promoting scientific innovation, industrial upgrading and preparing supporting facilities for emerging industries. It was put forward at the Executive Meeting of the State Council in June 2013 to enhance financial efficiency and stimulate the current capital stock, to adjust the directional flow of current capital and to channel the "lost capital" into the "arid" real economy. A government-trust cooperation model enables trust organizations to serve as a financial service adviser and a planning expert to support the government in property disposal, management, integration and recombination. Trust agencies invest in promising enterprises, launch industrial investment funds and optimize regional industrial structure through capital operation. They provide financial support for key projects, pillar industries and industrial upgrades. They strengthen the role of finance and support technology transformation and upgrades. All these efforts energize China's economic restructuring.

Corresponding to the different characteristics of enterprises of different scales in different industries and regions, the trust industry has developed diversified trust products and adopted tailor-made measures for credit enhancement accordingly. As enterprises vary in capital needs and creditworthiness, trust agencies launch combined-trust plans for projects with large capital needs such as building high-tech parks and commercializing high technologies. Social capital from varied sources becomes large-scale trust capital through integration. The differentiated trust product designs make precise positioning for real businesses and satisfy the diversified capital needs of the real economy. The trust industry encourages the accelerated development of emerging industries and the upgrading of pillar industries. It offers refined, differentiated and individualized financial products via trust projects. The trust industry also cooperates with export-oriented companies to carry out trade financing and export credit and enhances the international competitiveness of export-oriented innovative companies. The industry trust investment fund allows for equity investment for unlisted enterprises, design of combined investment trust products with shared benefits and responsibility, and investments in entrepreneurship, corporate restructuring and infrastructure. As a wealth management expert, the trust investment fund provides both financial support and other value-added services such as strategy management and asset operation, enabling the combination of financial investment and corporate management. The fund targets projects in the nonemployment fields. As direct financing investment in targeted enterprises, the fund gives support to real businesses and industry development through the operation of the asset market.

TRUSTS SUPPORT "FARMER, AGRICULTURE AND RURAL AREAS" AND PROMOTE NEW
URBANIZATION

Along with accelerated urbanization, China's rural land system is faced with many new problems, among which land circulation has become the focal point of the country's land transformation. The fundamental way of achieving agricultural modernization and urbanization is to make the best use of land resources. As land is the most essential agricultural element, any issue related to land concerns the trio of "agriculture, farmers and rural areas." It is of far-reaching significance to building a new socialist countryside to carry forward rural land circulation. Scientific land-use planning and management is urgently needed as a large number of rural labor forces leave the countryside for jobs and business opportunities in urban areas, leaving land in many regions fallow and desolated. Problems in land circulation at the current stage include restrained thoughts, scarcity of protective mechanisms and unregulated circulation methods; there is also an alarming tendency of land circulation for non-agricultural purposes. As a modern financial tool, a land trust carries through scientific land circulation, optimizes resource allocation and solves the problem of fragmentation and small scale. The traditional agricultural production mode has been changed and a number of benefits reaped, such as facilitating the agricultural restructuring and large-scale development, enhancing land management efficiency, increasing farmers' earnings, promoting labor force transfer and accelerating urbanization. The new type of land trust is able to assist new urbanization in a steady and vigorous way and protect rural land effectively in the long run. In this way, farmers' property rights get protected, they harvest added value with their land property and enjoy the benefits of modernization and urbanization. A land trust mechanism largely extends agricultural management scale and makes it possible to conduct a new round of scientific planning for agriculture and rural infrastructure. With the development of land trust circulation, agricultural production will realize scale management, and farmers will directly receive earnings from land trusts. The residual income will be devoted to the building of rural public services, infrastructure improvement and other social benefits. A property income trust is an effective way of linking land circulation and social security. While basic rural social security is provided by the government, part of the earnings from land trusts can be used to raise social benefits, overcome the resistance against rural reform, and maintain the rural reform momentum and stability.

Land trust circulation enables farmers to be directly involved in urbanization. A land trust features a stability of property and makes land a fortune that could be inherited for generations. A land trust mechanism protects land inheritance and rural stability and prevents farmers from losing land and becoming refugees. As land trust circulation is more regulated and stabilized over the long term, it releases farmers from seasonal restrictions on farming. While the scale management of land is achieved, farmers are able to free themselves from scattered land plots and to broaden their income channels, either by starting their own businesses or finding jobs. Farmers still have income through land rent. Land use rights held by farmers are concentrated on the trust platform; a trust clarifies legal relations and suffi-ciently protects farmers' rights. By playing its inherent institutional and financial advantages, trusts have facilitated effective land circulation and realized large-scale, intensive and capitalized management. It is a step that has not only increased land management revenue and intrinsic value but also implemented financialization and capitalization of farmers' rural land management rights. Consequently, a number of goals have been reached: the financing channels for agriculture and farmers are broadened, people-oriented urbanization is implemented and farmers' incomes see steady increases. With the arrangement of land trusts, rural land resources have been effectively put to use, entered the market as factors of production and gener-ated earnings. In summary, an accelerated land circulation further facilitates the transfer of the rural surplus labor force and creates a larger development space for large-scale, intensive and efficient agriculture management.

TRUST BOOSTS DEVELOPMENT OF STRATEGIC EMERGING INDUSTRIES AND USHERS
IN CHINA'S REJUVENATION

Although strategic emerging industries are backed up by emerging technologies and innovation, technologies themselves are far from enough. The development of emerging industries needs a combination of technology and capital, that is, scientific innovation and financial innovation. Globally speaking, of the emerging industries in the United States, such as computer science, the Internet and bio-logical medicine, none is able to survive without support from the capital market. An advantageous cycle is formed as innovation facilitates high-tech development which in return stimulates a new round of scientific innovation. The development of the emerging industries requires long-term and enormous capital investment through the capital. However, due to the features of large investment, high risk and good returns, investment in innovative industries faces a relatively high threshold. Financing is a universal problem for emerging industries all over the world. The development track of strategic emerging industries is not a linear one. Because of tremendous uncertainties, upgrading technology moves fast, "soft assets" such as intellectual property abound and traditional security for loans such as fixed assets is insufficient. Technical features and capital needs vary in different industries and development phases, which also differ significantly from traditional financ-ing conditions. Thus, strategic emerging industries impose demanding require-ments on financing schemes and risk guarantees. Traditional financing industries don't have corresponding risk analysis mechanisms and means of financial tech-nology. Trust institutions have innovative management modes, flexible product designs and rigorous risk control measures to fulfill the financial needs of tech-nical enterprises through multiple channels and modes and support the devel-opment of strategic emerging industries. The trust industry vigorously promotes the combination of industry, science and capital, improves the investment system and constructs a complete investment chain of strategic emerging industries. Its financial innovative advantages are able to break through financing bottlenecks in strategic emerging industries. Financial instruments such as fund integration, finance leases, trusts and guarantees will provide more complete financial services for strategic emerging industries.

Trust improves people's livelihood, fulfills social responsibility and helps achieve common prosperity

Accelerating the development of industries related to people's livelihoods is impossible without powerful support from the financial industry. China's financial system and transformation should focus on improving people's livelihoods and achieving common prosperity. The fundamental function of a trust is to allocate resources to the industries that are most contributive to economic and social development at minimum cost and to keep systematic risks under control. Currently, a trust is becoming the frontier of financial innovation. Under the structure of separate operation and supervision, banks, securities and insurance are providers of traditional financial products. As flexible as a trust is, it naturally leads the way in China's financial innovation and has become the bridgehead and test field of China's financial system. A trust not only serves gold-collar workers in skyscrapers but also serves as a mighty instrument for promoting social development, improving people's livelihoods and helping ordinary individuals and families realize their dreams. On the one hand, trust companies provide multiple and personalized financial services for customers; on the other hand, they allocate financial resources and take advantage of diversified, multichannel and multi-layered financial services to strengthen financial support for industries related to people's livelihoods, including education, medical services, infrastructure, environmental protection, housing projects, social welfare, social security, poverty reduction and so on. By giving full play to its capability of capital integration and coordination, trusts break through financing bottlenecks and regulate and carry out investment and financing through market-based operations. By cooperating with government, trust companies implement systems of tax exemptions and government-funded interest discounts for loans from industries related to people's livelihoods. Financial support for these industries is to help disadvantaged groups and public welfare schemes with a very low rate of return. Government-funded interest discounts relieve debtor burdens and achieve double support from the public economy and finance. Risk compensation for loans from industries related to the people's livelihoods is established to offer compensation for losses, a move to activate the initiative of financial supply from other financial institutions.

Give play to institutional advantages of "common-ownership trust" and explore land circulation means

Theories and practices of "common-ownership trust"

A common ownership system merges together a number of ownership forms and realizes the coexistence of multiple property rights. This system is in line with socialism and the market economy, representing a new type of relationship. On this basis, a "common-ownership trust" gives play to its institutional advantages and makes up the deficiency of traditional financial services. It proves to be a borderless intermediate institutional arrangement which attaches importance to both equity and efficiency and helps bridge the gap between the rich and the poor.[2]

After more than thirty years' development and five major reorganizations, the trust industry has gradually entered its golden period with steadily increasing registered capital and net assets and spirally rising total income and net profits. In June 2012, management trust capital exceeded 9 trillion yuan. The rapid development of the trust industry is rooted in the harmony between trust and social development.

Taking trust as a means, "common-ownership trusts" cover the capital market, monetary market and industry market. It casts off the disadvantages of private production and private capital and transforms production modes and forms of capital. It ensures social production and social capital based on socialized mass production and a large-scale gathering of the means of production and labor forces and realizes the socialization of personal property, diversification of property rights elements and inclusiveness of property rights. In this way, we call a "common-ownership trust" a new type of relations of production.

History of industry development. A "common-ownership trust" is based on the separation of the three rights – use rights, property rights and rights to earnings. On the basis of clear property ownership, it continues to mix diversified economic development forms together, including state ownership, collective ownership, private ownership, individual management and foreign investment. It broadens the development space, raises capability and optimizes the structure of multiple productive forces. Furthermore, it gradually alters social conflict and achieves a perfect combination of socialism and a market economy.

Institutional design. Taking a trust as the basis and entrustment as the means, a "common-ownership trust" gives play to its institutional advantage and transforms the mode of production and the forms of capital. It also gets rid of the disadvantages and absorbs the advantages of private production and private capital and realizes the socialization of production means and labor forces. It steadily forms social production and social capital based on socialized mass production and the large-scale gathering of the means of production and labor forces. At the same time, on the basis of socialized property rights, it further clarifies property ownership and optimizes the distribution pattern and achieves capital sharing by the people and financial inclusion.

Supervision philosophy. A trust system is a rudiment of democratic decision-making. The nature of democratic decision-making is a decision made by people, which depends on their average level of social knowledge. The more knowledge the people possess, the more democratic a decision is. Trust, as an intermediate institutional arrangement, represents the interests of a trust settler and trustee and separates property rights and use rights. It gives consideration to both democracy and centralism and makes up the insufficient occupancy of social knowledge. In this way, it makes a democratic decision more scientific and offers the public services with maximized results.

"COMMON-OWNERSHIP TRUST" IS AN INTERMEDIATE INSTITUTIONAL ARRANGEMENT

The function of common ownership is to manage financial investments for others through entrustment. This institution boasts flexibility and efficiency and constitutes an effective form of corporate management structure in China. Through an organic combination of common ownership and a market economy, a "common-ownership trust" becomes a bridge between socialism and the market economy.

In practice, common ownership can be achieved through public ownership, collective ownership and a shareholding system, and they have somewhat boosted socio-economic development but also manifested some shortages such as low efficiency and blurred rights and liabilities. To sustain the development of a socialist market economy and conform to both socialism and a market economy, China should try new forms of ownership and establish a thorough modern property order by adjusting the relationship among the state, the collective and individuals and drawing proper borders among them. China also needs to confirm individual ownership of the means of production and to reflect the attributes of a common ownership of the means of production. Any system should give consideration to both common ownership and private ownership. Taking trust as the means, a "common-ownership trust" brings about reforms in the structure of the property rights of enterprises and ensures the socialization of individual property and diversity of property elements. It constitutes a modern corporate system and proves to be an effective form of common ownership.

Take rural land circulation as an example. In rural land circulation, the most realistic issue is how to make farmers retreat from the land and how to transfer, transact, transform and benefit from the management rights of contracted land. A trust mechanism clarifies land ownership and land use rights and achieves a diversity of land ownership. It divides land ownership to three levels – the state, the collective and the individual – and establishes state ownership of national land, ownership by farmers of collective land and household ownership. A diversified land property rights system makes it clear that land property rights belong to the state, the collective and the individual and realizes the unification of ownership, management rights and use rights.[3] Under the new land system, the relationship between the government and the land, the relationship between farmers and the land and the relationship between land owners and land users are reconstructed, which ensures rural stability and promotes the development of the rural relations of production. While land circulation links up to social security, part of the earnings from a land trust can be used to improve social security standards and reduce resistance against rural reform, which will help safeguard development and stabilization and give play to the institutional advantage of a "common-ownership trust."

A "COMMON-OWNERSHIP TRUST" ENABLES CAPITAL, KNOWLEDGE AND SOCIAL
RELATIONS TO RECEIVE SHARED GOVERNANCE, OWNERSHIP AND BENEFIT

A "common-ownership trust" takes trust as a platform, demonstrates the population's intelligence and transforms liquid assets into investment properties. It gives
consideration to both common occupation and individual possession of knowledge and most importantly fosters social relations.

First, taking trust as a tool, a "common-ownership trust" interacts with the capital market, monetary markets and industry markets, gathers scattered capital and
integrates social resources. It then makes use of its capital advantage, transforms
capital forms by turning liquid assets into investment ones and provides an effective capital arrangement for socialist economic development. Second, a "common-
ownership trust" uses institutional advantages and gives full consideration to the
duties, rights and interests of the trust settler, trustee and beneficiary. Trustees
(trust companies) build management teams, give play to team advantages, accumulate knowledge and make up for the insufficient knowledge of trust settlers
(investors) to provide financial services for trust settlers and meet the diversified
and multilayered needs of a socialist market economy. Last, the fundamental point
of shared governance, ownership and benefit of a "common-ownership trust" lies
in social relations. Karl Marx defined human nature as formed by the totality of
"social relations." The most obvious manifestation of social relations is that when
a trust project runs into a problem, the trustee will work to solve the problem at
once. The fundamental reason of this phenomenon is that under this arrangement,
social relations are freed and reconstructed.

Here is one more example. When the capital of a trust settler (investor) comes
into a trust company, a project is set up before the fund is ready, which means
when a trust company makes an investment, projects are already there, and the
trust company will then collect the money. This smart setup achieves the unification of knowledge, capital and social relations. When an investor chooses a trust
product, he is making an intellectual decision. When a trust goes through this
selection process, the trust management company gains an opportunity to gather
knowledge. When an investor invests his money into a trust platform, the investor
actually turns the liquid asset into an investment asset and gathers funds. When a
project runs into problems, all investors will gather together to discuss solutions,
which realizes the integration of social relations on the trust platform.

Clearly, the trust system achieves the integration of capital, knowledge and
social relations, which is naturally in line with China's special institutional
arrangement. Since socialism requires a planned economy, while a market economy obligates the thorough liberation of human individuality, it is rather difficult
to balance the two. As an intermediate institutional arrangement, a trust system
creates an organic combination of socialism and a market economy, proving to be
a convertor of interests and bridging the gap between the rich and the poor. This
integration and sharing system practically realizes financial inclusion and capital
sharing by the people, avoiding a monopoly of surplus value and realizing the
rational and universal benefit of distribution.

Practices of a "common-ownership trust"

In 2011, profits after tax in the Chinese banking industry achieved 1.25 trillion yuan, and 85 percent of the money in the market was concentrated in the hands of 5 percent of the population. The institutional design behind the facts is against common prosperity. People are deprived of equal opportunities to fortune, which goes against the purpose of a socialist market economy. But the practice of a "common-ownership trust" proves that a trust is a mechanism where the trust settler's interest is the top priority, the trust settler's supervision is in effect, and the trust settler is likely to receive maximized interest. It somewhat promotes the development of a socialist economy with Chinese characteristics.

CHINESE PRACTICE OF A TRUST

According to statistics of the Chinese trust industry, by the end of June 2013, the scale of assets managed by trust companies has broken through the 9 trillion yuan mark.

In a comparison between the trust industry and other financial industries, the capital scale of trusts exceeded that of public offerings of funds in 2010, and that of the insurance industry in 2012, and became the second-largest financial industry next only to the banking industry.

A TRUST IS IN LINE WITH A SOCIALIST ECONOMY MARKET WITH CHINESE
CHARACTERISTICS

A trust gives consideration to both socialism and the market and achieves the perfect combination of equity and efficiency. On the one hand, it conforms to market laws and creates social wealth; on the other hand, it takes common prosperity as the greatest common ground and helps the public reap maximum interest.

The effectiveness of a "common-ownership trust" can be seen as follows:

- Trust companies have created an annual rate of return for beneficiaries of 4.63 percent, 4.30 percent and 6.33 percent from 2010 through 2012.
- Trust companies have contributed, respectively, 36.6 billion yuan, 70.5 billion yuan and 186.1 billion yuan to beneficiaries from 2010 through 2012, the total of which reached 293.2 billion yuan.[4]
- The rewards trust companies have received from 2010 through 2012 were 2.78 billion yuan, 3.88 billion yuan and 14 billion yuan, accounting for about 10 to 14 percent of the total earnings from the trust property managed by trust companies.[5] This means that 86 to 90 percent of the earnings have been allocated to beneficiaries.

The superiority of a "common-ownership trust" can be seen from the following:

According to the statistics from the banking industry and trust industry, from 2009 to 2012, banks have taken 41.3 to 49.1 percent of total earnings,[6] while the earnings gained by trust companies only accounts for 10.7 to 17.5 percent of the total. Compared with banks, trust companies allocate the major part of their earnings to beneficiaries and are left with a small part (see Table 5.1 and Table 5.2 for detailed information).

The features of a "common-ownership trust" – shared governance, ownership and benefit – touches upon the fundamental issue of ownership, proving to be an effective form for the implementation of common ownership. Common ownership is a new form of ownership. Compared with other forms, it features clear property rights, explicit duties and liability and distinct boundaries. Common ownership combines state ownership, collective ownership and individual ownership and crosses regions and industries. It also features the socialization of capital and realizes the coexistence of the diversified subjects of property rights. By drawing clear borders, it solves the defect of blurred property rights in public and collective ownership, by which rights are protected and duties are made clear. Practice has shown that the effectiveness and flawless performance in the socialist market comes from the reality that a trust is effective for implementing common ownership.

Let's take a look at a specific trust project. When a project collects funds from ten people, it is owned by the ten; when a project collects funds from a thousand people, it is owned by the thousand; it is also true for 1.4 billion people, and this illustrates diversified property rights and the inclusiveness of a trust. In this way,

Table 5.1 Bank earnings and investor earnings[7]

Year	Bank earnings (100 million yuan)	Investor earnings (100 million yuan)	Total earnings (100 million yuan)	Percentage of bank earnings (%)
2009	7,328.24	9,492.39	16,820.62	43.6
2010	9,943.50	10,295.10	20,238.60	49.1
2011	12,945.77	16,173.59	29,119.36	44.5
2012	15,348.13	21,858.41	37,206.54	41.3

Table 5.2 Trust company earnings and beneficiary earnings[8]

Year	Trust company earnings (100 million yuan)	Beneficiary earnings (100 million yuan)	Total earnings (100 million yuan)	Percentage of trust company earnings (%)
2009	169.81	1,115.38	1,285.20	13.2
2010	235.48	1,286.45	1,521.93	15.5
2011	318.56	1,499.91	1,818.47	17.5
2012	462.44	3,877.23	4,339.68	10.7

it adjusts interest circulation routes, makes up for the deficiency of allocation from enterprises owned by the people and realizes the financial inclusion and capital sharing of the people. Introducing a trust system to state-owned business will effectively overcome the drawback of state-owned companies by drawing explicit boundaries and making clear the property rights of market entities. It draws a clear boundary among different companies and defines the subject of ownership and the subject of enterprise property. Under the precondition of not changing state ownership, a trust helps separate government functions from enterprise management and reduces the loss from inefficiency of such management and irrational decision-making. Introducing a trust to private enterprises will urge them to improve fairness, abide by the law and be more disciplined, not to mention improving their financial structure.

Moreover, a "common-ownership trust" is able to solve social problems and ease social conflicts. Introducing a trust system to land circulation will effectively solve the current problems without creating new ones. A trust system is based on the separation of the three rights, making sure that ownership of trust settlers (farmers) will not change and then regulating the use right of trustees (trust companies) legally. The institutional arrangement of a trust circulates rights of use and protects rights to earnings. Trust companies, serving as an agent, a bridge and a converter, combine the right to use land and the right to earnings.

The framework of a land trust

A land trust is about creating a free but also regulated land market. A land trust needs a legalized market to replace administrative authorities and take the place of government to participate in land transactions. It is to eliminate power from the market and end corruption resulting from land transactions. A land trust will eliminate the concept of land privatization.

A trust system establishes a macro framework for a land trust with a trust settler, trustee and beneficiary as the fundamental elements and the separation of the three rights. This macro framework presents a new logic and new order and also a new method and new route. Surrounding the three fundamental elements, the macro framework is also an assembler of values, which can lengthen its business chain and broaden its business scope, as it can be associated with banking and agriculture insurance, and develop an education trust, a profession training trust, an intellectual property trust, a pension trust and an administration trust.

Definition of land trust

Land trust is a new type of land system established in line with "common-ownership trust," which features clear property rights, direct interest, shared risk, remarkable benefits and easy operation. Based on collective ownership, land trust makes use of the multilayered property rights structure of common ownership and divides land into value assets and real assets. While sticking to the collective ownership of land, land trust further separates the rights of possession, use rights, rights to earnings, and disposal rights to meet the requirements of market economy. Farmers possess rights to earnings and the final disposal rights; trust companies have management rights and carry out scale management of the land.

*Land trust makes clear the property rights owner and represents a
new type of productive relations*

Based on the national authority's regulations, the rights and functions of collective land ownership are stipulated. Farmers' rights over the collective land are also made clear and gain government recognition and legal protection. These efforts break down institutional barriers and establish a distinct property structure that is able to meet the demands of socialist economic market.

*Land trust turns land resources into asset, with physical possession
of land no longer counting so much*

In the land trust system, farmers, as the beneficiaries, participate in the allocation of land earnings. It helps liberate farmers' minds from the physical occupation of land and make farmers more willing to give up their contracted land and invest their labor force and capital in non-agricultural industries, which facilitates better planning and use of the land.

Land trust improves land management mode and land use

Land trust doesn't undermine the household responsibility system; instead, it diversifies land management modes. In the land trust system, farmers are still allowed to rent land from trust agencies with each household as a unit, or households cooperate and carry out large-scale land management. It gives the competent ones preferential access to land management rights. In this way, the land's potential is released.

Nature of land trust: introducing intellectuality to land

Chinese farmers' knowledge level

Knowledge possession is an indicator for people's intellectuality, which hereby refers to people's ability to understand and solve problems with knowledge and experience and includes their cultural and technical competence and management capability. The low knowledge levels among Chinese farmers can be seen from the following aspects:

Overall low cultural competence: Farmers' cultural competence refers to their cultural knowledge and educational levels, which is reflected from the quality and quantity of cultural knowledge held by farmers. A main indicator is farmers' educational levels. Over the past five decades, China's illiteracy rate has declined by 64.12 percent, but the overall cultural competence of Chinese farmers still remains low. Of the 490 million rural labor forces, farmers receiving a high school diploma or even higher only account for 13 percent, while 49 percent finished junior middle school education and 38 percent primary school education. The number of illiterate farmers still accounts for 7 percent.[9] This is a huge gap against some Western developed countries: in France, more 7 percent of farmers hold university degrees, and 60 percent of young farmers hold an occupational secondary school certificate; in Japan, 5.9 percent of farmers hold university degrees, 74.8 percent of farmers finished high school education and 19.4 percent completed junior middle school education.

Overall low technical competence: Farmers' technical competence can be reflected from the quantity and quality of their technological knowledge and their agricultural proficiency. Due to farmers' low cultural competence, little agricultural knowledge involved in secondary school curriculum and insufficient professional education, most farmers have difficulties in reading agricultural technology books and grasping advanced farming skills. Many of them are still used to the traditional smallholding land management.[10] What's worse, there is high turnover among agricultural technicians, and more than half of them have switched to non-agricultural sectors.

Weak operations management capability: Having long been influenced by a planned economy and feudal traditions, Chinese farmers lack market awareness and the ability of grasping market economy laws.[11] They have weaknesses in operating, managing and coordinating large-scale social production. Without a strong sense of business management and scientific management, they often flinch from risks and competition and find it difficult to grasp market information and dynamics. Their weak communication skills result in a lack of sound interaction with the government. Plus, a majority of them receive little professional education or training on agricultural management. All these factors make them unable to accommodate to large-scale modern agriculture.

Farmers' intellectuality is an unavoidable issue

Farmers' knowledge insufficiency has become a bottleneck against China's sustainable agricultural development, makes them prone to be marginalized by the market and thus unable to enjoy the fruits of reform and opening up, and acts as a drag on achieving common prosperity. The unavoidable issue of farmers' intellectuality directly influences the sustainable development of agriculture and improvement of farmers' living standards.

Farmers' low knowledge levels hinder the sustainable development in agriculture. First, low knowledge levels make farmers lack the ability to improve and create new production methods. Second, uneducated farmers are unqualified for service sector jobs, which is a requirement for China's industrial structure adjustment. Finally, the low knowledge levels of farmers also worsen the brain drain in agriculture. Farmers' low knowledge levels undermine the efforts to achieve harmony between man and nature. First, it makes farmers blind to future gains and only conscious of immediate benefits. And the consequent environmental degradation, such as water and soil erosion, poses a severe threat to sustainable agricultural development. Second, it entails farmers' slow response to changes in nature. Last, the low knowledge level is also a factor for unlimited population increases. Together with disease and poverty, their low knowledge level leads to a vicious circle: the poorer they are, the more kids they have, and then they get even poorer. This worsens the disharmony between man and nature.

Farmers' low knowledge levels lead to their low income and make them prone to be marginalized by the market. Their conservative approaches and crowd mentality make them rely upon experience to cope with new situations and less adaptive to market changes. This is unfavorable for fair income distribution and common prosperity.

Land trust achieves an organic combination of intellectuality and land

Land trust combines intellectuality and land together and offsets farmers' knowledge insufficiency based on its integrating and sharing mechanism. To help achieve the industrial management of agriculture, land trusts make the following contributions: promoting agricultural technologies, adjusting agricultural industry structure, transferring rural surplus labor force and enhancing farmers' knowledge levels and incomes.

PROMOTE AGRICULTURAL TECHNOLOGIES, AND MAKE TECHNOLOGICAL PROGRESS

Scientific technologies are a fundamental means to facilitate agricultural modernization and rural economic development. By adopting a modern organization system, establishing professional teams and accumulating talent resources, land trusts will make great contributions to agricultural development. It upgrades productive tools and technologies and will accelerate the adoption of new agricultural f technologies to raise labor productivity.

ADJUST AGRICULTURAL INDUSTRY STRUCTURE

Any industry is based on a structure which plays an important role in its development and requires constant structural adjustment to adapt to the latest industrial development. When it comes to Chinese agriculture, land trust initiates a restructuring of agricultural production factors such as labor forces, land and capital to increase agricultural benefits and optimize its structure. Land trusts are able to defuse the conflicts between farmers and the market, explore market demands in a timely manner and move toward a whole industrial chain instead of single industries such as crop cultivation and aquaculture.

TRANSFER RURAL SURPLUS LABOR FORCE

The increasing level of agricultural resource utilization and labor transforms the extensive management mode into an intensive one and produces a large number of rural surplus labor force. Land trusts facilitate the transfer of rural surplus labor force and accelerate urbanization of rural areas by stimulating the development of township and village enterprises and raising farmers' incomes. With land trusts, farmers achieve effective land circulation and turn land into portable assets. On the one hand, it ensures fair revenue allocation for farmers; on the other hand, it releases rural surplus labor force and transfers them to secondary and tertiary industries.

ENHANCE FARMERS' AVERAGE KNOWLEDGE LEVELS AND INCOMES

Land trust ensures steady growth of farmers' income. With land trust, farmers do not have to face the market directly but will enjoy the fruits of reform and opening up. The income growth enables them to afford better education for themselves and their children. Generally speaking, a higher knowledge level leads to higher income. From the perspective of income structure, farmers' incomes from secondary and tertiary industries take an increasing proportion and are becoming an important source of farmers' incomes. Higher-qualified farmers have stronger market economy awareness and adapt better to market competition and therefore more choices of employment. They are able to earn more non-agricultural income from secondary and tertiary industries.

REALIZE LARGE-SCALE MANAGEMENT OF AGRICULTURAL INDUSTRY

The industrial management of agriculture is an important means to modernize traditional agriculture, which on the one hand relieves the contradictions between small-scale operations and big markets and, on the other hand, poses higher requirements on agricultural production operators. Land trust promotes the large-scale and intensive management to deepen the development of agriculture, which can be seen from the integrated operation, socialized service and adoption of a business management pattern. It enhances the proficiency of product producer, processor, seller, and technology and information service provider and improves the agricultural industry chain.

Operation of land trust: dual agent mechanism

Based on agent entrustment and trust, land trust practices a dual agent mechanism. It protects farmers' legal rights and interests and achieves land marketization. The precondition of the dual agent mechanism is that the owner, as a trust settler, is fully motivated to supervise the use of his capital, which means a complete and motivated trust settler. If there is no such a trust settler, the whole agent entrustment system won't work from the beginning, which demonstrates how trust companies play their roles.

First-time agency: commission

For first-time agency, members of a village collective, on a voluntary basis, commission their village committees or some public institutions with governmental relations to manage their contracted land. Members of the village collective are the owners of village land, the implied property relationship of which is that each legal individual in the village collective enjoys equal and equivalent rights towards the collectively held land, so no one has any privilege. Against this background, a unified public institution that is different from a specific individual must be established to be a representative (agent) of the rights of use and exercise the undifferentiated rights given by society. This explains the basic logic of first-time agency, and it is where the legality bases.

Second-time agency: trust

Second-time agency refers to the process that village committees or some public institutions with governmental relations entrust the land to trust companies. The entrustment relationship between trust companies and village committees equals to the relationship between the owner of land use rights and trust companies. In this way, farmers, as the owners of land use rights, are able to exercise their supervision rights over the agents (trust companies). Trust companies manage the assets in a market-oriented and highly effective manner. It also ensures appreciation of rural land and avoids misjudgment on the market resulting from lack of knowledge. Relying on trust companies' mature management, farmers are able to gain sufficient information and have their rights protected. As for profit distribution, trust companies distribute the fixed return and incremental benefit of land to farmers directly, not through a village committee or a public institution. It ensures that farmers practically receive the earnings in time.

6 "Cloud trust + land trust" – interpretation of the profit model for land trust

As the financial industry gradually integrates with the Internet, the innovation and development of Internet finance and financial Internet will dramatically change the whole financial ecology. It will intensify financial market competition, improve the efficiency of capital allocation and unprecedentedly accelerate capital flows. Furthermore it will promote the marketization of interest rates, reform financial supervision and open up the banking industry. In Internet finance, Internet service providers use new technologies and new trading modes to expand by penetrating from the information intermediary to the credit intermediary. This is done by means of low cost and efficient overflow of information transmission, collection and analysis. While financial Internet depends on financial and capital functions, this in turn fuses Internet technologies to provide clients with more efficient, convenient, personalized, inclusive and diversified financial services. It implies a "natural" impulse to penetrate and expand from the information intermediary to the credit intermediary. The two-way penetration and fusion of information mediation and credit intermediary is a challenge but also generates unlimited new patterns and new business opportunities.

Land trust is based on financial Internet logic, with common prosperity as the greatest common ground. Relying on the trust of the circulation of contracted land use rights, it forms the "Internet of things (IoT)" of land. While it brings scale advantages and integrates and shares knowledge and capital, it also reconstructs production relations to realize the intensive and overall development of land. It combines science and technology with land and breaks down barriers between the upstream and downstream enterprises related to land. Furthermore, it extends the industrial chain and realizes inclusive benefit sharing under the premise of using the trust certificates to determine the rights on average for the scattered lands with differences. Both theoretical and practical applications of land trust have proven the effectiveness of the trust system and the feasibility of land trust. This chapter, based on trust practice, will interpret the operation approach and profound content of the cloud trust + land trust.

Ideological basis of land trust

The universe is a totality of universal connections among all sorts of things. Engels in *Anti-Dühring* pointed out: "When we consider and reflect upon nature at large or the history of mankind or our own knowledge activity, at first we see the picture of an endless entanglement of relations and reactions in which nothing remains what, where and as it was, but everything moves, changes, comes into being and passes away."[1] Engels argued that the material world is universally connected and moves perpetually, and the unity of the two features constitutes the historical evolution process of the world. Land trust, based on the Internet thinking, takes the land as the subject matter and the trust as the platform. It both gives consideration to the Internet and the IoT to practice cloud trust + land trust mode and realizes the harmonious development of farmers, agriculture and rural areas. Based on this, one needs to explain the cloud trust + land trust mode. The cloud trust mode uses information intermediary to realize a wider range of connections among things, while the land trust uses a credit intermediary to connect scattered and isolated values and gives financial and capital attributes. The fundamental purpose of the combination of credit intermediary and information intermediary is to make up for the asymmetric integrity and unmatched efficiency between the two. Information transfer will lose its fundamental meaning if it cannot solve the credit problem. Credit advantage will lose competitiveness if it cannot be converted into efficiency value. The operation logic of the cloud trust + land trust also lies in this.

Internet thinking

The Internet is an organic whole formed by human individuals based on network infrastructure. Connections and communications among individuals are an important premise for the existence and development of the Internet. Importantly the Internet cannot leave material production of network equipment and other technologies; it is on this basis that it forms "the sum total of social relations." Concerning the Internet in a sense of material existence, it must exist on the condition of common activities by many individuals through space and time and by the continuous activities of many individuals within time. This interaction and continuity of such activity reflect the universality and objectivity of the organic connections of things. Karl Marx said: "[S]ocial history of men is never anything but the history of their individual development, whether they are conscious of it or not. Their material relations are the basis of all their relations. These material relations are only the necessary forms in which their material and individual activity is realized."[2]

Through these material relations, various social interactions happen on the Internet, including spiritual communication. Spiritual communication between individuals is a communication form which is far from the production process. It largely goes beyond the direct production process and economic interest relations but has never been separated from material activities and economic interests. Marx and Engels pointed out: "The production of ideas, of conceptions, of consciousness, is at first directly interwoven with the material activity and the material intercourse of men – the language of real life. Conceiving, thinking, the mental intercourse of men, appear at this stage as the direct efflux of their material behavior."[3]

The emergence of the Internet has revealed the independent form and characteristics of spiritual communication and has produced certain adverse effects on the material production modes. This reflects the complex and changeable characteristics of the mutual movement of various things in the objective world. Engels pointed out that mental activity shows a picture of an endless entanglement of relations and reactions. But even in this case, the spiritual communication still can't exist without material production and material interests. Marx emphasized a basic principle of Marxism: "The mode of production of material life conditions the social, political and knowledge life process in general. It is not the consciousness of men that determines their being, but, on the contrary, their social being that determines their consciousness."[4]

As a new mode of existence for social relations, the Internet was created and used by people to serve people. Along with the nature of man is the meaning of existence of the Internet. The nature of man is the coupling of materiality, sociality and intellectuality. The Internet is a byproduct of interactions among people. The spiritual communication produced among people based on the Internet is not isolated from material communication but is a deeper level of material activity and material communication. It is a common conscious action based on the consciousness. In this sense we can say that the Internet realizes the unity of people's materiality, sociality and intellectuality. Marx once analyzed: "Both have the need to breathe; for both the air exists as atmosphere; this brings them into no social contact; as breathing individuals they relate to one another only as natural bodies, not as persons."[5]Therefore, only when "man's consciousness of the necessity of associating with the individuals around him is the beginning of the consciousness that he is living in a society."[6] "If man is social by nature, he will develop his true nature only in society, and the power of his nature must be measured not by the power of the separate individual but by the power of society."[7] And "like all human thought, and social relations only exist among human beings to the extent that they think, and possess this power of abstraction from sensuous individuality and contingency."[8]

The Internet, based on the material basis like network equipment and relying on people's materiality, intellectuality and sociality, enables "public of productivity,"[9] "public of intellectuality"[10] and "public of creativity"[11] to achieve comprehensive development in an extremely vast domain.

Information intermediary: information

The existence and movement of anything in the objective world are both interdependent and interconnected; they are thus conditioned by each other and are connected with other surrounding things and maintain certain relations, relations found in nature from elementary particles to the motion of celestial bodies, from the inorganic world to the organic world and from stillness to motion. Relations in the social life from material life to spiritual life, from a class society to a classless society and between sectors of a national economy, all of these are under universal connections and mutual restrictions. Universal connections and mutual restrictions among objective things are the basic principle of materialist dialectics.

Engels once pointed out: "[D]ialectics as the science of universal inter-connection." These universal connections mentioned by Engels differ in thousands of ways but can be divided into three categories. The first category, horizontally speaking, is spatial connections. In the uniform material world, from cosmic objects to the micro field, all of them are associated with each other and form the endless totality. Inside the totality, there are lots of large and small parent systems and subsystems of different categories and levels that are connected with each other to form the complex, interwoven, ever-changing and universally related net, some of which are dominant, while some are recessive. In this universally connected net, there are endless and diverse intermediary links. We will focus on some intermediary links. For example, let's take a look at the connections between man and nature. People are composed of various kinds of cells, and these cells need to absorb nutrients and metabolize; nutrients come from plants and animals; animals cannot survive without plants, and plants can only grow with water, soil, air and sunlight for photosynthesis. This is the connection totality that involves a very wide range of aspects and includes all kinds of large and small systems. This connection totality includes diverse intermediate links. We should choose the links that are most important for people to examine and study.

The second category is, vertically speaking, temporal connections. Space is infinite, and time is also infinite. The development of all things is inevitably characterized by the passage of time, which reflects correlation and exchange among things. Things themselves inherently contain other things, which determines that the process of their development inevitably changes from one thing to another and then from another to something else, and finally form the connections of things between yesterday, today and tomorrow as well as connections between their origin and derivation, the former generation and future generation, and the old thing and the new thing. We need to take these connections seriously. Connections between things of yesterday, today and tomorrow, between their origin and derivation, between their former generation and future generation and between the old and the new all contain corresponding intermediary things, intermediary states or intermediary links. Only by carefully examining and studying these intermediary things can we correctly understand the existence and development of things and thus prevent errors and rigidity.

The third category is the social connections in human society. Such kinds of social connections are also diverse. They include the connections among different countries, among parties, among families, among various units, among individuals, and among individuals, collectives and their country. The connections of social affairs are quite striking; many social revolutionaries, economists, and philosophers have studied it. What is the main point of these kinds of connections? As Stalin observed, "The superstructure is not directly connected with production, with man's productive activity. It is connected with production only indirectly, through the economy, through the basis."[12] The Internet, based on big data, and with information as the intermediary, realizes the organic connection of subjects and objects and builds a dynamic system of "people, information, and the real economy."

Information originates and coexists with materials. It is a result of the interactions among materials. Information that is not material does not exist. It is a sign of the presence of material. In the Internet intermediate system, in addition to the elements of computer and information technology such as the network, which is the basic "hardware," information is also an essential basic element that contacts the intermediary system of subject and object bodies.

It is proved by the philosophy of information that information is the representation of the attribute, relation and meaning of an object but not the object itself. Information, due to its relative independence from the source material carrier, can flow between one man and another and function as a link connecting man and the material world. Seen from the generation mechanism of the Internet, besides certain material means and spiritual means, information intermediary is also necessary for man to have a conceptual grasp of the material world. For the material world, first, the information of the material world is transmitted to people via certain material and electrical intermediaries, and then people select, receive and process the information from the material world by their own sensorium and cognitive structures. The material world has already been touched by man's practice. First, men act on the object and send out messages to the object by certain tools and means; then the material world shows its own information to men under the action of men's information and then transmits the information to men via corresponding material and energy carriers, which then, after being selected, received and processed by men's related physiological structures and cognitive structures, forms the cognition of the material world. It requires special attention that what is selected, received and processed by men's physiological structures and cognitive structures is merely the information from the material world rather than the material world itself. Furthermore, the cognitive result or cognition that men have obtained is the transformed form of information from the material world rather than the material world itself. The material world can by no means go directly into man's cognitive structure; what thereby goes into men's cognitive structure can't be anything but the information of the structure, attribute and nature which reflects the material world itself. In this sense, it is "information" that is the essential factor and even the most important factor in the intermediate system connecting man and the material world. Without information flow, cognition can never occur merely by material means and spiritual means. This is just like in the Internet world, where without transmission of concrete information flow, realistic and authentic cognition will never occur merely with hardware such as computer and information networks.

Seen from the cognitive function of information, information meets the basic requirements as cognitive intermediary. For men, cognitive intermediary means "the stuff to depend on and rely on" to learn about the material world and "the stuff by virtue of which to grasp the attribute, relation and meaning of the object." For the object, it means the stuff to transmit the attributes, relations and meanings of the object to the subject to represent those of the material world. Information has such properties and functions. It is information that allows the attributes, relations and meanings of the material world to be transmitted to men. At the same time, it is the information of the object obtained by men, by certain material means and spiritual means, that makes it possible for the subject to conceptually grasp the material world. Therefore, it is information that connects men's cognition and the material world. Without the concurrence of the attributes, relations and meanings of the material world being transmitted to the physiological structure and cognitive structure of the subject in the form of information, man can by no means conceptually grasp the material world from reality. It is only by the material and spiritual means by which men act on the material world. In this sense, on the Internet, it is based on practice, by material means and spiritual means and via information transmission that men realize the communication and exchange between mankind and the material world and between one individual and another.

Land trust profoundly corresponds to the characteristics of the Internet era such as hierarchy, structuralization and openness. It achieves multiple integration of land, resources, knowledge and information on a uniform platform of trust and unleashes the potential value and ensures farmers' income growth.

Cloud trust + land trust model

The concept of "symbiosis" was initially raised by the German biologist Anion De Bary in 1879, meaning that, out of the need for survival, two or more kinds of creatures inevitably depend on and interact with each other through a certain pattern and coexist and coevolve in a symbiotic relationship. In the last decade or so, this symbiosis theory has been gradually expanded to economics and sociology. In practice, trust, as an effective institutional arrangement and relying on its intermediate function, has achieved the exchange and symbiosis of knowledge, data and information of industry factors. Cloud trust + land trust is just a practical paradigm conforming to this theory.

Cloud trust

"Cloud trust," based on big data and by means of trust, achieves the symbiosis of information supply chain between agriculture and agriculture-related industries.

"Cloud trust" achieves information exchange between agriculture and agriculture-related industries with land as the object. It follows codes of conduct in different industries, and an obvious information symbiosis relationship exists between members of an agriculture community and agriculture-related factors. Information is both the input of knowledge innovation by the agriculture community and agriculture-related factors. It is also the link to maintain the symbiosis between the agriculture community and agriculture-related factors. It relies on the information activities of community members to realize the conversion of data, information, knowledge and ability, that it may conduct effective management of each subject, factor and link of information activities and their interaction interface to build a seamless connection of information. It is the internal requirement to form an information supply chain within the agriculture community and agriculture-related factors.

"Cloud trust" builds the information requirement interaction
mechanism between agriculture and agricultural production factors

In reality, there is a shortage of information and asymmetry between agriculture and agriculture-related factors, subjects and the ineffective flow of information requirements that obstruct the progress of agricultural industrialization. "Cloud trust" meets barrier-free information requirements between agriculture and agriculture-related factors. On the one hand, information requirements of community members are consistent and have similarities in seeking information on technology, market, policy and economy. They rely on "cloud trust" to ensure information exchange and sharing, accumulate the market information of enterprises onto the trust intermediate platform and take advantage of information aggregation to reduce the information acquisition cost, meet the common information requirements and gain the value appreciation of information cooperation between agriculture and agriculture-related industrial players. On the other hand, "cloud trust" can adapt to the professional differences among community members and meet the heterogeneous information requirements of cooperative members. Furthermore, with the deepening of member cooperation, "cloud trust" timely and effectively adapts to the information requirement changes of each member to ensure the information equilibrium of the whole community. By virtue of the advantages of trust, "cloud trust" establishes a flexible response mechanism, makes quick response to the changes in information requirements and timely adjusts the information exchange pathways. In addition, by establishing an effective information supply chain, it can reconcile institutional interests and achieve the Pareto optimality of information gains between community members while meeting personalized information requirements.

"Cloud trust" builds the information production supplementation
mechanism between agriculture and agricultural production factors

Information production is oriented to meeting the information requirements of agriculture and agriculture-related entities and provides standardized information products by collecting, processing and organizing information. The information production of agriculture and agriculture-related entities depends on external information and the information input by each community member. This in turn helps agriculture-related entities improve their decision-making and make more input for better information production. Relying on cloud data, "cloud trust" gives consideration to both personalized information requirements and standardized information production and creates information supply chains that build an open information resource sharing platform. It facilitates professional information integration and information discovery for multi-domain intersection of agriculture and agriculture-related factors and enriches the information resources input in technological innovation. The information production of "cloud trust" involves knowledge of various fields. This helps accurately reflect the in-depth correlation among different kinds of information and intelligently support information comprehension. An information database will be used to store and manage the existing standardized and modular information for better reuse or improvement while meeting personalized information requirements.

"Cloud trust" builds the information collaboration mechanism for agriculture and agricultural production factors

Information collaboration is an interest re-equilibrium process based on information sharing among agriculture-related entities. The asymmetry in factor input, information ability and information occupation among them inevitably causes gaps in information gains and contractions inside the community. Scarcity of effective organization and coordination will obstruct the sustainable progress of cooperative innovation and information exchange, which presses for the integration advantage of "cloud trust" to build an information supply chain within the community of agriculture and agriculture-related factors and gives play to its role in collaborative management, overall planning and decision-making. Thus, efforts should be made to enhance the self-learning and information aggregation ability of agriculture and agriculture-related entities while also accelerating the community's organizational restructuring. We should establish a reasonable interest distribution mechanism and a conflict management mechanism under the principle of equality and mutual benefit. It further encourages the openness and transparency of private information and strengthens information quality control to reduce information cost, reconcile the interest demands of each party and enhance cooperation and mutual trust.

Land trust

A land trust refers to a network structure formed with the land as the object on the basis of forward and backward correlations in the agricultural industry.

Land trust integrates resources

A land trust represents an industrial relationship based on trust, the essence of which is the relationship between supply and demand and input and output in the industry. A land trust, as a network made up of enterprises or units, connects the resource market with the demand market and offers different service functions over the entire process of agricultural production. As a basic element, land has a close technical and economic relationship with other elements or parts. A complete chain of agricultural production regarding a land trust covers many processes including seedling cultivation, field management, the processing of agricultural and animal products, preservation and distribution, and marketing. They can be further segmented into four parts: pre-production, that is, the seedling industry, feed industry, information-based guidance and product planning; in-production, that is, field management, technical guidance, farm inputs and fertilizer; post-production, that is, product grading, packaging and processing, preservation, food processing and storage; and consumption, that is, variety and quality supply, consumption guide, marketing and promotion.

A land trust helps integrate enterprise resources, expand the agricultural supply chain and optimize its industrial scale. Allyn Young stressed in 1928 that

> the mechanism of increasing returns is not to be discerned adequately by observing the effects of variations in the size of an individual firm or of a particular industry, for the progressive division and specialization of industries is an essential part of the process by which increasing returns are realized. What is required is that industrial operations be seen as an interrelated whole. . . . [Yet] the scale of their operations (which is only incidentally or under special conditions a matter of the size of the individual firm) merely reflects the size of the market for the final products of the industry or industries to whose operations their own are ancillary."[13]

Thus, expanding the scale of agriculture will definitely drive the development of individual firms which will in turn further extend the supply chain of the agricultural industry.

Land trust is the result of multiple factors

Decentralized land ownership is of great significance in China. However, at a certain developmental stage of forces of production, it will become inevitable to adopt land circulation as an important measure for upgrading the agricultural industry.

Land circulation is subject to the combined influence of a number of factors, such as the development level of rural markets, social security, government financial support, financial services, agricultural technology as well as the knowledge of farmers, while land resource endowment, agricultural infrastructure and the development path of various subjects determine the direction of land circulation. (For details see the analysis that follows.)

Compared with subcontracting, transfer, shareholding, rent or other forms of land circulation, a land trust allows a more flexible arrangement of rights and can meet the different needs of all stakeholders to jointly serve the overall development of agriculture.

As an important form of land circulation and agricultural organization, a land trust can help farmers become more organized. The issue of organization is internally connected with the extension of the agricultural supply chain. By virtue of financial means, a land trust solves the issues of economies of specialization and added transaction fees caused by the extension of the industrial chain, as when a specialized economy is higher than the added transaction fees, the industrial chain will extend. Reducing transaction fees is an important function in the organization of farmers. As farmers become more organized, transaction fees will be cut down, which is conducive to the extension of an agricultural industry chain.

The establishment and evaluation of the nationwide comprehensive system of rural land circulation

Define the indicators of a comprehensive system of rural land circulation

We have selected ten Level I indicators closely associated with land circulation, that is, land circulation, land resource endowment, average knowledge of farmers, level of market development, level of farmer organization, agricultural technology, infrastructure, social security, financial service and financial support. Each of the Level I indicators contains three quantifiable Level III indicators, which are further categorized into corresponding Level II indicators. These indicators as a whole constitute a rural land circulation system. Among them, every Level I indicator consists of two to four Level II indicators, and every Level II indicator consists of two to six Level III indicators, with twenty-seven Level II indicators and ninety-two Level III indicators as illustrated in Table 6.1.

Comprehensive system of indicators of rural land circulation

As the Level III indicators have different units of measurement, we first render them dimensionless to ensure the comparability and additivity of them. The details are as follows:

Among them, k and j stand for Level I, II and III indicators, respectively; m_k stands for the number of Level II indictors under the No.k indicator of Level I; n_{ki} stands for the number of Level III indicators of the No.i Level II indicator under the No.k Level I indicator; x_{kij} stands for the score of the Level III indicators of No.i Level II indicator under the No.k; S_{kij} refers to the standard deviation of X_{kij}; φ $(\cdot)$ refers to standard normal distribution function and R_{kij} refers to the score of x_{kij} after dimensionless treatment.

When using Level III indicators to calculate the score of Level I and Level II indicators, the weight of different indicators has a direct bearing on the results of the assessment. As we stress the balanced contribution of all factors, we adopt the method of equal weighting in the calculations. The method of calculation for the Level I and Level II indicators is as follows: F_{ki} stands for index score of the No.i Level II indicator under the No.k Level I indicator; E_k stands for the index score of the No.k Level I indicator.

Assessment results of the comprehensive system of indicators of rural land circulation

Based on the described method of calculation and data from the Second National Agricultural Census, we first calculated the score of the ninety-two Level III indicators of the thirty-one provinces, autonomous regions and municipalities of China; then we obtained the index score of their Level I and Level II indicators. These scores can be used to describe land circulation in China's rural areas.

Table 6.1 System of indicators of rural land circulation

Level I indicators	Level II indicators	Level III indicators	Unit	Level I indicators	Level II indicators	Level III indicators	Unit
Land circulation	Methods of circulation	Proportion of household with farmland leased, subcontracted or transferred to others	%	Organization level of farming	Institutions or enterprises	Proportion of enterprises of agricultural production and operation units	%
		Proportion of household with farmland rented, contracted or transferred from others	%			Proportion of public institutions from agricultural production and operation units	%
	Area of farmland circulation	Area of farmland rented, subcontracted or transferred from the actually managed farmland	%			Proportion of government organs from agricultural production and operation units	%
		Proportion of contracted farmland, private plots and reclaimed wasteland of the actually managed farmland	%			Proportion of social organizations from agricultural production and operation units	%
					Industry unit	Proportion of multi-industry legal entities	%
Land resources endowment	Type of farmland	Proportion of paddy fields	%			Proportion of single-industry legal entities	%
		Proportion of irrigable land	%			Proportion of unregistered units	%

		Indicator	Unit
Average knowledge of farmers		Proportion of dry land	%
	Location	Less than 5 km away from the nearest station or wharf	%
		6–10 km away from the nearest station or wharf	%
		More than 10 km away from the nearest station or wharf	%
	Landform	Proportion of 0–15° arable land	%
		Proportion of 15–25° arable land	%
		Proportion of 25° arable land and above	%
	Education	Proportion of permanent labor with schooling less than a primary education	%
Agricultural technology	Professional organization	Proportion of villages with professional agricultural cooperative organizations	%
		Proportion of villages with professional agricultural cooperative entities	%
	Scale of agricultural technology extension	Average number of agricultural technology extension agencies in each village	
		Average number of people served in agricultural technology extension agencies in each village	
		Number of people served in agricultural technology extension agencies	
	Agricultural technology popularization	Proportion of villages offering lectures on agricultural technology in 2006	%
Agricultural technology	Agricultural technology popularization	Proportion of villages producing and marketing agricultural products through "company + farmers" in 2006	%

(Continued)

Table 6.1 (Continued)

Level I indicators	Level II indicators	Level III indicators	Unit	Level I indicators	Level II indicators	Level III indicators	Unit
		Proportion of labor with a junior high education	%			Proportion of farmer households participating in "company + farmers" at the end of the year	%
		Proportion of labor with a junior high education	%				
		Proportion of labor with a junior college education and above	%				
	Technicians	Proportion of junior agricultural technicians	%				
		Proportion of intermediate agricultural technician	%		Practical application of agricultural technology	Proportion of machine-ploughed farmland	%
		Proportion of senior agricultural technicians	%			Proportion of mechanically and electrically irrigated farmland	%
Market development level	Number of markets	Proportion of villages with a comprehensive market	%			Proportion of farmland using sprinkling irrigation	%
		Proportion of villages with a specialized market	%			Proportion of farmland using drip irrigation	%

Category	Indicator	Unit
	Proportion of villages with a specialized market for farm produce	%
	Proportion of villages with a specialized grain market	%
Market size	Number of comprehensive markets with an annual trade volume of more than 10 million yuan	
	Number of specialized markets with an annual trade volume of more than 10 million yuan	
	Number of specialized markets for farm produce with an annual trade volume of more than 10 million yuan	
	With a specialized grain market with an annual trade volume of more than 10 million yuan	
	Proportion of farmland mechanically sowed	%
	Proportion of farmland mechanically harvested	%
Infrastructure	Proportion of villages with a highway	%
Transportation	Proportion of natural villages with a highway	%
	Proportion of villages with street lights on major roads	%
Farm machinery	Average number of large or medium tractors owned by each village	Unit/village
	Average number of ancillary farm tools for large or medium tractors owned by each village	Unit/village

(Continued)

Table 6.1 (Continued)

Level I indicators	Level II indicators	Level III indicators	Unit	Level I indicators	Level II indicators	Level III indicators	Unit
	Marketing channels	Proportion of farmers in agricultural production and management with united sales by cooperative organizations	%			Average number of small tractors owned by each village	Unit/village
		Proportion of farmers in agricultural production and management selling to retailers	%			Average number of ancillary farm tools for small tractors owned by each village	Unit/village
Market development level	Marketing channels	Proportion of farmers in agricultural production and management selling to companies	%			Average number of combine harvesters owned by each village	Unit/village
		Proportion of farmers in agricultural production and management selling to the market	%	Infrastructure	Water conservancy facilities	Villages guaranteed water safety in normal years	%
Financial service	Farmer credit	Proportion of farmers borrowing from banks or credit cooperatives	%			Proportion of villages with electric-mechanical wells	%
						Proportion of villages with access to ponds or reservoirs for irrigation	%

Category	Indicator	Unit
	Proportion of farmers lending from other channels	%
	Average amount of loan borrowed from banks or credit cooperatives by permanent residents in rural areas	Yuan/household
	Average amount of loan borrowed from other channels by permanent residents in rural areas	Yuan/household
Enterprise finance	Average fixed assets of legal entities in farming	RMB 10,000/unit
	Average annual fix assets investment by agricultural legal entities	RMB 10,000/unit
	Average annual balance of loans of agricultural legal entities	RMB 10,000/unit
Social security	Proportion of villages with drainage and irrigation stations	%
Dependency ratio	Total dependency ratio	%
	Children's dependency ratio	%
	Aged-dependency ratio	%
Basic education	Enrolment rate of children of school age (7–12)	%
	Enrolment rate of children of school age (13–15)	%
Old-age medical service	Proportion of rural permanent residents participated in a rural old-age insurance scheme	%

(Continued)

Table 6.1 (Continued)

Level I indicators	Level II indicators	Level III indicators	Unit	Level I indicators	Level II indicators	Level III indicators	Unit
						Proportion of rural permanent residents who participated in a new rural cooperative medical system	%
		Average annual operating revenue of agricultural legal entities	RMB 10,000/unit			Proportion of rural permanent residents participated in urban basic social old-age insurance	%
		Average annual business tax of agricultural legal entities	RMB 10,000/unit			Proportion of rural permanent residents who have received a collective old-age pension	%
		Imbalance between revenues and expenditures	RMB 10,000		Housing	Total area of house owned	Square meter
Financial support	Rural government fund	Asset–liability ratio	none			Area of house of per household	Square meter/household
	External funds	Proportion of villages with such funds from the state	%				
		Proportion of villages with collective funds	%			Proportion of permanent residents with house valued over RMB 100,000	%
		Proportion of villages receiving funds from other sources	%				
		proportion of villages without funds	%				

Table 6.2 shows the final index score of the ten Level I indicators of the thirty-one jurisdictions nationwide.

First, we had an overview of the average index score of the ten modules to make a comparison of different regions in the system and identify the key factors as well as weaknesses affecting rural land circulation. Among them, we carried out further discussion and comparison of five modules, including land circulation, average knowledge of farmers, market development level and financial services and social security, with the aim of evaluating the conditions of different regions and providing some guidance in formulating effective land circulation policies.

Nationwide the scores for social security, average knowledge of farmers and land resource endowment are the highest, indicating that apart from location and other natural attributes, the dependence ratio, education, medical care and housing are the major factors affecting land circulation. Financial services and market development levels register the lowest scores, which are weaknesses constraining rural land circulation and widening the gap between urban and rural areas. Due to a lower rural market development level, the agricultural products produced by farmers can reach customers only by going through many intermediate agencies, with the profits carved up in the process. Therefore, the value created by farmers is not left in the hands of farmers. Due to scarcity of financial services, land cannot receive sufficient funds, which further limits land revenues and renders the price of rural land severely underestimated, thus causing a shortage of liquidity. As a result, the key to breaking the bottleneck of rural land circulation and implementing the strategy of new-type urbanization lies in developing to the full extent rural trading markets and attracting investment.

Fujian, Zhejiang, Chongqing, Heilongjiang, Sichuan and Jiangxi score the highest in terms of land circulation, with an index score more than fifty-five. These regions are featured by a transfer of rural labor. Among them, commerce, the small commodity manufacturing and food processing industries are relatively advanced in Fujian and Zhejiang, attracting rural labor to transfer to secondary and tertiary industries, which contributes to the supply and demand of land circulation. Chongqing and Sichuan, major provinces that export labor, have large rural populations that migrated to the first-tier cities of Beijing, Shanghai, Guangzhou and Shenzhen and left behind plenty of vacant land. What's more, these people tend to be more open-minded with a sense of business, which helps speed up rural land circulation. On the other hand, some provinces feature a much lower degree of land circulation, such as Qinghai, Shaanxi, Hebei, Tibet, Gansu, Shandong and Henan. Farming in these major agricultural provinces still features scattered operations.

In terms of average knowledge of farmers, Beijing, Shanghai and Tianjin have the highest index scores, while Sichuan, Chongqing, Guizhou and Tibet have the lowest. With relatively advanced economies, the former provinces featured more education for farmers, a higher level of agricultural technology and more technicians. On the other hand, Sichuan, Chongqing and Guizhou are home to less education for farmers, a lower level of agricultural technology and more households with non-farming occupations.

Table 6.2 Assessment results of land circulation-related indicators of thirty-one provinces, autonomous regions and municipalities nationwide

	Land circulation	Market development level	Land resource endowment	Average knowledge of farmers	Social security	Financial services	Financial support	Infrastructure	Level of farmer organization	Agricultural technology
Beijing	54.12	33.15	41.75	62.06	53.87	30.41	47.19	56.66	64.30	50.93
Tianjin	46.75	29.77	42.96	57.21	47.92	46.22	47.72	67.04	45.40	37.04
Hebei	34.08	55.51	44.60	53.74	48.50	43.77	47.47	62.40	36.32	47.90
Shanxi	40.18	47.09	50.55	51.45	43.92	43.51	42.24	38.80	40.39	28.12
Inner Mongolia	54.10	39.03	48.28	52.98	32.43	71.02	46.11	44.83	50.80	59.71
Liaoning	45.08	40.26	43.44	48.22	43.28	43.27	50.97	52.78	48.83	49.28
Jilin	54.46	43.39	45.15	45.90	26.03	50.97	50.22	65.00	59.78	55.78
Heilongjiang	61.34	31.29	45.07	48.38	24.89	70.43	54.29	64.93	50.48	52.25
Shanghai	56.57	52.58	42.82	59.46	60.95	31.85	53.36	55.21	53.46	51.71
Jiangsu	39.48	82.68	42.73	51.53	73.94	26.85	61.34	68.55	63.61	71.81
Zhejiang	65.38	61.82	45.02	50.56	73.85	30.21	48.58	56.24	56.36	49.25
Anhui	46.41	67.73	45.18	48.51	56.24	32.90	58.82	65.04	58.73	55.99
Fujian	68.39	40.92	49.25	46.45	52.95	40.65	48.84	48.19	41.41	42.31
Jiangxi	57.27	51.91	50.28	49.50	54.11	32.41	60.94	47.65	43.90	32.85
Shandong	33.46	67.83	43.61	54.15	59.07	26.74	36.57	80.15	54.15	58.07
Henan	33.23	79.30	45.08	54.15	61.10	40.48	42.21	62.26	44.65	64.18
Hubei	46.75	63.31	52.48	50.25	52.30	40.12	47.37	55.36	49.57	43.89
Hunan	56.47	48.90	48.09	51.79	59.95	33.26	50.99	45.66	49.07	33.03

Guangdong	52.33	54.85	47.32	54.02	61.60	33.26	51.70	50.06	39.36	29.32
Guangxi	49.98	43.22	51.97	45.25	52.69	35.70	45.80	38.01	41.76	56.25
Hainan	40.40	37.47	49.25	44.31	48.50	50.65	48.15	44.04	35.11	29.03
Chong qing	63.09	38.89	56.59	39.88	58.94	27.38	59.96	44.68	58.35	54.54
Sichuan	57.61	50.34	54.18	41.26	54.78	37.00	58.79	41.13	44.74	47.02
Guizhou	49.96	36.49	58.68	38.73	49.97	37.38	37.18	26.21	38.28	42.09
Yunnan	48.13	47.73	59.10	43.02	43.61	55.94	44.38	37.73	47.14	68.56
Tibet	33.80	26.87	45.48	36.78	38.00	73.97	30.84	16.64	38.46	14.29
Shannxi	35.03	34.94	55.82	56.09	43.55	55.91	41.61	27.49	41.76	36.55
Gansu	33.60	42.10	55.77	47.88	41.03	58.92	39.57	23.38	47.41	51.93
Qinghai	36.16	24.03	52.25	45.21	29.58	83.03	31.77	25.34	33.83	29.63
Ningxia	44.93	37.06	49.36	47.23	42.96	59.90	55.97	41.38	64.97	56.14
Xinjiang	56.31	36.10	46.69	49.33	42.41	71.19	38.83	43.98	34.84	71.31
Average	*48.22*	*46.66*	*48.67*	*48.93*	*49.45*	*45.65*	*47.73*	*48.28*	*47.65*	*47.44*

In terms of level of market development, the provinces with the highest scores are Jiangsu, Henan, Shandong and Anhui; and those with the lowest scores are Beijing, Heilongjiang, Tianjin, Tibet and Qinghai. The reason is that the former are major agricultural provinces with relatively developed agriculture, larger market sizes and more sales channels, where the rural market can offer sales and exchange platforms for farm produce and other elements related to agricultural production. With land as the most crucial element of agricultural production, a mature rural market can help the land circulate with higher prices, thus protecting the rights and interests of farmers.

Due to unfavorable geographic conditions, the scale of agricultural production is relatively small in Tibet and Qinghai, thus the development of rural markets there lags behind other regions, resulting in lower index scores; while for Beijing and Tianjin, as developed regions, their low scores are attributed to a small area of farmland and accordingly fewer sales channel and markets for trade in farm produce. Therefore, they scored lower based on the three-level indicators used to assess the development level of agricultural markets.

In terms of financial services, the provinces with the highest scores are Qinghai, Tibet, Xinjiang and Inner Mongolia, while those with the lowest scores are Shanghai, Beijing, Zhejiang, Chongqing, Jiangsu and Shandong. Agricultural development of the western provinces lags behind other regions due to their geographical location and historical factors. In recent years, guided by the strategy of Western development, agricultural development in these provinces is high on the agenda. Yet due to limited revenue there are insufficient funds for these provinces to achieve agricultural industrialization. The result is that farmers and enterprises take large-scale loans, highlighting an urgent need for financial services. In contrast, in the more developed jurisdictions of Shanghai, Beijing, Zhejiang and Jiangsu, farming is not in urgent need of financial services, for they have high-level rural finance and sound township finances that encourage local agricultural development. Land circulation will inevitably involve capital injection, so better financial services can effectively reduce the cost of funds for land circulation.

In terms of social security, the provinces with the highest index scores are mostly located in China's southeast coastal areas such as Jiangsu, Zhejiang and Guangdong; those with the lowest scores are the inner provinces such as Tibet, Inner Mongolia, Qinghai, Jilin and Heilongjiang. With better basic education, medical services and housing, the coastal provinces score high in terms of social security, while Tibet and Qinghai are remote provinces with unfavorable geographical conditions and limited local financial revenue and thus with insufficient social security. In addition, due to the export of labor and an aging rural population, the economic burdens are heavy for farmers relying on their farmland. Therefore, land circulation needs to assume more social functions.

Analysis of factors influencing an inclination by farmers toward land circulation

In reality, the decision-making regarding land circulation by farmers is a complex process, which is subject to the influence of a number of factors, such as their knowledge levels, the development of agricultural industry and financial services. To further explore the relations among these underlying factors and the willingness by farmers to move toward land circulation, we established a structural equation model based on the data of the Second National Census of Agriculture and analyzed the correlative mechanism of different internal factors centered on willingness for rural land circulation. Based on the research conclusions of the existing literature, we propose the following hypothesis, as shown in Table 6.3, which is to be tested by an empirical study.

Data was obtained by applying the Structural Equation Modeling (Amos 20.0), as shown in Table 6.4.

From Table 6.4, we can see that in terms of the direct influence from various factors, the organizational level of farming and social security have no significant impact on land circulation, so hypotheses 5 and 6 are invalid. Land resource endowment, market development level and financial support have a certain positive impact on land circulation, with path coefficients of 0.120, 0.242 and 0.306, respectively. Although the positive impact is not highly significant, it confirms the validity of hypotheses 1, 3 and 9. The average knowledge level of farmers has a negative impact on land circulation, with the path coefficient of −1.450. Such a strong negative effect proves the invalidity of hypothesis 2. The reason is that when

Table 6.3 Hypothesis on the correlative mechanism of internal factors affecting farmers' willingness for rural land circulation

No.	Hypothesis
1	Sound endowment of land resources is conducive to land circulation.
2	Better education of farmers is conducive to land circulation.
3	More developed markets are conducive to land circulation.
4	Better financial services are conducive to land circulation.
5	A higher level of organization among farmers is conducive to land circulation.
6	Advanced agricultural technology is conducive to land circulation.
7	Better infrastructure is conducive to land circulation.
8	Social security level is in positive correlation with land circulation.
9	Stronger financial support is conducive to land circulation.
10	More education for farmers is conducive to land circulation.
11	Social security level is in positive correlation with market development.
12	Social security level is in positive correlation with the organization of farmers.
13	Social security level is in positive correlation with the growth of farmers' knowledge.
14	Better financial services are conducive to the improvement of agricultural technology.
15	Stronger financial support is conducive to the improvement of agricultural technology.
16	A higher market development level is conducive to the improvement of financial services.
17	Better infrastructure is conducive to the improvement of the market development level.
18	Better infrastructure is conducive to the improvement of the organization of farmers.

Table 6.4 Test results of the correlative mechanism of internal factors affecting farmers' willingness for rural land circulation

Hypothesis	Latent variable	Path	Latent variable	Estimated value	Standard deviation	Standardized coefficient
1	Land resource endowment	→	Land circulation	0.120	0.248	0.179
2	Average knowledge level of farmers	→	Land circulation	−1.450	0.137	−0.357
3	Market development level	→	Land circulation	0.242	0.007	0.898
4	Finance services	→	Land circulation	0.435	0.195	0.046
5	Organizational level of farming	→	Land circulation	0.162	0.145	0.006
6	Agricultural technology	→	Land circulation	1.001	0.061	0.928
7	Infrastructure	→	Land circulation	0.392	0.025	0.301
8	Social security	→	Land circulation	−0.009	0.041	−0.005
9	Financial support	→	Land circulation	0.306	0.135	0.193
10	Average knowledge level of farmers	→	Organizational level of farming	−0.624	0.22	−0.491
11	Social security	→	Market development level	0.808	0.164	0.320
12	Social security	→	Organizational level of farming	0.818	0.069	0.072
13	Social security	→	Average knowledge level of farmers	0.118	0.017	0.657
14	Finance services	→	Agricultural technology	0.072	0.187	0.972
15	Financial support	→	Agricultural technology	0.045	0.234	0.742
16	Market development level	→	Finance services	0.412	0.026	0.599
17	Infrastructure	→	Market development level	0.819	0.012	0.849
18	Infrastructure	→	Organizational level of farming	0.797	0.182	0.549

farmers have more knowledge on average,[14] they tend to manage their farmland by themselves. Financial services, agricultural technology and infrastructure have a strong positive impact on land circulation, with path coefficients of 0.435, 1.001 and 0.392, respectively, which confirms the validity of hypotheses 4, 6 and 7.

In terms of the indirect influence of the relations among different factors, we can see that infrastructure exerts a significantly positive impact on the level of rural market development and farming organization, with path coefficients of 0.819 and 0.797, which confirms the validity of hypotheses 17 and 18. Social security demonstrates a positive correlation with the level of rural market development and farming organization as well as farmers' average education, with path coefficients of 0.808, 0.818 and 0.118, respectively, which confirms the validity of hypotheses 11, 12 and 13. The result also shows a significant negative effect exerted by the average knowledge of farmers on the organizational level of farming, with a path coefficient of –0.624, which confirms the invalidity of hypothesis 10. Fully developed financial services can greatly promote the development of agricultural technology, with a path coefficient of 0.072, which proves the validity of hypothesis 14. However, financial support by the government has no significant impact on the development of agricultural technology. The level of rural market development fosters the need for financial services, with a path coefficient of 0.412, which to a large extent confirms the validity of hypothesis 16.

The empirical results fall into four categories: (1) a valid hypothesis showing a strong positive correlation between variables, such as hypotheses 6, 7, 11, 12, 13, 14, 16, 17 and 18; (2) a valid hypothesis showing weak correlation between variables, such as hypotheses 1, 3 and 9; (3) a hypothesis whose validity cannot be confirmed, such as hypotheses 5, 8 and 15; (4) and an invalid hypothesis showing negative correlation between variables, such as hypotheses 2 and 10.

Therefore, there is much inconsistency between the correlation of land circulation-related factors and a number of hypotheses, with plenty of uncertainty and instability; even when a correlation is confirmed, its effect is either insignificant for some variables or even negative for other variables. Thus, we can conclude that land circulation is more of a social problem, and the desired effect cannot be attained by relying solely on economic means.

Understanding cloud trust + land trust

A cloud trust + land trust model constitutes an integrated network with the land as the contract object and the support of cloud data. Based on a certain geographic information system, it consists of two or more market entities, with trust as the intermediary agent and agriculture as the bond. To be specific, under the influence of agricultural policy and ecological variables, a cloud trust + land trust model is an integrated system combining business flow, logistics, capital, technology, value and supply flow.

A cloud trust + land trust model through information and big data can realize the exchanges and extension of the virtual and physical worlds. It fills the gap between information and the real economy and the digital divide in the development of the supply chain by land and builds the bridge between information and people, and land and other factors of production, which enables information and credit to effectively integrate the virtual and physical worlds.

A cloud trust + land trust model can lead to a more intelligent development of the land supply chain. It helps us develop a comprehensive understanding of the chain and the world. With the application and development of big data, we will be able to behold the processes of a land trust. In such a land trust industrial chain, we can integrate various factors, such as people, a land supply chain, information and credit based on big data.

Cloud trust + land trust can extend the agricultural supply chain, enrich the modes of land circulation and broaden the marketing channels for farm products, thus improving the efficiency of agricultural development and changing the ecology of the land. Cloud trust + land trust can ensure an effective flow of things, widen the scope of communication and render the face-to-face communication unnecessary. It is a part of the IoT which connects not only people but also objects in an interdependent network.

The cloud trust + land trust model offers a new mode of agricultural development, extends supply chains and changes the population's way of living. It can not only enhance the quality of life but also productivity, thus pushing forward the development of social productive forces.

Objective, value and effect of cloud trust + land trust

More and more evidence proves that a land trust has many advantages compared with other means of land circulation, such as contracting, transferring, shareholding, cooperation or exchanges. Cloud trust + land trust, as a two-way mode, has specific aims, a distinctive value pattern and an irreplaceable mechanism for action.

Target mechanism of cloud trust + land trust

Cloud trust + land trust ensures the capital chain for agricultural development

A cloud trust + land trust model can fill the capital gap for agricultural enterprises and ensure constant capital flows. A capital chain is essential to the production and operation of any enterprise as part of the cash-assets-cash (value-added) chain. The smooth running of an enterprise depends on this chain. In general, a capital chain is prone to rupturing when problems occur in the value-added process. Therefore, the continuity of a capital chain is fundamental to an enterprise. For most agricultural enterprises in their start-up stages, they have sufficient funds, and their business scopes are yet to be fully expanded, and so a smooth capital chain is in place. As the enterprise grows, with new types of business and an increasingly complicated capital chain (in Zhejiang and Jiangsu, the production value of RMB 300 million is the dividing line between big and small enterprises), fund management will easily grow disorderly, resulting in the non-continuity of the capital chain. The capital chain rupture finally leads to enterprise bankruptcy, which can be attributed to the inability to manage financial risks and control cash flow. Cloud trust + land trust, with specialized financial institutions as trustees, can extend the agricultural supply chain and provide funds for the sound development of enterprises.

Cloud trust + land trust ensures supply flow for agricultural development

Cloud trust + land trust together ensures the supply flow for agricultural development and the stability of the upper, middle and lower parts of the chain.

Upstream stability means that in the context of an open market economy, the demand for farm produce constantly grows, while the supply is restricted by the production environment and elasticity of supply. Cloud trust + land trust can ensure a sustainable supply of agricultural products as well as the agricultural supply chain. Mid-stream speed up means that in the face of fierce competition in domestic and overseas markets, the cloud trust + land trust combo can integrate the mid-stream portion of procurement, processing, transportation and sales as well as rapidly develop new and deep processing technologies for farm products to meet market demand. Downstream penetration aims to assist downstream organizations to produce diversified, high-quality products and offer all-dimensional services to meet the demands of different markets and customers. The downstream organizations are directly linked to consumers and form the final part of the value-added chain of agriculture production. Therefore, the core strategy is to penetrate into a larger consumer base.

Cloud trust + land trust builds an information network for the agricultural industry

Cloud trust + land trust can integrate processes and make rational use of information for agricultural development. Compared with the progressive control of information in traditional agricultural development, this new mode can ensure a comprehensive exchange of information and easier management, accelerate the flow of information and reduce information pollution and distortion.

A combined network regarding information supply chain will lead to the rapid spread of information and more frequent horizontal and multilevel information exchanges, thus realizing the convenient, interactive communication of the organization's members with increased point-to-point cooperation. With an efficient exchange of information, the goals and tasks of various agricultural industries can be actively defined. The information supply chain network built from a cloud trust + land trust model can form many closely connected information centers with its openness and flexibility.

The exchanges of different information centers are interwoven and interactive, forming an information network of members of the organization. As a result, the sources of internal and external information from the agricultural industry form an integral whole, avoiding fragmentation or distortion. To adapt to the information exchange of high efficiency, the organizational structure of the agricultural industry must be a flexible network instead of a rigid chain to ensure lower trading costs and higher management efficiencies. It not only meets the requirement of being information driven but also accelerates information exchanges, reduces information pollution and improves the efficiency of an organization.

Cloud trust + land trust value mode: building a symbiotic agriculture value chain

Cloud trust + land trust, through integrating various intermediate demands of the agricultural supply chain, merges the pre-production supply system, production system, post-production sales and service systems, and the ultimate consumers into a rational value chain, all in a bid to seek proper channels to reduce trading costs and enhance the overall market competitiveness of the product supply chain.

With the development of modern agriculture, a buyer's market of farm products has been established. It has become an irresistible trend for farm production to shift from being quantity oriented to value oriented. The cultivation and processing of farm products should not only meet the need for quantity but also pursue the added value of final products. It has become a new type of management mode to pursue added value and value realization of different parts of the product supply chain. As a result, the "symbiotic" agricultural value chain, underpinned by the long-term cooperation and the sustainable development of different supply chain parts, aims to build a value-sharing mechanism of agricultural organization and management where all stakeholders share interests and risks.

Michael Porter's value chain theory also believes that an enterprise and its upstream and downstream counterparts have their respective interconnected value chains. Yet he stressed the relationship between the value chain within the enterprise and its upstream and downstream counterparts; the symbiotic agriculture value chain built by the cloud trust + land trust model, on the other hand, is a value chain of the whole agricultural industry in essence. It reflects the underlying value transfer, creation and distribution of an agricultural industry chain and effectively pushes for the value realization of different parts of the agricultural product supply chain.

The symbiotic agricultural industry chain is a process of supply chain value integration. All suppliers along the chain take the value realization of ultimate consumers as their goal, and the added value of the supply chain is only an additional product of the goal, yet the two are mutually reinforcing. The key issue is how to coordinate the action of stakeholders along the industrial chain and overcome the drawbacks of the traditional industrial chain where stakeholders attach undue emphasis on maximum profits for themselves at the expense of upstream or downstream enterprises, which affects the market competitiveness and sustainable development of the whole supply chain of agricultural products.

The management of the symbiotic agricultural supply chain is, in essence, the process of value adding the final products jointly produced by upstream and downstream enterprises, which covers the whole process of value creation of farm products from raw material to final product or, as we say in China, from the field to the dining table.

Mechanism of cloud trust + land trust

Cloud trust + land trust enables wealth flowing and unleashes man's creativity

Land is the basic means for human subsistence and "the source of all production and existence."[15] As the English economist William Petty said, "Labor is the Father and active principle of Wealth, as Lands are the Mother."[16] The essence of land circulation is the flow of wealth. Cloud trust + land trust can realize the flow of wealth, which is the only way out for the comprehensive development of agriculture. Land reflects mankind's wisdom, connects the productive forces and relations of production and serves the all-around development of human beings. In practice, the cloud trust + land trust model is inspired by the Internet and integrates knowledge and information to realize the evolution of a social form of wealth.

Cloud trust + land trust realizes the large-scale and intensive development of land

According to Karl Marx, "Ownership of the land is the foundation of individual independence and the necessary transition stage for the development of agriculture itself."[17] It means to realize the transition from fragmented management to large-scale intensive management. In practice, "Proprietorship of land parcels, by its very nature, excludes the development of social productive forces of labor, social forms of labor, social concentration of capital, large-scale cattle-raising, and the progressive application of science."[18] Therefore, the large-scale management of rural land can lead to increased incomes for farmers and those in rural areas. Facts show that the 1,301 trusts of transferring land use rights by the CITIC Trust in Suzhou, Anhui Province, based on traditional land circulation patterns, incorporates a financial element to integrate fragmented land resources and factors of production such as capital, technology and labor. In particular, within the framework of a land trust, we are able to make reasonable use of rural land to add income from it, push for the adjustment of the agricultural industrial structure to shift from grain crops to diversified cash crops and enable the agricultural industry to embark on a more rational path of development, thus changing the rules of proprietorship of land parcels; put forward by Karl Marx, that is "perpetual fragmentation of means of production and separation of producers."[19]

Cloud trust + land trust builds an Internet-based trust of rural land circulation

The cloud trust + land trust model realizes the separation of land ownership, right of management and usufruct. Without changing ownership attributes, such a new pattern not only avoids the emergence of new landlords but also reasonably changes farmers' ways of land ownership from the actual possession of land to the possession of trust capital, thus freeing them from the attachment to the land and unleashing their power. On this ground, we can further take advantage of the trust system, build an Internet-based trust of rural land circulation and improve the socialized division of labor in agriculture and the organizational level of bringing rural land into the market. In this way, we can extend the agricultural supply chain, create more value to serve the market needs and sharpen the competitiveness and market adaptability of rural land. Take the CITIC Trust's rural land circulation trust program in Anhui for instance. The program has built a new model of "grain production and supply chain management" to meet the needs of big grain production households, agricultural cooperatives and land-reclamation enterprises. It ensures agricultural production through the "integrated platform of productive factors of grain production and supply chains." It also established the Anhui Tianhe CITIC Farming Service Co., Ltd, applying grain production, supply chain management and farming service capabilities to agricultural production practice. The company also launched the CITIC Tianhe Modern Agriculture Service Development Fund to finance agriculture development and the CITIC Tianhe Agriculture Professional Mangers Business School to train traditional farmers to become modern agricultural entrepreneurs. The program is actively exploring effective ways to solve the problems of fund shortages, aging farming labor and a lack of agricultural management knowledge.

Cloud trust + land trust: a realization of shared interests

A land trust accommodates multilevel productive forces and various forms of ownership. Through contracting and the marketization of property, the average person can participate in such an investment, achieving a sharing of interests, fairness and efficiency. The cloud trust + land trust model, with land as the contract object, establishes a trust relationship for the contractual management rights of rural land. Among them, the farmers as trustors have the dual identity of laborer and owner of the means of production. Their enthusiasm can reach great heights as this mechanism combines a distribution based on work and capital, enabling farmers to gain income from their work as well as returns on their assets through their trust capital ownership. Therefore, such a mechanism conforms to the socialist distribution system of the sharing of interests. In the process of income distribution, the separation of value assets and real assets balances fairness and efficiency; in terms of the management of the land's real assets, the large-scale operation can increase economic returns, create added value and enhance efficiency. In this way, we can maximize benefits while ensuring the usufruct of farmers.

Accordingly, cloud trust + land trust, based on the Internet and the principle of common prosperity, balances fairness and efficiency through a circulation trust of rural land management rights. It realizes the intensive and large-scale development of land by taking advantage of the integration of knowledge and capital, and technology and land, hence removing the barriers between upstream and downstream enterprises, extending the industrial chain and achieving the sharing of interests.

Overview: the practice and profit model of the CITIC's cloud trust + land trust

A rural land circulation trust is based on financial and Internet logic, with land as the contract object, which can take advantage of credit platforms and the banking system, extend the industrial chain and build an all-dimensional land circulation trust service system. This specific operation model ensures the separation of ownership, rights of management and usufruct through the circulation trust for contractual rural land management rights without changing the rural collective land ownership. In this way, we can connect the upstream and downstream industries of agriculture and extend the industrial chain. We can integrate different factors of production including the agricultural order, agricultural finance, agricultural insurance and farming services (farm machinery, means of production and agriculture technology), encourage rational land use and take on intensive and large-scale land management. While protecting farmers' usufruct, we should ensure that they have access to the added value of land, which will yield not only sound economic results but also social effects. In land circulation, a "consumption trust," with the trust company as the trustee and in accordance with the willingness of the consumers, purchases designated farm products with the trust capital and monitors the whole process of the performance of the trust products as required in the trust instrument to protect consumer rights and the interests of the beneficiaries.

The whole industrial chain of the cloud trust + land trust model covers the whole agricultural production and adds value to land in many aspects, such as natural features, productive competence, technology and customization. Through intensive procurement, the cost is significantly reduced, which realizes the sharing of benefits among different stakeholders and helps form a win-win pattern for farmer households, industrial organizations and trust companies.

Land trust: the practice of a circulation trust for a contractual right of land

Rural land trust circulation is a new form for common ownership which represents a profound change of the rural land system and exerts a far-reaching impact on achieving the large-scale, specialized and intensive management of agriculture and fostering the transition from traditional to modern agriculture. It further represents the transfer of farmers from secondary to tertiary industries to diversify employment and increase income through multiple channels and to capitalize on rural land resources and attract urban capital, enterprise capital and financial capital to flow to rural areas. Finally, it realizes the coordinated development of urban and rural areas as well as the industrial and agricultural sectors and the accelerated building of a new socialist countryside along with advancing the country's urbanization.

Circulation trust for rural land contractual rights

As stipulated in China's constitution, rural land includes the land for agricultural production and collective construction. The land for agricultural production includes farmland, forest land, garden plots and grassland; the collective construction includes non-commercial land and commercial land.

A circulation trust for rural land contractual rights (the person with the right to contract the land management rights), in a certain period of time, entrusts the contractual right of the land to the trustee, who then transfers the land management rights to other citizens or legal persons engaged in agriculture development and management on the basis of collective land ownership and in accordance with the law and requirements of the market through standardized procedures.

Building a circulation trust for rural land contractual rights by applying the "dual agency" model

A circulation trust for rural land contractual rights is based on the dual agency of agency by agreement and a trust agency to ensure the legitimate rights and interests of farmers and the market-oriented management of the land. The premise for dual agency is the existence of a motivated principal to monitor the use of capital. Without such a principal, the principal-agent relation in the later part of the system cannot be ensured. This entails the existence of the trust company.

"FIRST-TIME AGENCY": COMMISSION

The first-time agency refers to the procedure where members of a village collective, on a voluntary basis, commission the village committee or a public institution with government relations to manage their land use rights.

In practice, whether farmers are willing to carry out land circulation is a complex process of decision-making, which is subject to the average knowledge level of farmers, the development level of rural markets, financial services and many other factors. While the capability of land circulation is affected by the natural endowments of land resources and the characteristics of farmer households (including an urban-rural disparity), farmers' understanding of and willingness for a land trust is determined by their average knowledge level, the government's financial support and the quality of financial services they receive. When farmers decide to change from cultivating farmland by themselves to earning income from other economic means, they are more likely to decide in favor of land circulation. With a good trust operation system as the catalyst, there will be motivation for closing a land trust deal. In the CITIC's land trust practices, this is realized through the "second-time agency."

Members of a village collective share the ownership of the rural land, which implies that every member of the rural population equally shares the rights to the property, with no privilege for anyone. Accordingly, we need to endow or "externalize" the rights to a unified public authority to exercise the rights to use (agency), which is the basic logic of the first-time agency in the dual agency mechanism.

"SECOND-TIME AGENCY": TRUST

The second-time agency refers to trust relations between a village committee or a related public institution and the trust company, the essence of which is the relationship between the owner of the land use rights and the trust company. In this way, farmers (the owner of the land use rights) can effectively monitor the trust company through the village committee or a related public institution; at the same time, the trust company can manage the property with high efficiency through market-oriented operations, eliminating the needs for farmers to directly face the market. In this way, we can make up for the low average knowledge level of farmers, realize market-oriented management of the land, ensure added value of rural land and avoid market misjudgment by farmers due to a lack of knowledge. The trust company, with a mature mode of business operation, can ensure that farmers gain sufficient information and protect their interests. In the distribution of interests, the trust company directly allocates a constant return and incremental benefit to farmers, bypassing the village committee or a related public institution, thus guaranteeing the timely and efficient distribution of earnings for farmers.

The circulation trust for contracted land management rights

The trade of the circulation trust for contracted rural land management rights is structure oriented and divided into three categories, that is, A, B and T. Category A is calculated by discounting basic earning cash flows from the land trust; the prospective earnings of category A are divided into basic earnings and excess earnings, in which the basic earnings are the basic land rent from the land trust, and excess earnings are the remaining part by deducting the basic rent, land consolidation investment capital and earnings that need to be withdrawn from real land rent. Category B is subscribed by qualified investors with cash, which is used for land trust consolidation and relevant agricultural infrastructure construction. Category T is also subscribed by qualified investors with cash but used for providing liquidity support for the distribution of category A's basic earnings and category B's trust interest.

DESCRIPTION

(1) A structural collective trust plan is adopted. The trust property of the trust plan consists of category A trust property delivered by category A settler, category B beneficial interests issued by the trustee and trust capital raised from category T beneficial interests.

(2) During the existence of the trust plan, the trustee, according to the demand of the land trust consolidation investment, is entitled to issue the category B trust units to raise the needed capital. The issue price of a category B trust unit is one yuan, whose existence period, prospective earnings and so on, are specified in trust instrument upon its issuance.

(3) During the existence of the trust plan, if category A's basic earnings, category B's prospective earnings or category B's investment capital cannot be paid due to a temporary shortage of funds, the assignee can issue a corresponding scale of category T trust units to raise capital to provide liquidity support. The issue price of a category T trust unit is one yuan, whose existence period,

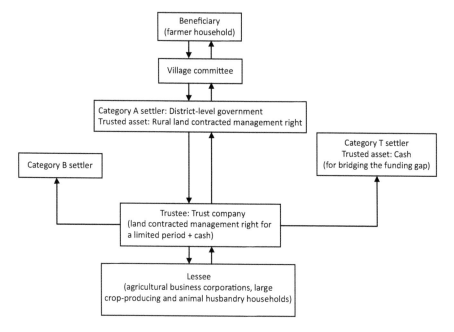

Figure 6.1 Structure chart: the circulation trust for contracted land management rights

prospective earnings, redemption and so on, are specified in a trust instrument upon its issuance.

(4) If the trust capital is involved in the land trust consolidation investment, the land consolidation investment capital and land consolidation earnings should be withdrawn from the land trust rent. Land consolidation earnings are earnings calculated from land consolidation capital according to the benchmark interest rate (floating upward not more than 100 percent) published by the People's Bank of China of the same period. The specific earning rate is determined by the sum of prospective earnings, fixed trustee revenue and trust fee paid by the trustee in issuing category B trust units for raising capital necessary for the land consolidation investment according to the trust plan.

RIGHTS AND OBLIGATIONS OF THE ASSOCIATED PERSONS OF THE TRUST PLAN

Major associated persons involved in the trust plan include: farmers, the government, the CITIC Trust and agricultural companies. The relations, rights and duties of these four parties are connected and defined in the trust plan through relevant agreements and are further bound together in one trust plan through signing relevant legal agreements. Farmer households are defined as the final beneficiaries;

the government is defined as the representative of settlers and beneficiaries of trust plan category A; the CITIC Trust is defined as the trustee, property manager and knowledge capital introduction organization; agricultural enterprises are defined as lessees and users for large-scale, intensive and modern land operations. Through the trust system, such contracting form defines rights and obligations of each party. See Table 6.5.

EXPLANATION OF APPLICATION STRUCTURE

The trust property under the trust plan includes the contracted land management rights of the land trust entrusted by the category A settler, category B trust capital provided by the category B settler, category T trust capital provided by the category T settler, as well as other trust properties arising from the management, application, disposal or other forms of category A property and category B and category T trust capital.

The trustee will in whole or in part rent the contracted land management rights turned over by the category A settler after integrating them and organize the land consolidation and investment to the construction of irrigation and infrastructure for water conservancy ("land consolidation"). The trustee can hire service providers to carry out a land evaluation and circulation according to the

Table 6.5 Introduction of rights and obligations of trust parties

Trust party	Rights	Obligations	Duties
Farmer households	Basic earnings + excess earnings	Transfer the contracted land management rights through a trust	Supervise land use
Government	Obtain trust income on behalf of farmer households	Entrust the land rights to be centralized to the CITIC Trust for management	Supervise land use, distribute earnings to farmer households and mediate disputes among them
CITIC Trust	Manage land trust in a centralized way, and carry out land consolidation and investments in agricultural facilities according to the actual situation	Rent the land to professional companies; raise trust capital for facility construction and liquidity support	Balance interests of each party, and introduce knowledge capital
Agricultural enterprises	Land use	Pay land rent, and refund loans	Push forward with agricultural modernization

trust plan, and the service providers make commitments to the income of the contracted land management rights and other performances according to the service provider contract.

The idle fund in the trust plan account can be invested by the trustee in financial products with high liquidity and low risk. To improve production conditions and rental income from the land trust, the trustee is entitled to issue category B trust units to raise trust capital for a land consolidation investment. If the trust capital is involved in the land trust consolidation investment, the land consolidation investment capital and land consolidation earnings should be obtained from the land trust rent. Land consolidation earnings are calculated from land consolidation capital according to the benchmark interest rate (floating upward not more than 100 percent) released by the People's Bank of China during the investment period. The specific earning rate is determined by the sum of prospective earnings, fixed trustee revenue and trust fee paid by the trustee in issuing category B trust units for raising capital necessary for the land consolidation investment according to the trust plan.

Cloud trust: the practice of consumption trust

A consumption trust is a single assigned trust whereby a trust company acts as a trustee; based on the will of the consumers, it applies the trust fund to gain designated consumer rights and interests from industrial organizations. It should also monitor and manage the whole operation chain of trust products as stipulated in the trust documents to meet the special consumption needs of consumers and their rights and interests.

Consumption trust in land circulation

In the case of land circulation, apart from the aforementioned process, the trust fund is specially used to purchase designated farm products or to gain consumer rights and interests from agriculture-related industrial organizations.

Design of consumption trust transaction structure

TRANSACTION STRUCTURE CHART FOR A CONSUMPTION TRUST

This trust plan consists of four steps: first, consumers buy trust products from the trust company; second, the trust company delivers the capital from selling trust products to an industrial organization; third, the industrial organization uses part of the capital to pay the cost and expense for agricultural products and agriculture-related services and entrusts the trust company to invest the rest of the capital; and fourth, the trust company pays the consumers investment capital and earnings which act as a cash deposit, and the trust plan ends.

THE DIFFERENCE BETWEEN A CONSUMPTION TRUST PRODUCT AND SINGLE-
PURPOSE COMMERCIAL PREPAID CARD

In terms of a consumption trust transaction structure and product mode, a single-purpose commercial prepaid card (SPCPC) is a certificate of consumer interests; however, a consumption trust product doesn't mean a SPCPC.

(1) A consumption trust product is similar to an SPCPC in three aspects: first, for consumers, both of them should be prepaid before consumption; second, they define the consumption content and scope; and third, they require commercial banks to supervise the prepaid capital.
(2) The differences between a consumption trust product and an SPCPC include the following: first, a consumption trust product is supervised by the China Banking Regulatory Commission (CBRC), while an SPCPC is supervised by the Ministry of Commerce; second, the sum of the capital prepaid by the settler is determined according to trust contract instead of the *Measures for the Administration of Trust Companies*, which limits the sum for consumers to buy the single-purpose cards; third, the consumption of the single-purpose card is clearly defined, while the products of consumption trust are much wider; fourth, the capital prepaid by the settler of consumption trust products can be invested to produce trust estate income, most of which is paid back in the form of cash deposits, but providers of single-purpose cards cannot offer such content.

Unique advantages of consumption trust: an integration of industry and finance

The integration of industry and finance in our country has gone through four development stages. In the first stage, the industrial organizations themselves set foot in the financial industry and raised funds by themselves due to the difficulty in acquiring financing, but the case of D'Long International Strategic Investment Company tells us that this road is not easy; in the second stage, the industrial organizations invested the stock rights of financial institutions to facilitate their asset allocation; in the third stage, industrial organizations developed their businesses depending on financial methods. For example, Sany Heavy Industry and Zoomlion Heavy Industry sold their products in the forms of finance leases, guarantees and insurance. The fourth stage saw the development of Internet finance. Customers from the traditional financial industry, including enterprises and individuals, depended more on the Internet for information and asset management.

Before a consumption trust, the traditional pillars of finance served the real economy in only two ways, that is, direct financing and indirect financing, while its role of asset allocation was not fully exerted. According to statistical data from the All-China Federation of Industry and Commerce, 90 percent of below-scale enterprises had no debtor-creditor relationship with the banks, and 95 percent of small and micro businesses also had no debtor-creditor relationship with the banks. Enterprises faced many difficulties in issuing stocks through listings. Although trust loans and private equity investment funds provided some financing, the financing costs also put great pressure on enterprises. The important and objective reason for these phenomena is that small and micro businesses lack complete and true credit records, which leads to higher costs for loan audits and larger loan risks. Another important reason is that the financial industry fails to actively and deeply understand the enterprises and the industries to which they belong.

In terms of industry, costs are always an important factor in determining the feasibility of a transaction. Persistently high transaction costs are closely related to the failure of direct interaction between industrial organizations and consumers, that is, business to customer (B2C). Thus industrial organizations cannot accurately grasp consumer preference in producing their products. Currently, e-commerce companies like Alibaba have established such platforms. But after opening up the market, the financial support needed has become a constraint for the development of industrial organizations. Alibaba's MicroCredit has emerged at the right moment. Although Alibaba's MicroCredit provides some loan funds through issuing small loan asset securitization products and is also preparing to introduce strategic investors in the future, such integration of finance and industry is only limited to financing; establishing e-commerce platforms to help industrial organizations directly interact with consumers is actually an integration of business (industrial organization) and business (e-commerce companies) instead of an integration of industry and finance.

In August 2012, the China Finance 40 Forum (CF40) predicted in a research report that Internet finance models would replace existing finance models. Mobile payment would replace traditional payment methods, peer-to-peer lenders would replace traditional loans, and crowd funding would replace traditional securities businesses. The report predicted that modern information technologies represented by the Internet, especially mobile payment, social networking services, search engines, cloud computing and so on will have a fundamental impact on finance models. A third Internet financial model that is different from both indirect financing through commercial banks and direct financing in the capital market may appear. Such a model offers convenience in payment and is less asymmetric in market information; capital suppliers and demanders can direct trade without banks, securities traders, exchanges or other financial intermediaries; the transaction cost for duration matching, risk pricing and so on will be reduced and the process simplified. Already in the past year these processes have begun to take shape. Based on Internet technology and big data innovation, Internet finance is creating more and more forms and models, and the confrontation with traditional finance has already begun.

The trust industry is also being challenged by Internet finance, and its competition with the traditional finance industry is intensifying. According to *The Coming Transformation of China's Trust Industry – China Trust Industry Report 2013*, released by the McKinsey & Company and the Ping An Trust, the business channel that contributes 39 percent of trust industry income will shrink or even die out, while the private place and investment bank businesses that contribute 49 percent will be scrambled by banks, security companies and fund companies.

Risk control measures against consumption trusts

A consumption trust is a trust product which takes consumption as the object and trust as the means based on the rights and obligations of consumers, industrial organizations and trust companies. In actual operation, we may face credit, sales, policy, cost control and operation risks, but we will seek effective control measures in advance based on the content of the risks. See details in Table 6.6.

Table 6.6 Risk control content and measures of consumption trust

Risk	Explanation	Control measures
Credit risk	This is the possibility that the industrial organization is unable to continuously provide agricultural products and agriculture-related services as promised.	Control the use rights of the sales capital of trust products, special tracking of each project and timely communication with manufacturers or service providers.
Sales credit	The trust income obtained by the beneficiary is within the consumer's rights and interests, which is different from the capital income paid by trust products. Therefore there is the risk of a lack of market awareness and dull sales in the marketing terminals.	Control product launching scale, and expand sales channels.
Policy risk	The adjustment of the national macro economy and related policies, laws and regulations may influence the operation and payment ability of consumption service providers, which will further prevent customers from enjoying their due rights and interests.	(1) Operate in strict accordance with related documents and fully reveal related risks to the settler. (2) Reserve sufficient space for the growth of operational costs to hedge the risk of the rise of partial revenue. (3) Optimize payment process and the response plan against policy adjustment to reduce related policy risks.
Cost control risk	The possibility of operational and human costs rises during a consumption service provision, which will have a direct influence on the profit and loss balance of the products.	(1) Have in-depth, in-width and careful understanding of the cost of the industrial organization at the initial stage of product design to let the partner realize that this is an important basis for cooperation. (2) Reserve sufficient space for the growth of operational costs and human costs in the financial measurement of the products.

(Continued)

Table 6.6 (Continued)

Risk	Explanation	Control measures
Operational risk	As the number of customers will far exceed general trust products, there may be transactional risks in contract management, account management, information disclosure and so on.	(1) Optimize the contract signing process, and increase contract management efficiency. (2) Establish a supervision mechanism for strict capital application. (3) Establish a consumer rights and interests registration system inside the trust company, and establish regular interaction and a mechanism to issue updates within the customer system of the industrial organization.
Capital investment risk	There may be risks that the management of the capital pool formed by product sales may fail to achieve the expected return, or there may even be a capital loss.	(1) Measure the method of investment and expected earnings according to the scale and service life of the estimated capital at the initial stage of product design. (2) Timely adjust a capital allocation plan according to the situation of the invested object. (3) Reserve "loan loss provisions."

Profit model for cloud trust + land trust

A cloud trust + land trust combination involves four stakeholders – farmer households, consumers, the industrial organization and the trust company. The four stakeholders integrate industry and finance by the contracted trusteeship to achieve a win-win result.

Farmer households

In the cloud trust + land trust mode, farmer households are both the settlers in a land trust and possibly the consumers in a consumption trust under a cloud trust, and the identity of the consumer may be superimposed, which may be both the consumer of land outputs, agriculture-related products and services like seedlings, agricultural machinery services and agricultural information training.

In this mode, the earnings of farmers mainly include: (1) fixed land rent (five hundred kilograms of Level III wheat of a national standard or cash of one thousand yuan); (2) agricultural subsidies appropriated by national finance; (3) economic income obtained by providing labor for the industrial organization; (4) gains in yield due to technical inputs in the trust projects; (5) improvement of social security environment brought by trust projects.

Taking Suzhou (Anhui) Project of the CITIC Trust, for instance, 54 million shares of category A trust units were issued when the trust was established. The contracted management right per mu (fifteen mu = one hectare) held by farmer households corresponds to ten thousand shares of trust units. Trust income is obtained according to the shares of trust unit per year. The trust income has two parts: the base component is the land rent of five hundred kilograms of Level III wheat of a national standard per mu paid by the agricultural company involved in the project (on the basis of the lowest procurement price in 2013, which is equivalent to about 1,180 yuan, and if its market price is below 1,000 yuan, it is still calculated as 1,000 yuan). The general market price for local land circulation is the price of three hundred kilograms of wheat); on this basis, the CITIC Trust makes a commitment to local governments that in the net return of appreciation after the transformation of land through infrastructure upgrading capital raised by them, 70 percent will be returned to the farmer households, and the remaining part will belong to the CITIC Trust.

In conclusion, a cloud trust + land trust model can lead to solid earnings for farmer households.

Consumers

A consumption trust can effectively centralize the scattered funds of consumers for centralized purchasing and therefore allow consumers to enjoy the best agricultural products and agriculture-related services at optimal prices. Consumers who participate in this plan can enjoy prices 20 percent lower than the market, and within the effective life of consumer rights and interests, the price paid for consumption remains unchanged, which in fact prevents the decreasing of purchasing power caused by inflation.

Under the current transaction mode, as an individual, consumers find it difficult to equally negotiate with providers of agricultural products and related services due to limited knowledge, capital scale and information resources. Therefore, most of them are disadvantaged in signing named or unnamed consumption agreements; when disputes occur due to consumers' dissatisfaction with agricultural products and agriculture-related services, plenty of time and effort will be required, even though outside help can be sought for rights protection. The trust company, as an organization trustee, has stronger negotiation ability and can not only get more favorable prices for the consumers as the beneficiary but also better supervise commercial tenants' use of customers' capital.

In a consumption trust under a cloud trust, consumers usually have specific expectations for related agricultural products based on their demands for food safety, special dietary requirements and green agriculture. In this consumption trust model, they can shake off the burden of producer selection, supervision of agricultural product manufacturing, processing, storage and sales and can directly purchase the agricultural products they need. In addition, backed by the credit of a trust company, product liability retrospect is assured.

Industrial organizations

For industrial organizations, the business model in which the production, sales, logistics and other links are separated from each other enables the organizations to focus on agricultural products and agriculture-related services themselves, but it also gradually takes them away from the consumers. More distribution links not only increase consumer costs but also make the industrial organizations increasingly unable to clearly understand neither the real demand of consumers nor the size of consumer groups. The problem of consumers' "authenticity" is even difficult for the more prosperous e-commerce companies to solve. This is the advantage of traditional finance, including trust companies. After screening potential investors, the trust company's customers are not only a group of high consumption ability but also must be real customers. The positive effect of such an advantage for industrial organizations can be well reflected in a consumption trust. The industrial organizations participating in a consumption trust can directly interact with consumers with the aid of the issuance and marketing channel of the trust products, which means that they can understand the demands of consumers in a timely manner and grasp the scale of consumer groups to produce according to sales, minimize the inventory and save the cost of production.

For a consumption trust under a cloud trust, consumption trust products use a consumer card as the certificate of consumer rights and interests. Consumers must prepay the expenses to gain their rights and interests. Therefore, the industrial organizations who issue the products can get the immediate income with no need to wait for the return of the sale fund. Because a service life is arranged for the realization of consumer rights and interests, the collected funds for the issuance of trust products – whether returned to the industrial organizations in the current period or after a certain time following a freezing of assets – contain the future earnings of industrial organizations, which means that the consumption trust actually ensures certain future earnings for the industrial organizations. The settler and the beneficiary of the consumption trust should first become the investor of trust products, and then they can enjoy specific consumer rights and interests. This means that issuing consumption trust products can actually share part or all of the marketing workload for industrial organizations. The savings therein in manpower, material and other sales costs can not only reduce financial pressure on the industrial organizations but also enable consumers to benefit indirectly.

Still using the CITIC Suzhou Land Trust Project as an example, the industrial organization (an unnamed biotechnology company in Anhui Province) has a clear profit plan for the project:

First, the circular agriculture is to split the existing 5,400 mu of arable land into five pieces for use. The largest piece with an area of nearly 4,000 mu is used as basic farmland for the cultivation of wheat, corn, soybeans and other traditional crops. The unnamed agricultural company turned it over to a state farm to operate. The state farm gains profit with the high efficiency brought by large-scale mechanical means and other intensive production, through which it ensures a land transfer fee payment or a slight surplus. The CITIC Trust also tries to cut its circulation cost for production materials by strengthening its cooperation with Bayer and other partners.

The second piece of land is used to build greenhouses to facilitate agriculture production, where out-of-season fruits and vegetables and herbs are planted. Profits are expected to be about 12 million yuan each year.

The third piece is used for the construction of a livestock and poultry slaughtering base. The aforementioned agricultural company has signed a cooperation agreement with an unnamed group company, agreeing that the former will finance the establishment of a modern breeding farm and lease it to the latter, while the latter will pay 13 percent of the construction costs as rent to the former each year.

The crops straw and waste produced in these three pieces of land will be processed into methane and other products through a "biomass energy harmless disposal center" and "large organic fertilizer and machine-made fertilizer production base" on the fourth piece. After meeting the needs of the farm, the remaining portions of the products will be sold. According to estimates, biomass energy can generate an annual output of 30 million cubic meters of biogas, of which, 40 percent is used for grid-connected power generation with a revenue of about 16 million yuan each year; 60 percent is purified as civil methane gas, with an annual sales income of 20 million yuan; biogas residue and slurry are used for making organic fertilizer, which can bring in a sales revenue of 6 million yuan in addition to demand for self-use.

The aforementioned agricultural company obtains external financing support from the CITIC Trust, with an annual interest of 10 percent as the cost; the CITIC Trust will share part of the company's operating income.

At present, the multiple means of financial support by the local government will also become an important profit channel for the aforementioned agricultural company. It can enjoy a subsidy for building conservation projects, of which the most important is the subsidy equivalent of two hundred kilogram of wheat per mu that will be given by the local government to encourage the implementation of the project.

This is the first part of the profit chain for the aforementioned agricultural company. In addition, the company also plans to work with the Israel Chamber of Commerce to develop agricultural facilities and create a digital processing center integrating the IoT, the Internet and a physical network, in which the Israeli side is responsible for production management. The agricultural company would enjoy dividends through a shareholding ratio. At the same time, it also plans to enter the upstream and downstream fields to make a profit through the production of related equipment, seedlings and so on.

After deducting the rent given to farmers each year, and taking into account project construction and operation and financing costs, the agricultural company told the media that the whole project would be profitable next year, gradually mature in the next three years and eventually copied to the surrounding 26,000 mu of land. It's expected that the annual operating profit per mu will reach 6,500 yuan.

Trust company

The cloud trust + land trust model belongs to a transactional trust under active management. Relying on its strong negotiation skills, the trust company can obtain the active management rights of the capital pool formed by the sale of trust products, while consumers and industrial organizations only need to pay a fixed income. This means that the trust company can get a high-risk premium and thus change the revenue pattern of general trust products which is dominated by fixed incomes and supplemented by fluctuating incomes.

The trust company can also use the high-quality customer resources accumulated through general trust products. These customers enjoy greater spending power than the national average. They have a certain degree of faith in the professional ethics of trust companies and also generally have a higher requirement for product quality and experience than lower income groups. The loyalty of existing customers will be naturally enhanced if consumption trust products can meet the lifestyle demands of customers from Fast Moving Consumer Goods (FMCG) to luxury, from maintaining health to nursing, and many other aspects, and enable the customers of general trust products to easily find quality products and services. Eventually customers would trust and even rely on the relevant businesses of the trust company, whether or not they have investment or consumption demands. In addition, through the development of consumption trust businesses, personnel will better understand related industries; the interaction and feedback of knowledge also contributes to the development and control of the trust company regarding other trust products, thus forming a mutually beneficial virtuous cycle between a consumption trust and other trust businesses.

Bibliography

Ashby, William Ross, trans. *An Introduction to Cybernetics*. Beijing: Science Press, 1965.

Bai, Junchao. "A Study on China's Rural Land System Reform." PhD diss., Northwest A&F University, 2007.

Basu, Kaushik, trans. *Beyond the Invisible Hand: Groundwork for a New Economics*. Beijing: Oriental Press, 2011.

Chai, Qiang. *Land Systems and Policies of Countries and Regions*. Beijing: Beijing Economics College Press, 1993.

Chen, Baiming, Zhou Xiaoping, Hu Yecui, and Wang Xiufen. *Land Resource Science*. Beijing: Beijing Normal University Press, 2008.

Chen, Xiwen. *China's Rural Reform: Review and Outlook*. Tianjin: Tianjin People's Publishing House, 1993.

Crosland, Anthony, trans. *The Future of Socialism*. Shanghai: Shanghai People's Publishing House, 2001.

Dai, Weijuan. *A Study on Rural Land Circulation in Urbanization*. Shanghai: Shanghai Academy of Social Sciences Press, 2010.

Deng, Xiaoping. *Selected Works of Deng Xiaoping*, vol. 2. Beijing: People's Press, 1993.

Department of Rural Economic System and Management of the Ministry of Agriculture, "The Practice and Exploration of the Reform and Innovation of the Rural Economic System in China." *Strategy and Management* 5 (2013).

Department of Science and Technology Dissemination of State Land and Resources Administration. *An Introduction to Agricultural Economies around the World*. Shanghai: Science and Technology Literature Press, 1988.

Dong, Daye. "Did the Enclosure Movement Mean Occupying Farmers' Own Land?" *History Learning* 11 (2003).

Du, Hongmei. "Study on the Coupling Mechanism of Green Supply Chain for Agricultural Products in China." PhD diss., Hunan Agricultural University, 2010.

Duan, Zhengliang. "Some Thoughts on Several Land-Related Concepts." *China Land Sciences* 4 (2000).

Duan, Zhengliang, Zhang Weiran, and Ye Zhenfei. "On the Contents, Sources and Features of the Value of Land." *Tongji University Journal Social Science Section* 2 (2004).

Engels, Friedrich. *Dialectics of Nature*. Beijing: People's Press, 1987.

Fan, Lanzha. *Appraisal and Planning on Rural Land Circulation*. Beijing: China Agricultural Science and Technology Press, 2011.

Fang, Wen. *Institutional Environment, Farmers' Behavior and Innovation Mechanism in China's Rural Land Circulation*. Hangzhou: Zhejiang University Press, 2012.

Feng, Zhendong, Huo Li, and Shao Chuanlin. "Research Review of the Land Circulation Issue in China's Rural Areas." *Journal of Northwest University (Philosophy and Social Sciences Edition)* 2 (2010).

Fromm, Erich. *To Have or to Be*. Beijing: SDX Joint Publishing Company, 1989.

Guo, Jianxiong. *Agricultural Development: A Three Sector Analysis Framework*. Beijing: China Social Sciences Press, 2008.

Guo, Jianxiong, and Wang Yansheng. "Rechoosing Yan'an's Agricultural Development Pattern." *The Journal of Yanan University (Philosophy and Social Science Edition)* 4 (2000).

Guo, Xiaoming. *Urban-rural Integration Development and Land Circulation System Reform: An Empirical Research Based on the Pilot Area in Chengdu*. Beijing: Science Press, 2012.

Hong, Zenglin. *A Study on the Collectively-owned Land Circulation System in China*. Beijing: Science Press, 2008.

Hu, Angang. *2020: A New Superpower*. Hangzhou: Zhejiang People's Publishing House, 2012.

Hu, Rong'en. *The Flowing Land: A Survey of the Land Circulation Situation in Tongren Region, Guizhou*. Beijing: Peking University Press, 2010.

Huang, Dingfang. "The New Development of Chinese Communist Party's Revolutionary Ideas during the Period of Liberation War." *Journal of Wuxi University of Light Industry (Social Science Edition)* 1 (2001).

Huang, Hewen, and Wu Dan. "A Study on the Education Support of Modern Agriculture Development." *China Agricultural Education* 5 (2010).

Jiang, Ailin. "A Brief Account of the Chinese Communist Party's Land Policy during the Period of Liberation War." *Journal of Beihua University (Social Sciences)* 3 (2001).

Jiang, Boqian. "The Birth and Operation of Land Bank under the Perspective of Transaction Expense Theory – Taking the Land Bank of Pengzhou, Sichuan as an Example." *Journal of Southwest University (Social Science Edition)* 4 (2010).

Jian, Pu. "Land Trust Circulation: Headstone of Steady Progression in New Socialist Countryside." *Study and Research* (2012).

Jian, Pu. "Trust Has a Bright Future in Serving Real Economy." *Red Flag Manuscript* 11 (2012).

Jian, Pu. "Trust Is a Realization Form of Public Ownership." *Red Flag Manuscript* 11 (2013).

Lai, Zeyuan et al. *A Comparison of Farmland Systems*. Beijing: Economic Administration Press, 1996.

Li, Bo. "Land Bank: The Fresh Troops of the New Rural Construction." *Journal of Finance and Economics* 1 (2007).

Li, Wei. "The International Practices of Land Ownership Reform and Agricultural Growth." *Issues in Agricultural Economy* 4 (1995).

Li, Zhenyuan. "A Study on the Circulation of Rural Farmland and Its Guarantee of Rights and Interests." PhD diss., Agricultural University of Hunan, 2010.

Liao, Luyan. "The Great Victory of the Land Reform Movement in the Past Three Years." *Materials of the History of the Communist Party of China*, vol. 7. Beijing: People's Press, 1980.

Lin, Yifu. *Institution, Technology, and the Development of Chinese Agriculture*. Shanghai: Shanghai Joint Publishing Company, 1992.

Liu, Fang. "A Study on the Arrangement and Innovation of Rural Land in China." PhD diss., Southwestern University of Finance and Economics, 2008.

Liu, Hui. "A Study on the Property Rights of Agricultural Technology Innovation." PhD diss., Agricultural University Of Hunan, 2009.

Liu, Lijun. "A Comparative Study on the Performance of Land Circulation Pattern in Rural Areas." PhD diss., Central South University, 2010.

Liu, Lijun. "A Comparative Study on the Performance of Land Circulation Pattern in Rural Areas." PhD diss., China Economic Publishing House, 2012.

Liu, Runqiu. *A Study on the Land Circulation System in China's Rural Area: From the Perspective of the Harmony of Interests*. Beijing: Economic Science Press, 2012.

Liu, Weibai. "A Dissection of the Innovation of Current Rural Land Circulation Patterns in China." *China Value* 6 (2012).

Lizhi, Duan. "Study on the Issue of Rural Land Transfer in China." PhD diss., Chongqing University, 2011.

Luo, Guangqiang. "A Study on Food Security and Its Realization Mechanism in Major Production Provinces." PhD diss., Agricultural University of Hunan, 2010.

Mao, Zedong. *On Coalition Government*. 1945.

Mao, Zedong. *Selected Works of Mao Zedong*, vol. 7. Beijing: People's Press, 1999.

Marshall, Alfred. *Principles of Economics*. Beijing: Huaxia Publishing House, 2006.

Marx, Karl. *Das Kapital*. Beijing: People's Press, 2004.

Marx, Karl, and Friedrich Engels. *Collected Works of Karl Marx and Friedrich Engels*, vol. 1. Beijing: People's Press, 1975.

Marx, Karl, and Friedrich Engels. *Collected Works of Karl Marx and Friedrich Engels*, vol. 2. Beijing: People's Press, 1995.

Marx, Karl, and Friedrich Engels. *Collected Works of Karl Marx and Friedrich Engels*, vol. 4. Beijing: People's Press, 1972.

Marx, Karl, and Friedrich Engels. *The Complete Works of Karl Marx and Friedrich Engels*, vol. 21. Beijing: People's Press, 1988.

Marx, Karl, and Friedrich Engels. *The Complete Works of Karl Marx and Friedrich Engels*, vol. 23. Beijing: People's Press, 1972.

Marx, Karl, and Friedrich Engels. *The Complete Works of Karl Marx and Friedrich Engels*, vol. 32. Beijing: People's Press, 1975.

Marx, Karl, and Friedrich Engels. *The Complete Works of Karl Marx and Friedrich Engels*, vol. 46. Beijing: People's Press, 1995.

Mei, Lin. "A Study on the Land Circulation Patterns in China's Rural Areas." PhD diss., Fujian Normal University, 2011.

Menger, Carl. *Principles of Economics*. Shanghai: Shanghai Century Publishing (Group) Co., Ltd, 2005.

Mill, John Stuart. *Principles of Political Economy with Some of Their Applications to Social Philosophy*. Beijing: The Commercial Press, 1991.

National Rural Fixed Site Survey Office of the Ministry of Agriculture, "An Empirical Analysis of the Farmers' Income during the Ninth Five-Year Period." *Issues in Agricultural Economy*, 2000.

North, Douglass C., trans. *Understanding the Process of Economic Change*. Beijing: China Renmin University Press, 2008.

Pang, Li. "A Study on the Public Finance System Aiming to Ensure Equitable Access to Basic Public Services in Urban and Rural Areas." PhD diss., Agricultural University of Hunan, 2010.

Ricardo, David. *On the Principles of Political Economy and Taxation*. Beijing: Guangming Daily Press, 2009.

Romer, David. *Advanced Macroeconomics*. 2nd ed. Shanghai: Shanghai University of Finance & Economics Press, 2009.

Solow, Robert M. *Growth Theory: An Exposition*. Beijing: The Commercial Press, 2003.

Soto, Hernando de, trans. *The Mystery of Capital*. Beijing: Huaxia Publishing House, 2012.

Xenophon. *A Discourse upon Improving the Revenue of the State of Athens*. Quoted in Arthur Eli Monroe, *Early Economic Thought: Selections From Economic Literature Prior to Adam Smith*. Beijing: The Commercial Press, 1985.

Notes

Prologue

1 Karl Marx and Friedrich Engels, *Collected Works of Karl Marx and Friedrich Engels*, vol. 2 (Beijing: People's Press, 1995), 24.
2 Karl Marx, *Das Kapital*, vol. 1 (Beijing: People's Press, 2004).
3 Karl Marx and Friedrich Engels, *The Complete Works of Karl Marx and Friedrich Engels*, vol. 32 (Beijing: People's Press, 1975), 503.
4 Karl Marx and Friedrich Engels, *Collected Works of Karl Marx and Friedrich Engels*, vol. 2 (Beijing: People's Press, 2009), 591–592.

Chapter 1

1 Erich Fromm, *To Have or to Be* (Beijing: SDX Joint Publishing Company, 1989).
2 Karl Marx and Friedrich Engels, *Collected Works of Karl Marx and Friedrich Engels*, vol. 7 (Beijing: People's Press, 2009), 912.
3 Karl Marx and Friedrich Engels, *Collected Works of Karl Marx and Friedrich Engels*, vol. 7 (Beijing: People's Press, 2009), 912.
4 Karl Marx and Friedrich Engels, *Collected Works of Karl Marx and Friedrich Engels*, vol. 7 (Beijing: People's Press, 2009), 912.

Chapter 2

1 Karl Marx and Friedrich Engels, *Collected Works of Karl Marx and Friedrich Engels*, vol. 1 (Beijing: People's Press, 1995), 56.
2 Karl Marx, *Economic and Philosophic Manuscripts of 1844* (Beijing: People's Press, 2006), 57.
3 Karl Marx and Friedrich Engels, *The Complete Works of Karl Marx and Friedrich Engels*, vol. 12 (Beijing: People's Press, 1962), 4.
4 Karl Marx and Friedrich Engels, *The Complete Works of Karl Marx and Friedrich Engels*, vol. 2 (Beijing: People's Press, 1975), 64.
5 Karl Marx and Friedrich Engels, *The Complete Works of Karl Marx and Friedrich Engels*, vol. 42 (Beijing: People's Press, 1979), 123.
6 John R. Commons, *Institutional Economics*, vol. 1 (Beijing: The Commercial Press, 1962).
7 Karl Marx and Friedrich Engels, *The Complete Works of Karl Marx and Friedrich Engels*, vol. 1 (Beijing: People's Press, 1979), 344.
8 Karl Marx and Friedrich Engels, *The Complete Works of Karl Marx and Friedrich Engels*, vol. 1 (Beijing: People's Press, 1979), 80.
9 Karl Marx and Friedrich Engels, *The Complete Works of Karl Marx and Friedrich Engels*, vol. 4 (Beijing: People's Press, 1979), 532.

10 Douglass C. North, *Institutions, Institutional Change and Economic Performance* (Shanghai: Shanghai Joint Publishing Company, 1994), 3.
11 Karl Marx and Friedrich Engels, *The Complete Works of Karl Marx and Friedrich Engels*, vol. 1 (Beijing: People's Press, 1979), 411.
12 Karl Marx, "Chapter 48," in *Das Kapital* (Beijing: People's Press, 2004).
13 Karl Marx, "Chapter 48,"in *Das Kapital* (Beijing: People's Press, 2004).
14 Erich Fromm, *To Have or to Be* (Beijing: SDX Joint Publishing Company, 1989), 82.
15 Karl Marx and Friedrich Engels, *The Complete Works of Karl Marx and Friedrich Engels*, vol. 46 (Beijing: People's Press, 1979), 473.
16 Robert J. Shiller, *Finance and the Good Society* (Beijing: CITIC Press, 2012).
17 Karl Marx, *Das Kapital*, vol. 3 (Beijing: People's Press, 2004), 97.
18 Karl Marx and Friedrich Engels, *Collected Works of Karl Marx and Friedrich Engels*, vol. 3 (Beijing: People's Press, 2009), 575.
19 Karl Marx, *Das Kapital*, vol. 3 (Beijing: People's Press, 2004), 120.
20 Friedrich Engels, *Dialectics of Nature* (Beijing: People's Press, 1987), 144.
21 Karl Marx and Friedrich Engels, *The Complete Works of Karl Marx and Friedrich Engels*, vol. 23 (Beijing: People's Press, 1972), 669.
22 Karl Marx and Friedrich Engels, *The Complete Works of Karl Marx and Friedrich Engels*, vol. 42 (Beijing: People's Press, 1972), 123.
23 Karl Marx and Friedrich Engels, *Collected Works of Karl Marx and Friedrich Engels*, vol. 4 (Beijing: People's Press, 1972), 321.
24 Mao Zedong, *On Coalition Government*, 1945.
25 Douglass C. North, trans., *Understanding the Process of Economic Change* (Beijing: China Renmin University Press, 2008), 75.
26 Douglass C. North, trans., *Understanding the Process of Economic Change* (Beijing: China Renmin University Press, 2008), 75.
27 Friedrich Engels, *Dialectics of Nature* (Beijing: People's Press, 1971), 144.
28 Mao Zedong, *Selected Works of Mao Zedong*, vol. 7 (Beijing: People's Press, 1999), 102.
29 Howard W. French, "Letter from China: What if Beijing Is Right," *International Herald Tribune* (November 2007), quoted in Hu Angang, *2020: A New Superpower* (Hangzhou: Zhejiang People's Publishing House, 2012), 4.
30 William Ross Ashby, trans., *An Introduction to Cybernetics* (Beijing: Science Press, 1965), 123.
31 Sun Yat-sen, *The Three Principles of the People* (Changsha: Yuelu Publishing House, 2001), 200.
32 Henry George Liddell, *Progress and Poverty* (Beijing: The Commercial Press, 1995), 347.
33 Vladimir Lenin, trans., *Philosophy Notes*, 2nd ed. (Beijing: People's Press, 1993), 85.
34 Friedrich Hegel, *Science of Logic*, vol. 1 (Beijing: People's Press, 2002), 122.
35 Vladimir Lenin, trans., *Philosophy Notes*, 2nd ed. (Beijing: People's Press, 1993), 85.
36 Meng Mei and Zhang Yunhui, "A Study on the Matching between Residual Control Right and Residual Claim in Incorporated Enterprises," *Scientific and Technological Information* 4 (2008): 194.
37 Modern enterprise theories which support the matching between residual control rights and residual claims are inclined to think that they should match with each other. According to Milgrom, control rights mean that the owner of the enterprise has the right to prohibit those who fail to pay the required price to use the property.
38 Wang Hui, *An Introduction to Resource and Environment* (Beijing: Chemical Industry Press, 2009), 73.
39 Karl Marx and Friedrich Engels, *Collected Works of Karl Marx and Friedrich Engels*, vol. 1 (Beijing: People's Press, 1979), 153.
40 Karl Marx, *Das Kapital*, vol. 3 (Beijing: People's Press, 1975), 830.
41 Wang Hui, *An Introduction to Resource and Environment* (Beijing: Chemical Industry Press, 2009), 73.
42 Duan Zhengliang, "On the Contents, Sources and Features of the Value of Land," *Journal of Tongji University 1* (2004): 35.

43 Duan Zhengliang, "Some Thoughts on Several Land-Related Concepts," *China Land Science* (2000).
44 Chai Qiang, *Land Systems and Policies of Countries and Regions* (Beijing: Beijing Economic College Press, 1993).
45 Wang Hui, *An Introduction to Resource and Environment* (Beijing: Chemical Industry Press, 2009), 74.
46 Hernando de Soto, *The Mystery of Capital* (Beijing: Huaxia Publishing House, 2012), 185.
47 Land under the ownership of the whole people is referred to as land owned by the state, or "state-owned land." Its proprietary rights belong to the State Council, as representative of the state. The second article of *Land Management Law* says: "The proprietary rights of land under the ownership of the whole people, or state-owned land, belong to the State Council, as representative of the state." Land in urban areas of cities belongs to the state. It has been explicitly stipulated by the *Constitution of the People's Republic of China* and the *Property Law of the People's Republic of China* that urban land belongs to the state.
48 Farmers' collectively owned land, abbreviated as collectively owned land, includes the following three forms: 1) village collective; 2) two or more villager groups under the village; and 3) township collective. The tenth article of *Land Management Law of the People's Republic of China* gives relevant stipulations.
49 Karl Marx, *A Critique of Political Economy* (Beijing: People's Press, 1972), 103.
50 Vladimir Lenin, *Philosophy Notes* (Beijing: People's Press, 1956), 125.
51 Deng Xiaoping, *Selected Works of Deng Xiaoping*, vol. 3 (Beijing: People's Press, 2001), 374.

Chapter 3

1 Rites of Zhou.
2 Xumu and Zhang Xiaohua, *History of Land Arrangement and Utilization in China* (Beijing: China Agricultural Science and Technology Press, 1995).
3 "The Major Odes: North Mountain," in *The Book of Songs.*
4 Dayu Ding.
5 Bai Junchao, "A Study on China's Rural Land System Reform" (PhD diss., Northwest Agriculture & Forestry University, 2007).
Xumu and Zhang Xiaohua, *History of Land Arrangement and Utilization in China* (Beijing: China Agricultural Science and Technology Press, 1995). The quotation is edited.
6 Li Wenzhi and Jiang Taixin, *A Study on Chinese Feudal Landlord Economy: The Development and Change of Feudal Agrarian Relations* (Beijing: China Social Sciences Publishing House, 2005).
7 Bai Junchao, "A Study on China's Rural Land System Reform" (PhD diss., Northwest Agriculture & Forestry University, 2007). The quotation is edited.
8 Xumu and Zhang Xiaohua, *History of Land Arrangement and Utilization in China* (Beijing: China Agricultural Science and Technology Press, 1995).
9 Bai Junchao, "A Study on China's Rural Land System Reform" (PhD diss., Northwest Agriculture & Forestry University, 2007).
Xumu and Zhang Xiaohua, *History of Land Arrangement and Utilization in China* (Beijing: China Agricultural Science and Technology Press, 1995). The quotation is edited.
10 Zheng Jianmin, "On the Land Policy of Chinese Communist Party during the New Democratic Revolution Period," *Journal of Southwest China Normal University (Philosophy & Social Sciences Edition)* 4 (2003): 133–137.
11 Zheng Jianmin, "On the Land Policy of Chinese Communist Party during the New Democratic Revolution Period," *Journal of Southwest China Normal University (Philosophy & Social Sciences Edition)* 4 (2003): 133–137.
12 Jiang Ailin, "A Brief Account of the Chinese Communist Party's Land Policy during the Period of Liberation War," *Journal of Beihua University (Social Sciences)* 3 (2001): 23–25.

13 Huang Dingfang, "The New Development of Chinese Communist Party's Revolutionary Ideas during the Period of Liberation War," *Journal of Wuxi University of Light Industry (Social Science Edition)* 1 (2001): 12–16.
14 Liao Luyan, "The Great Victory of the Land Reform Movement in the Past Three Years," *Materials of the History of the Communist Party of China*, vol. 7 (Beijing: People's Press, 1980).
15 Bai Junchao, "A Study on China's Rural Land System Reform" (PhD diss., Northwest Agriculture & Forestry University, 2007).
16 Lin Yifu, *Institution, Technology, and the Development of Chinese Agriculture* (Shanghai: Shanghai Joint Publishing Company, 1992), 55.
17 Chen Xiwen, *China's Rural Reform: Review and Outlook* (Tianjin: Tianjin Peoples Publishing House, 1993).
18 Bai Junchao, "A Study on China's Rural Land System Reform" (PhD diss., Northwest Agriculture & Forestry University, 2007). The quotation is edited.
19 Zhou Qiren, Du Ying and Qiu Jiancheng, *Single Trip in Development* (Chengdu: Sichuan Renmin Press, 1985).
20 Tang Zhong, *A Comparison of Rural Land System* (Beijing: China Agriculture Science and Technique Press, 1999).
     Bai Junchao, "A Study on China's Rural Land System Reform" (PhD diss., Northwest Agriculture & Forestry University, 2007).
21 According to TheFreeDictionary.com, *cadaster* means "[a] public register showing details of ownership of the real property in a district, including boundaries and tax assessments").
22 "Unified management of rural and urban land administration affairs": urban and rural land should be managed by the land administration department as a whole. The land administration department is in charge of making land-related guidelines, policies and regulations and supervising their implementation. It manages land resources and land registration. It addresses disputes on land rights ownership and manages land transfer and requisition matters in urban and rural areas. It is in charge of the grant of the land use rights of state-owned land; the organization, coordination, investigation, and approval of land-use rights granting; as well as the implementation of land transfer programs. It also regulates the matters on land use rights, land lease and mortgage.
23 "Combination of regional and central systems while giving priority to regional": The State Council establishes the Ministry of Land and Resources. The land management department of local people's governments at or above the county level is responsible for the unified management of land within its administrative regions. In regard to institution setting, it shall be adjusted by the provinces, autonomous regions and municipalities directly under the central government. In practice, provincial governments generally establish provincial departments of land resources; municipal governments establish city land resources bureaus; governments at county and district level establish institutes of land management, all of which are in charge of the land administrative work within their administrative regions. All the land managing departments are under the governance of the government at the same administrative level and are responsible for them. Between the superior and subordinate departments, there are no other relations other than operational guidance. And among the five-level governments, the county level's government management is the most important part.
24 National Rural Fixed Site Survey Office, "An Empirical Analysis of the Farmer Income Situation during the Ninth Five-year Plan Period," *Issues in Agricultural Economy* (2000): 2.
25 Xiang Guohui and Yan Ming, "Ways to Reform the Rural Land Tenure System," *Journal of Beijing University of Posts and Telecommunications (Social Sciences Edition)* 2 (2005).
26 Yan Yunqiu and Wang Zehui, "Nationalization: to Reform the Collective Ownership of Rural Land in China," *Journal Of Xiangtan University: Philosophy and Social Sciences* 2 (2005).
27 Liu Fengqin, "Protection of Rural Land Rights and the Three Rural Issues," *Comparative Economic & Social Systems* 1 (2005).

28 Yan Yunqiu and Wang Zehui, "Nationalization: to Reform the Collective Ownership of Rural Land in China," *Journal of Xiangtan University: Philosophy and Social Sciences* 2 (2005).
29 Liu Rongcai, "The Literature Review of the Current Rural Land Ownership System Reform in China," *Commercial Times* 18 (2006).
30 Sun Xiaojun, "On the Economic Logic of Rural Land Contract Law," *Fujian Tribune (The Humanities & Social Sciences Bimonthly)* 4 (2004).
31 Li Changping, "Caution against the Privatization of Rural Land," *China Land* 9 (2004).
32 Liu Rongcai, "The Literature Review of the Current Rural Land Ownership System Reform in China," *Commercial Times* 18 (2006).
33 Zhang Xinguang, "On the Fundamental Guarantee of the Privatization of Rural Land," *Rural Economy* 12 (2004).
34 Zeng Qing, Tang Tao, ed., *Property Law: Analysis on Legislation and Dissection of the Essential* (Chengdu: Sichuan Renmin Press, 2006), 243.
35 Liu Haiyun, *Marginalization and Differentiation: A Research on the Problem of Land-losing Farmers* (Beijing: China Agriculture Press, 2007), 152.

Chapter 4

1 William Petty, *A Treatise of Taxes and Contributions* (Beijing: The Commercial Press, 1963), 71.
2 Karl Marx and Friedrich Engels, *The Complete Works of Karl Marx and Friedrich Engels*, vol. 30, 2nd ed. (Beijing: People's Press, 1979), 479–480.
3 Rural land circulation: it is a process of detaching the land management rights from the contracted rights and transferring it to other farmers or operators with the land ownership remaining unchanged. It can also be seen as the circulation of the rural area's contracted land management rights.
4 Department of Rural Economic System and Management of the Ministry of Agriculture, "The Practice and Exploration of the Reform and Innovation of the Rural Economic System in China," *Strategy and Management* 5 (2013): 6.
5 Liu Weibai, "A Dissection of the Models Innovation of Current Rural Land Circulation in China," *China Value* 6 (2012). The quotation is edited.
6 Liu Weibai, "A Dissection of the Models Innovation of Current Rural Land Circulation in China," *China Value* 6 (2012). The quotation is edited.
7 In the socialization model, the specialized farm, agricultural cooperatives and grain cooperatives provide one-stop services for food production. They may also provide paid services in one link of the whole industrial chain.

Chapter 5

1 Richard Edwards and Nigel Stockwell, *Trust and Equity* (Beijing: Law Press), 6.
2 Jian Pu, "Trust Is A Mechanism for Realizing Public Ownership," *Red Flag Manuscript* 11 (2013): 24.
3 Xu Guoyuan, "Building a Diverse Land Property Right System," *China Reform* 11 (2005).
4 The calculation is based on the scale of the trust projects in those years.
5 The total revenue of trust companies' trust assets under administration = the beneficiaries' effective rate of return + the trustee's gained return.
6 Data source: The bank returns and the investors' returns are collected from the banks' annual report and have been processed.
7 Data source: The revenue of the trust companies and the investors' returns are collected from the trust companies' annual report and have been processed.
8 The earnings of the banks, trust companies and the investors during 2009–2012. (For trust companies, it is called "beneficiaries' earnings.")
9 Data source: *China Population Statistics Yearbook*.

10 Jian Xiaoying, "On the Cultural Trait of Agriculture Modernization Process," *Research of Agricultural Modernization* 9 (1996).
11 Gu Wei, "The Influence of Chinese Farmers' Qualities on Agriculturalization," *Journal of China Agricultural University* 1 (2000).

Chapter 6

1 Karl Marx and Friedrich Engels, *Collected Works of Karl Marx and Friedrich Engels*, vol. 3, 2nd ed. (Beijing: People's Press, 1995), 359.
2 Karl Marx and Friedrich Engels, "Anti-Dühring," in *Collected Works of Karl Marx and Friedrich Engels*, vol. 3, 2nd ed. (Beijing: People's Press, 1995), 359.
3 Karl Marx, "Marx to Pavel Vasilyevich Annenkov," in *Collected Works of Karl Marx and Friedrich Engels*, vol. 4, 2nd ed. (Beijing: People's Press, 1995), 532.
4 Karl Marx, "Critique of Political Economy," in *Collected Works of Karl Marx and Friedrich Engels*, vol. 2, 2nd ed. (Beijing: People's Press, 1995), 32.
5 Karl Marx, "The Grundrisse (1857–1858)," in *Collected Works of Karl Marx and Friedrich Engels*, vol. 46 (Beijing: People's Press, 1979), 194.
6 Karl Marx, "The German Ideology," in *The Complete Works of Karl Marx and Friedrich Engels*, vol. 3 (Beijing: People's Press, 1960), 35.
7 Karl Marx, "The Holy Family," in *The Complete Works of Karl Marx and Friedrich Engels*, vol. 2 (Beijing: People's Press, 1957), 167.
8 Karl Marx, "The Grundrisse (1861–1863)," in *Collected Works of Karl Marx and Friedrich Engels*, vol. 46 (Beijing: People's Press, 1979), 194.
9 Public of productivity: everyone is a producer of final products. By employing information and credit means, relying on the land platform and extending the industry chain, everyone in the industry chain can actively participate in and supervise the process of production.
10 Public of intellectuality: everyone's wisdom and intellectual potential can be utilized in the industry chain. For instance, when dealing with land trust, we can connect the seed supply with the relevant equipment in advance and leave the rest to the people, who can promote the proficiency in crop cultivation according to their own areas of expertise. During the production process, they can create more demands and hence speed up the optimization of seeds and equipment.
11 Public of creativity: everyone's intellectual potential can be utilized by using the credit medium via Internet platforms for the ultimate purpose of innovation.
12 Joseph V. Stalin, *Marxism and Problems of Linguistics* (Beijing: People's Press, 1964), 4.
13 Lester G. Telser, "A Theory of Self-Enforcing Agreements," *Journal of Business* 22 (1980).
14 The data sample used in this book is for analyzing the average knowledge level of the permanent rural population. However, the "empty-nest family" phenomenon in rural China is quite severe. Many young, capable and educated people have left the countryside to work in cities; hence they are not included in the evaluation system. However, when making major decisions during the land transfer process, this group of people plays an important role.
15 Karl Marx and Friedrich Engels, *Collected Works of Karl Marx and Friedrich Engels*, vol. 2 (Beijing: People's Press, 1995), 24.
16 Karl Marx, *Das Kapital*, vol. 1 (Beijing: People's Press, 2004).
17 Karl Marx and Friedrich Engels, *Collected Works of Karl Marx and Friedrich Engels*, vol. 7 (Beijing: People's Press, 2009), 912.
18 Karl Marx and Friedrich Engels, *Collected Works of Karl Marx and Friedrich Engels*, vol. 7 (Beijing: People's Press, 2009), 912.
19 Karl Marx and Friedrich Engels, *Collected Works of Karl Marx and Friedrich Engels*, vol. 7 (Beijing: People's Press, 2009), 912.

Index

For Product Safety Concerns and Information please contact our EU
representative GPSR@taylorandfrancis.com
Taylor & Francis Verlag GmbH, Kaufingerstraße 24, 80331 München, Germany

www.ingramcontent.com/pod-product-compliance
Ingram Content Group UK Ltd.
Pitfield, Milton Keynes, MK11 3LW, UK
UKHW020952180425
457613UK00019B/641